Automated Detection of Media Bias

Timo Spinde

Automated Detection of Media Bias

From the Conceptualization of Media Bias to its Computational Classification

Timo Spinde
Informatik
Universität Göttingen
Witten, Germany

ISBN 978-3-658-47797-4   ISBN 978-3-658-47798-1   (eBook)
https://doi.org/10.1007/978-3-658-47798-1

This work was supported by the Lower Saxony Ministry of Science and Culture and the VW Foundation, through Prof. Dr. Bela Gipp, Georg-August-Universität Göttingen.

© The Editor(s) (if applicable) and The Author(s) 2025. This book is an open access publication.

Open Access This book is licensed under the terms of the Creative Commons Attribution 4.0 International License (http://creativecommons.org/licenses/by/4.0/), which permits use, sharing, adaptation, distribution and reproduction in any medium or format, as long as you give appropriate credit to the original author(s) and the source, provide a link to the Creative Commons license and indicate if changes were made.
The images or other third party material in this book are included in the book's Creative Commons license, unless indicated otherwise in a credit line to the material. If material is not included in the book's Creative Commons license and your intended use is not permitted by statutory regulation or exceeds the permitted use, you will need to obtain permission directly from the copyright holder.
The use of general descriptive names, registered names, trademarks, service marks, etc. in this publication does not imply, even in the absence of a specific statement, that such names are exempt from the relevant protective laws and regulations and therefore free for general use.
The publisher, the authors and the editors are safe to assume that the advice and information in this book are believed to be true and accurate at the date of publication. Neither the publisher nor the authors or the editors give a warranty, expressed or implied, with respect to the material contained herein or for any errors or omissions that may have been made. The publisher remains neutral with regard to jurisdictional claims in published maps and institutional affiliations.

This Springer Vieweg imprint is published by the registered company Springer Fachmedien Wiesbaden GmbH, part of Springer Nature.
The registered company address is: Abraham-Lincoln-Str. 46, 65189 Wiesbaden, Germany

If disposing of this product, please recycle the paper.

Acknowledgements

My path through this dissertation thesis was largely affected by the Corona pandemic, caving me into my little room in Schliersee, Germany, my beloved home. During this work, I often felt as lonely as never before. I worked long and long hours while some things had a massive impact on my life, and I did not see any way out. I connected with my friends and colleagues over Zoom, but it was not the same as personal contact. I deeply want to express here, that whoever might ever read this: Don't give up. Things will be good.

In supporting and rooting for me in so many different ways, this thesis, which as a project has become my life by now, would not have been possible without the tremendous help and support from family members, friends, colleagues, supervisors, and several institutions, which I would like to thank in the following.

However, apart from all academic and professional work, I first want to mention the ones who helped me achieve this milestone on the most personal level, and without whom I would have never been able to make this happen. Especially, first and foremost, Bruno und Gilla, my grandparents and biggest idols. I especially want to thank my parents Michael and Ute Spinde, who stood behind me even in times when they struggled themselves. As much of a thank you goes out to my closest friends Fabi, Hansi, Sebastian, Sonja, Lukas, Jule, Lahevet, Rob, Laura, Anna, Karin, Julian, Angelika, Maria, and Andreas. I couldn't live without you. Even more, a massive thank you is in order for my media bias crew, who are the only thing making me give everything for the project: This goes out to Kanishka, Lada, Smi, Christoph, Annki, Anna, Martin, Jerome Wa, Jerome Wü, Fabi, Fabian (Haak), Lisa, Kathrin, Manu, David, Magda, Christin, and all other students I supervised. A special shoutout to Tomáš Horych, who made this entire journey just a bit more beautiful living next to me, and a big thank you to Caro, Anuschka, and Nicole, fighting in Konstanz, just as Sandra in Hattingen, to have my back. Also a big thank you to my big sister Verena, and a huge sorry for always being so occupied.

Apart from this project being so emotional for me, I would have never been able to finish it without the most professional and reliable backup: My first sincere wishes go to my prodigious doctoral advisers Bela Gipp and Michael Granitzer. Their continuous support and counsel enabled me to realize this thesis at marvelous places and together with numerous wonderful people from all over the world. Their enduring encouragement and assistance, Bela's strong optimism and creativity, and Michael's experience and always open ear. Without their guidance and inspiration, none of this would have ever been possible, and I will never forget all the doors they have opened for me.

Moreover, I am very grateful to my adviser and friend Terry Ruas: You are an absolute rockstar to me, and without your backup, I would also have not been able to pull it off. The same applies to Helge Giese and countless hours of statistical instructions. A special contribution goes out to Akiko Aizawa and Isao Echizen, who said yes to inviting me and my team to the NII in Tokyo, making a dream come true. I also want to name Anastasia Zhukova and her constant moral support, Norman Meuschke, who is the best proofreader on this planet. Even more, other professors supported me along the way, and I am forever grateful for the trust that you were willing to give for a young student: Philipp Schaer, Jelena Mitrović, Thomas Nygren, Karsten Donnay, Wolfgang Gaissmaier, Juhi Kulshrestha, Marc Erich Latoschik, Steffi Hußlein, and Franz Götz-Hahn. A special thank you and an apology are directed to Felix Hamborg. I also want to highlight Christina Elmer: Not only for your support but also for inspiring me to work on media bias in the first place.

I especially thank the one institution that really changed my life, and which I will pay back as much as I can, and as long as I live: The Hanns-Seidel-Foundation not only helped me out with funding, but it gave me the confidence to pursue my goals. A big thank you to Isabel Küfer, Andreas Burtscheidt, and Hanns-Peter Niedermeier. I am forever grateful for the support that Germany invests in young careers through the DAAD, which made going to Japan possible for me and even for students going with me. I will always keep that in mind in future career choices, and the experience has had a major impact on me.

For all the seminars and fruitful exchanges I thank Jo and Florian, as much as for the person who introduced me to the right way to work and followed me through all my endeavors: Verena Angerer. I finally want to thank the University of Konstanz, the University of Passau, the University of Wuppertal, and the University of Göttingen. The same applies to the National Institute of Informatics in Tokyo, the University of Haifa, and the Technion in Haifa. Lastly, I also want to thank all my friends for giving me feedback on my music, which kept me sane throughout the process and resulted in *Rainbows*, my debut album, portraying my emotional journey.

I dedicate this thesis to my lovely parents, my dear friends, and Bruno and Gilla.

Abstract

Ever since language has existed, the choice of words to express content influenced its perception. With the introduction of first written, then printed, and finally digital media, the quantity and impact of word choice increased, and, especially with digital media, also the possibilities to analyze language. Country, culture, background, and topics have a large impact on how any content can be depicted. Therefore, language is a complex entity. Among many other things, this leads to media bias research, especially in an automated form, to tackle the challenges of scalability in a world of strongly increasing availability of digital information. However, the research is still in an early stage. This thesis aims to take the next step within media bias research and specifically addresses the issue of automatically identifying media bias, especially media bias by word choice.

While media bias might be one of the topics most requiring interdisciplinarity, existing work usually only focuses on one perspective, creating classifications that are in some way only focussing on parts of the problem—and therefore being biased themselves. This is even more surprising since many different disciplines cover the topic: Bias research exists in areas such as linguistics, psychology, economics, social science, and computer science. Concepts and definitions in the different areas often overlap and are not organized in a structured way. Even more, concerning especially computer scientific research, the automatic identification of bias by word choice is challenging, primarily due to the lack of gold-standard data sets and high context dependencies.

To address the lack of reliable and comprehensive media bias analysis tools, this thesis makes the following five contributions. First, it provides the first large-scale literature overview of media bias research, introducing the media bias framework. In a systematic approach, we filtered and organized over 100.000 papers to define which concepts are targeted in the domain overall and to clarify how they overlap and relate to each other. This way, we set a common ground for future research on media bias.

Second, this thesis presents a standardized question set to assess media bias perception, to enhance evaluating future approaches. The perception of bias varies largely depending on a reader's personal background. Even though media bias has been the subject of many studies, previous assessment strategies are oversimplified and lack overlap and empirical evaluation. Without a profound evaluation, improving systems and understanding results is difficult. We condense over 824 questions into 25 final items and validate them empirically.

Third, we provide MBIC (Media Bias Including Characteristics) and BABE (Bias Annotations By Experts), two major media bias datasets. MBIC contains 1.700 sentences annotated for media bias both on the word and sentence level by crowdsource workers. MBIC is the first available dataset about media bias reporting detailed information on annotator characteristics and their individual background. BABE is a robust and diverse gold standard data set created by trained experts for media bias research. Comparing MBIC and BABE allows us to show why expert labeling is essential within this domain. BABE offers better annotation quality and higher inter-annotator agreement than existing work. It consists of 3,700 sentences balanced among topics and outlets, also containing media bias labels on the word and sentence level.

Fourth, based on our data, we also introduce a featured-based as well as two deep-learning approaches to detect bias in news articles automatically. For the feature-based approach, we identify and engineer various linguistic, lexical, and syntactic features that can potentially be media bias indicators and use them for training a classifier. We evaluate all of our features in various combinations and retrieve their possible importance both for future research and for the task in general. The first of our deep-learning approaches is a BERT-based model pre-trained on a larger corpus consisting of distant labels, achieving a macro F_1-score of 0.804 on BABE. Our second deep-learning approach, MAGPIE, is based on multi-task learning, incorporating many bias-related concepts into the approach. MAGPIE outperforms previous approaches in media bias detection on the BABE dataset, with a relative improvement of 3.3% F1-score. MAGPIE also performs better than previous models on 5 out of 8 tasks in the Media Bias Identification Benchmark (MBIB).

Lastly, the thesis opens up the wide field of how research about automated media bias detection could be used to support news reading and general decision-making processes. Effective communication that may counteract the potential negative effects of media bias still needs to be developed. We analyze how to facilitate the detection of media bias with visual and textual aids in the form of (a) a forewarning message, (b) text annotations, and (c) political classifiers. We also investigate how well automated classifications and expert bias ratings can help readers understand and perceive bias in greater detail. Finally, we take an outlook into the perception of bias from a different side, by analyzing whether or not biased news articles cause stronger reactions on social media.

Long-term, our vision is to devise a system that helps news readers become aware of media coverage differences caused by bias.

Zusammenfassung

Seit Sprache existiert, beeinflusst die Wortwahl zur Darstellung von Inhalten deren Wahrnehmung. Mit der Einführung von zuerst geschriebenen, dann gedruckten und schließlich digitalen Medien hat sich die Menge und Wirkung der Wortwahl erhöht und insbesondere bei digitalen Medien auch die Möglichkeiten zur Sprachanalyse erweitert. Land, Kultur, Grammatik, persönlicher Hintergrund und Themen haben großen Einfluss darauf, wie Inhalte dargestellt werden können, und machen Sprache zu einem komplexen Konstrukt. Unter anderem führt dies zur Forschung über Media Bias, insbesondere in automatisierter Form, um die Herausforderungen der Skalierbarkeit in einer Welt mit stark zunehmender Verfügbarkeit von digitalen Informationen anzugehen. Die Forschung befindet sich jedoch noch in einem frühen Stadium. Diese Dissertation zielt darauf ab, den nächsten Schritt in der Forschung zu Media Bias zu nehmen und sich insbesondere mit der automatischen Identifizierung von Media Bias, insbesondere von Media Bias durch Wortwahl, zu befassen.

Obwohl Media Bias ein stark interdisziplinäres Thema ist, konzentrieren sich bestehende Arbeiten meist nur auf eine Perspektive und erstellen Klassifikationen, die in gewisser Weise nur Teile des Problems fokussieren – und daher selbst voreingenommen sind. Dies ist umso überraschender, da viele verschiedene Disziplinen das Thema abdecken: Forschung zu Bias existiert in Bereichen wie Linguistik, Psychologie, Wirtschaftswissenschaften, Sozialwissenschaften und Informatik. Konzepte und Definitionen in den verschiedenen Bereichen überlappen oft und sind nicht strukturiert organisiert. Besonders hinsichtlich der computergestützten Forschung ist die automatische Identifizierung von Bias durch Wortwahl eine Herausforderung, hauptsächlich aufgrund des Fehlens von hochwertigen Datensätzen und aufgrund hoher Kontextabhängigkeiten.

Um den Mangel an zuverlässigen und umfassenden Tools zur Analyse von Media Bias zu beheben, leistet diese Dissertation die folgenden fünf Beiträge. Erstens bietet sie den ersten großangelegten Literaturüberblick über die Media Bias Forschung und führt das Media Bias-Framework ein. In einem systematischen Ansatz haben wir über 100.000 Artikel gefiltert und organisiert, um zu definieren, welche Konzepte insgesamt im Bereich genutzt werden und wie sie sich überschneiden und aufeinander beziehen. Auf diese Weise legen wir eine gemeinsame Grundlage für zukünftige Forschungen über Media Bias.

Zweitens präsentiert diese Dissertation einen standardisierten Fragenkatalog zur Beurteilung der Wahrnehmung von Media Bias, um die Bewertung zukünftiger Ansätze zu verbessern. Die Wahrnehmung von Bias variiert stark je nach persönlichem Hintergrund des Lesers. Obwohl Media Bias Gegenstand vieler Studien war, sind frühere Bewertungsstrategien vereinfacht und es fehlt an Überschneidungen und empirischer Auswertung. Ohne eine gründliche Bewertung ist es schwierig, Systeme zu verbessern und Ergebnisse zu verstehen. Wir verdichten über 824 Fragen zu 25 endgültigen Punkten und validieren diese empirisch.

Drittens stellen wir MBIC (Media Bias Including Characteristics) und BABE (Bias Annotations By Experts), zwei wichtige Media Bias-Datensätze, zur Verfügung. MBIC enthält 1.700 Sätze, die von Crowdsourcing-Mitarbeitern sowohl auf Wort- als auch auf Satzebene auf Media Bias hin annotiert wurden. MBIC ist der erste verfügbare Datensatz über Media Bias, der detaillierte Informationen über die Merkmale der Annotatoren und ihren individuellen Hintergrund berichtet. BABE ist ein robuster und vielfältiger Datensatz, der von ausgebildeten Experten für die Media Bias-Forschung erstellt wurde. Ein Vergleich von MBIC und BABE ermöglicht es uns zu zeigen, warum die Experten-Kennzeichnung in diesem Bereich unerlässlich ist. BABE bietet eine bessere Annotierungsqualität und höhere Übereinstimmung zwischen den Annotatoren als bestehende Arbeiten. Es besteht aus 3.700 Sätzen, die unter Themen und Outlets ausgewogen sind und ebenfalls Media Bias-Labels auf Wort- und Satzebene enthalten.

Viertens stellen wir auf Basis unserer Daten sowohl einen Feature-basierten als auch zwei Deep-Learning-Ansätze zur automatischen Erkennung von Bias in Nachrichtenartikeln vor. Für den feature-basierten Ansatz identifizieren und entwickeln wir verschiedene linguistische, lexikalische und syntaktische Merkmale, die potenziell Media Bias-Indikatoren sein können und verwenden sie zur Schulung eines Klassifikators. Wir bewerten alle unsere Merkmale in verschiedenen Kombinationen und ermitteln ihre mögliche Bedeutung sowohl für die zukünftige Forschung als auch für die Aufgabe im Allgemeinen. Der erste unserer

Zusammenfassung

Deep-Learning-Ansätze ist ein BERT-basiertes Modell, das auf einem größeren Korpus vorab trainiert wurde, bestehend aus entfernten Labels, und erreicht einen makro F_1-Score von 0,804 auf BABE. Unser zweiter Deep-Learning-Ansatz, MAGPIE, basiert auf Multi-Task-Learning, indem er viele Bias-bezogene Konzepte in den Ansatz einbezieht. MAGPIE übertrifft die vorherigen Systeme bei der Erkennung von Bias im BABE-Datensatz einem relativ 3,3% höheren F1-Score. MAGPIE schneidet auch bei 5 von 8 Aufgaben im Media Bias Identification Benchmark (MBIB) besser ab als frühere Modelle und ist damit deutlich diverser als die bestehenden Single-Task Ansätze.

Letztlich öffnet die Dissertation das weite Feld, wie die Forschung über automatisierte Media Bias-Erkennung zur Unterstützung des Nachrichtenlesens und allgemeiner Entscheidungsprozesse genutzt werden könnte. Eine effektive Kommunikation, die die potenziellen negativen Auswirkungen von Media Bias ausgleichen könnte, muss noch entwickelt werden. Wir analysieren, wie die Erkennung von Media Bias mit visuellen und textuellen Hilfsmitteln in Form von (a) einer Vorwarnmeldung, (b) Textannotationen und (c) politischen Klassifikatoren erleichtert werden kann. Wir untersuchen auch, wie gut automatisierte Klassifikationen und Experten-Bewertungen von Bias den Lesern helfen können, Bias detaillierter zu verstehen und wahrzunehmen. Schließlich werfen wir einen Blick auf die Wahrnehmung von Bias von einer anderen Seite, indem wir analysieren, ob Nachrichtenartikel mit Bias stärkere Reaktionen in sozialen Medien hervorrufen.

Langfristig ist unsere Vision, ein System zu entwickeln, das Nachrichtenleser dabei unterstützt, sich der durch Bias verursachten Unterschiede in der Medienberichterstattung bewusst zu werden.

Contents

1 **Introduction** 1
   1.1 Problem 2
   1.2 Research Gap 8
   1.3 Research Objective 10
   1.4 Thesis Outline 10
   1.5 Prior Publications 12
   1.6 Research Path 12
      1.6.1 Preliminary Work 13
      1.6.2 Media Bias Detection—Core Work 19
      1.6.3 Perception and Visualization 25

2 **Media Bias** 29
   2.1 Introduction 29
   2.2 Methodology 32
      2.2.1 Retrieving Candidate Documents 33
      2.2.2 Candidate Selection 34
      2.2.3 Finding Additional Conceptual Literature
            for the Media Bias Taxonomy 34
   2.3 Related Literature Reviews 36
   2.4 Related Work and Theoretical Embedding 37
      2.4.1 Media Bias 37
      2.4.2 The Media Bias Taxonomy 38
   2.5 Computer Science Research on Media Bias 43
      2.5.1 Traditional Natural Language Processing Techniques ... 45
      2.5.2 Machine Learning 48
      2.5.3 Graph-Based 54

		2.5.4	Bias in Language Models	56
		2.5.5	Datasets	57
	2.6	Human-Centered Research on Media Bias		58
		2.6.1	Reasons for Biased Media Perception	58
		2.6.2	Consequences of Biased Media Perception	59
		2.6.3	Recipient-Oriented Approaches to Reduce Media Bias	60
	2.7	Discussion		62
	2.8	Conclusion		64
3	**Questionnaire Development**			**67**
	3.1	Overview of Approaches		68
	3.2	Literature Collection		70
		3.2.1	Item Collection and Selection	70
		3.2.2	Design	73
		3.2.3	Survey Participants	73
		3.2.4	Article Selection	74
		3.2.5	Measures	75
		3.2.6	Exploratory Factor Analysis	75
	3.3	Analysis & Results		76
		3.3.1	Factor Analysis	76
		3.3.2	Validation	78
	3.4	Discussion		79
	3.5	Conclusion		81
4	**Dataset Creation**			**83**
	4.1	Overview		84
	4.2	MBIC		85
		4.2.1	Dataset Creation	85
		4.2.2	System Setup	86
		4.2.3	Study Execution	90
		4.2.4	Evaluation	92
		4.2.5	Results	94
		4.2.6	Conclusion	95
	4.3	Expert Dataset Creation		96
		4.3.1	Definition of Experts	97
		4.3.2	Dataset Creation	97
		4.3.3	Training Phase	98
		4.3.4	Study Execution	99
		4.3.5	Evaluation	100
		4.3.6	Conclusion	103

5	**Feature-based Media Bias Detection**		105
	5.1 Related Work		106
		5.1.1 Workflow Overview	107
		5.1.2 Biased Words Lexicon Creation	108
		5.1.3 Detection Methodology	110
		5.1.4 Feature Engineering	111
		5.1.5 Evaluation	113
	5.2 Experiments		114
		5.2.1 Lexicon of Biased Words	114
		5.2.2 Detection of Biased Words	116
	5.3 Conclusion		121
6	**Neural Media Bias Detection**		123
	6.1 Neural Classification With Distant Supervision		124
		6.1.1 Methodology	125
		6.1.2 Experiments	127
		6.1.3 Results	128
	6.2 Domain-Adaptive Pre-Training		129
		6.2.1 Related Work	130
		6.2.2 Domain-Adaptive Pre-Training Approaches	131
		6.2.3 Methodology	132
		6.2.4 Experiments	134
	6.3 Multi Task Learning		137
		6.3.1 Methodology	138
		6.3.2 Experiments	140
		6.3.3 Results and Discussion	142
7	**Visualization and Perception of Media Bias**		145
	7.1 Theoretical Background		146
	7.2 Survey A: Visualization Comparison		147
		7.2.1 Study Setup	148
		7.2.2 Results	150
		7.2.3 Conclusion	152
	7.3 Survey B: Automated Classification Assessment		153
		7.3.1 Study Setup	157
		7.3.2 Results	160
		7.3.3 Discussion	164
		7.3.4 Conclusion	166
	7.4 Twitter Comments and News Article Bias		166
		7.4.1 Research Gap	167
		7.4.2 Research Question and Hypotheses	168

	7.4.3	Methodology	169
	7.4.4	Results	177
	7.4.5	Discussion & Future Work	189
	7.4.6	Conclusion	192

8 Conclusion and Future Work ... 193
8.1 Summary ... 193
8.2 Contributions of the Thesis ... 199
8.3 Future Work ... 203
    8.3.1 Future Dataset and Task Developments ... 203
    8.3.2 Future Language Modeling Experiments ... 205
    8.3.3 Future Experiments on Visualization ... 206
    8.3.4 Ethical Implications ... 208

Glossary ... 211

Bibliography of Publications, Submissions & Talks ... 213

Bibliography ... 216

List of Figures

Fig. 1.1	Different images portraying the same event. Images by Jewel Samad/Getty	4
Fig. 2.1	Number of publications at each step of the literature retrieval and review of computer science publications	34
Fig. 2.2	Number of publications at each step of the literature retrieval and review for the Media Bias Taxonomy	35
Fig. 2.3	The Media Bias Taxonomy. The four subcategories of media bias consist of different bias types	39
Fig. 2.4	Classification of computer science methods for media bias detection we use in our analysis	44
Fig. 3.1	Item reduction process in four main phases	72
Fig. 3.2	Screeplot showing the number of factors	79
Fig. 4.1	Survey question requiring text annotation	89
Fig. 4.2	Example of a numeric input in TASSY	90
Fig. 4.3	Example of a slider input in TASSY	90
Fig. 4.4	Example of an extensible multi-select input in TASSY	91
Fig. 4.5	Differences in inter-coder agreement between annotators with different political ideology	93
Fig. 4.6	Data collection and annotation pipeline	98
Fig. 5.1	Workflow for the feature based automated identification of bias	108
Fig. 5.2	Pipeline for building bias lexicon semi-automatically	110

Fig. 5.3	Random sample of the semi-automatically extended dictionary of biased words	115
Fig. 6.1	Pipeline for building bias lexicon semi-automatically	132
Fig. 6.2	Outline of in-domain MTL model consisting of a shared encoder block and task-specific layers	140
Fig. 7.1	Excerpt from the news overview page	149
Fig. 7.2	Excerpt from one article with visually highlighted annotations of biased language	150
Fig. 7.3	Perceived level of political extremeness, fair perspective, and impartiality (each in one row) on a scale from 1 (least) to 5 (most), comparing the visualizations with the control group (columns). Red: C1, Green: C2, Blue: C3	152
Fig. 7.4	Example of the bias annotation "subjective term". Boxed annotation appeared by moving the cursor/finger over the highlighted text section	155
Fig. 7.5	Example of an article classification as being politically left-oriented	155
Fig. 7.6	Across all conditions, liberal articles were perceived to be more liberal and conservative articles more conservative. The interventions increased the differences between the two ratings. Dots represent means, and lines are standard deviations	161
Fig. 7.7	The forewarning message, as well as annotations, increased media bias awareness. Dots represent means, and lines are standard deviations	162
Fig. 7.8	Bias awareness increases when the article is not aligned with the persons' political position. Shades show 95% confidence intervals of the regression estimation	163
Fig. 7.9	Analysis pipeline used in the study	171
Fig. 7.10	The distribution of the articles' political bias scores (Fig. 7.10a) and reliability scores (Fig. 7.10b). The data was z-normalized, and the optimal number of bins (here: 28) was estimated by Rice's Rule	178

Fig. 7.11	The distribution of the articles' political bias scores (Fig. 7.11a) and reliability scores (Fig. 7.11b). The data was z-normalized, and the optimal number of bins (here: 28) was estimated by Rice's Rule	178
Fig. 7.12	Political bias vs. reliability for (a) articles and (b) outlets ...	179
Fig. 7.13	The distribution of the articles' (a) political bias scores and (b) reliability scores	180
Fig. 7.14	The distribution of the outlets' (a) political bias scores and (b) reliability scores	180

List of Tables

Table 1.1	Overview of the primary publications in this thesis	13
Table 1.2	Overview of the secondary publications in this thesis	14
Table 2.1	Results of the literature study on computer science methods used for media bias detection	44
Table 2.2	Overview of datasets found during our literature review	57
Table 3.1	Reliabilities of the final scales built for each factor and their correlations	77
Table 4.1	Widely used text annotation and survey tools	88
Table 4.2	The characteristics of the words annotated as biased	94
Table 4.3	Annotation results for the expert-annotated (SG1) and crowdsourced (MBIC) approach based on 1,700 sentences	101
Table 4.4	Class distribution for SG1's and MBIC's 1700 sentences	101
Table 4.5	Dataset annotation results for the expert-based approaches (left: eight annotators labeling 1,700 sentences (SG1); right: five annotators labeling 3,700 sentences (SG2))	102
Table 4.6	Dataset class distribution for the expert-based approaches (left: eight annotators labeling 1,700 sentences (SG1); right: five annotators labeling 3,700 sentences (SG2))	102
Table 5.1	Hyper-parameters for training word embeddings on HuffPost and Breitbart	111

Table 5.2	The complete set of features used in our approach for detecting biased words	112
Table 5.3	Characteristics and evaluation results of word embedding models	114
Table 5.4	Comparing the method of batches and the naive approach	116
Table 5.5	Performance of algorithms for bias word detection	117
Table 5.6	Excerpt of models and their performance	118
Table 6.1	Stratified 5-fold cross-validation results	128
Table 6.2	Stratified 5-fold cross-validation results	136
Table 6.3	Results of the McNemar test for statistical significance between baseline	137
Table 6.4	Auxiliary data sets incorporated in the MTL models ($n =$ number of instances)	139
Table 6.5	Results for all baseline models, i.e., the *huggingface* model or models obtained by TL, as well as the models trained using MTL considering only in-domain data sets or also incorporating cross-domain data. For each metric we have denoted the best performance in bold	143
Table 7.1	Participant-related variables presumed to influence bias perception	148
Table 7.2	Hyperparameters defined for the fine-tuning procedures for both sentiment and hate classification	173
Table 7.3	Results from the classification report obtained by fine-tuning XLNet for sentiment analysis (90% confidence intervals in brackets)	174
Table 7.4	Results from the classification report obtained by fine-tuning XLNet for hate speech detection (90% confidence intervals in brackets)	175
Table 7.5	Examples of how the fine-tuned XLNet_Sentiment classifies text into positive or negative sentiment. As described in subsubsection 7.4.3.3, the tweet text has been cleaned for a better text understanding	181
Table 7.6	Examples of how the fine-tuned XLNet_Hate classifies text into hate or non-hate. As described in subsubsection 7.4.3.3, the tweet text has been cleaned for a better text understanding	182

Table 7.7	Confusion Matrix showing the differences between manually annotated and XLNet_Hate's labels	183
Table 7.8	Description of the parameters in Equation 7.2	184
Table 7.9	Results for Level-1 and Level-2 Effects	185
Table 7.10	Results for Interaction Effects	188

Introduction 1

The court of public opinion moves much faster than the law.

T.E. Carter—*I Stop Somewhere*

This thesis addresses the issue of automatically identifying media bias, mostly linguistic bias (See Definition 1.1), in news articles[1]. A varying word choice in any news content may have a major effect on the public and individual perception of societal issues, especially since regular news consumers are mostly unaware of the degree and scope of bias. Detecting and highlighting media bias is generally a challenging task since it is context-dependent, can be expressed in many ways, and its perception even differs based on personal perception and background. To date, only a few research projects focus on media bias as a whole. In this work, I create a common ground for future bias research by giving and concluding an in-depth literature overview, creating new media bias datasets, providing state-of-the-art automated classification systems, and showing ways to evaluate bias detection systems reliably. Lastly, I look into possible applications and visualizations, making bias accessible in more day-to-day scenarios. In this chapter, I provide an introduction to the topic. **Section** 1.1 introduces my motivation and provides an overview of the problem. **Section** 1.2 summarizes the research gap. In Sect. 1.3, I define this thesis's

---

[1] Parts of the thesis were proofread with EditGPT and Grammarly, without adapting major changes.

Supplementary Information The online version contains supplementary material available at https://doi.org/10.1007/978-3-658-47798-1_1.

© The Author(s) 2025
T. Spinde, *Automated Detection of Media Bias*,
https://doi.org/10.1007/978-3-658-47798-1_1

research objective and tasks. **Section** 1.4 shows an outline of the thesis, including an overview of the publications that contributed to the goals of this thesis. Finally, **Sect.** 1.6 concludes with the research path that led to these publications.

> **Definition 1.1: Linguistic Bias**
> Linguistic bias, also known as lexical bias [139], is defined as "a systematic asymmetry in word choice that reflects the social-category cognition that is applied to the described group or individual(s)" [60]. In other words, biases of this type are introduced using lexical features such as word choice and sentence structure [60]. Linguistic bias can be subdivided into multiple concepts, which are detailed in Chap. 2.

1.1 Problem

News articles in online newspapers are considered a crucial information source that replaces traditional media like television, radio broadcasts, and print media (e.g., newspapers, magazines) [108]. Many people consider news articles a reliable source of information about current events [181]. However, these news outlets are also often biased [412]. Various reasons exist for media bias, e.g., the political and ideological view of any news producer or news outlet owner [181]. Another common reason for media bias is that opinion-based, entertaining, and sensationalist content are likely to reach a larger audience while being less expensive to produce [39, 88, 278]. While media outlets might tend to have a higher likelihood of a certain kind of bias, the bias permanently appears in everyday human communication. It usually depicts how someone perceives any given topic [412].

Depending on which words journalists select to describe an event, inflammatory or neutral, a reader can perceive the information differently. In turn, an author can manipulate a reader's perception by implying a particular opinion or perspective or inducing positive or negative emotions. The following two examples present instances of linguistic bias, respectively. In the first example, the author chooses the vaguer word "pro-life" to describe the very concrete "anti-abortion" position as positive. In the second example, labeling the coronavirus pandemic as "Chinese" implies China's fault in the pandemic.

1.1 Problem

1. Practicing **pro-life** litigators know that Trump judges are saving lives by permitting restrictions on abortion to go into effect.[2]
2. Tens of millions of children under 12 months are potentially at risk for diseases such as diphtheria and polio as the **Chinese** coronavirus pandemic interrupts routine vaccinations, according to data published by global public health experts on Friday.[3]

The following headlines exemplify how drastically the wording of news reports on the same event can differ:

1. Welcome to Germany! Thousands of refugees from Hungary will arrive in Munich [4]
2. Refugees are distributed all over Germany [5]
3. Islam invades Germany [6]

The complexity of bias can increase, for example, by visual features [207]. Among other things, pictures in news articles can affect bias in several ways. First, the selection of pictures can be biased. For example, an article about a protest may include pictures that depict only the most violent or disruptive participants, creating a biased impression of the event. Second, the captioning or placement of pictures can also be biased [207]. For example, an article about a political candidate may include a picture of the candidate in a flattering pose or surrounded by supporters. In contrast, a picture of their opponent may be unflattering or depict them alone [70]. Pictures can also be edited or manipulated to alter their meaning or support a biased narrative [70]. Two pictures can depict the same issue in different ways by showing different perspectives, angles, and emotions. For example, one picture may use vivid and emotive imagery to elicit strong emotional responses, while another may use more neutral and objective imagery to present the issue in a more factual manner. An example is given in Fig. 1.1.

---

[2] https://thefederalist.com/2020/04/24/david-french-needs-to-stop-slandering-trump-supporting-christians, accessed on 2020-10-31.

[3] https://www.breitbart.com/health/2020/05/22/report-over-80-million-children-at-risk-as-coronavirus-disrupts-vaccination-schedules/, accessed on 2020-10-31.

[4] https://www.bild.de/regional/muenchen/fluechtling/kommen-aus-ungarn-am-bahnhof-an-42466626.bild.html, accessed 2022-03-25

[5] https://www.zeit.de/politik/ausland/2015-09/ungarn-fluechtlinge-oesterreich-einreise?page=54, accessed 2022-03-25

[6] http://www.pi-news.net/2015/09/islam-invasion-nach-deutschland, accessed 2022-03-25

Fig. 1.1 Different images portraying the same event. Images by Jewel Samad/Getty

> **Problem A:** Media bias impacts decision-making but can be both complex and subtle, making it often hard to identify.

Media bias is widely recognized as having a potent influence on public perception of reported topics [108, 257]. It exacerbates the issue known as the filter bubble or echo chamber effect [14], where readers tend to consume news that aligns with their existing beliefs, views, or personal preferences [255, 257]. This behavior can lead to limited awareness of specific issues, a narrowed, one-sided perspective [10], and can even affect voting behavior [114, 124, 158, 395]. While completely eliminating bias might be an unrealistic goal, drawing attention to its existence by informing readers that content is biased allows them to compare content easily. Similarly, it could enable journalists and publishers to assess their work objectively [108]. In the following, I list some systems designed to help readers mitigate the effects of media bias on their decision-making. Most of them focus on aggregating articles about the same event from various news sources to provide different perspectives [257]. For example, news aggregators like Allsides[7] and Ground News[8] allow readers to compare articles on the same topic from media outlets known to have different political views. Various media bias charts, such as the Allsides media bias chart[9] or the Ad Fontes media bias chart[10] provide up-to-date information on media outlets' political slants. However, it is uncertain whether readers have the possibility and, more importantly, the desire to read several articles on the same topic and compare them.

---

[7] https://www.allsides.com
[8] https://ground.news
[9] https://www.allsides.com/media-bias/media-bias-chart
[10] https://www.adfontesmedia.com/

1.1 Problem

Media bias has recently experienced an increase in interdisciplinary research and, especially, in automated methods to identify bias. Still, as a concept and research area, media bias is only loosely defined in the literature [181]. Different subcategories and types of bias are used in existing work [15, 341], but authors often focus on one media bias subcategory while disregarding similar kinds of bias concepts. Publications on media bias usually work on similar concepts but assign different names to them. For example, some authors call word-based bias linguistic bias [341], and others call it bias by word choice [21], but the exact difference or overlap is undefined. Consequently, promising methods in the related areas are not found or adapted due to a missing framework of media bias as an area itself. Recent advances in Deep Learning show how using multiple inter- and cross-domain datasets and tasks exhibit potential for significant performance increases [37], but have not been incorporated for media bias research. Even more, specifically for media bias research, Spinde et al. [15] highlights the importance of interdisciplinary work by accounting for psychological effects and personal background when performing studies about media bias.

Problem B: No full overview of media bias concepts or detection methods exists, resolving in reduced efficiency and success of media bias projects.

Apart from a missing overview of concepts within the media bias domain, the reliable measurement of media bias poses another problem. Recent computer scientific research aiming to build automated media bias detection systems report that building a high-quality bias data set is difficult because readers struggle to agree on biased text documents [22], [21]. As briefly mentioned above, many individual factors affect the perception of bias, such as topic knowledge, political ideology, or simply age and education [22]. Phenomena like the Hostile Media Effect (HME, describing the tendency to perceive media coverage of an issue as biased against one's views [173]) might also play a role, making it hard to objectively determine whether and how an article or clip is biased. Various definitions and methods are used to measure media bias throughout the different studies on media bias perception and identification. Still, there is a major lack of agreement about how study participants or readers react toward bias depending on how they were asked. Most existing studies focus only on specific aspects, for example, the already mentioned HME [222, 246]. Some studies ask questions related to particular articles [171], while others choose a more general approach [162]. Some ask about bias directly (e.g., "Regarding the web page that you viewed, would you say the portrayal of the presidential candidates was strictly neutral or biased in favor of one side or the other?" [195]), and some indirectly [10–12] (e.g., "How likely is it that you would read a news story by the same author again?" [303]). Some researchers try experiments [104], while others use surveys [162]. While there is some overlap in questions across multiple studies (for example, questions similar to "Would you say that the content in this article was strictly neutral, or was it biased in favor of one side or the other?" [172] were used in different studies [195, 225, 277]), there is a large variety in methods and definitions used in prior research that limits studies' comparability on media bias perception. Furthermore, a standard of assessing media bias of articles as a general construct is essential to train automated classifiers or build data sets: Without a precise measurement of the construct, no classifier in the related areas can reach its full potential[11].

> **Problem C:** No standardized evaluation of questions to access media bias perception exists, making it difficult to evaluate survey, dataset and classification quality in detail.

Even though bias embodies a complex structure, contributions often neglect the annotator background and use crowdsourcing to collect annotations [18, 21]. Existing data sets exhibit low annotator agreement and inferior quality. Therefore, one of the challenges in the automated detection of media bias is the lack of a gold standard large-scale data set with labeled media bias instances. The existing data sets[12] either do not allow for the analysis of media bias on the word level or can induce drawbacks due to the following limitations:

1. A small number of topics [256, 257].
2. No annotations on the word level [257].
3. Low inter-annotator agreement [21, 55, 256, 257].
4. No background check for its participants [55, 139, 256, 257].
5. Some related papers focus on framing rather than on bias [55, 139], and results are only partially transferable.

---

[11] Additionally, the same even applies for datasets or surveys executed in research outside of computer science, which equally lacks a standardized measurement of media bias perception.
[12] I will give a detailed overview about existing datasets in Chap. 4.

1.1 Problem

Two central problems exist concerning datasets: firstly, the available datasets largely lack high-quality bias annotations. Secondly, there is no comprehensive overview of these datasets, making their in-depth analysis and utilization a challenging task.

> **Problem D:** No full overview of media bias datasets exists. Also, available datasets do not offer sufficient quality by seldom containing a reliable inter-annotator agreement and not checking the personal background of annotators.

The linguistic subtlety of slanted news coverage is known to be a tremendous challenge for automated classification methods [18]. Still, several studies tackle the automated detection of media bias (e.g., [12, 92, 200]). They usually focus on sentence-level bias, describing it as the lowest meaningful level that can be aggregated to higher levels, like the document level. Most of them use manually created features to detect bias [200], and are based on traditional machine learning models [22]. I will give a detailed overview of existing models and approaches in Chap. 5 and Chap. 6, but to summarize, most approaches use manually created features, leading to lower performance and poor representation but higher explainability. The few existing contributions on neural models are based on naive data sets (cf. Chap. 4). The Transformer architecture [390] has shown superior performance in several downstream tasks, such as text classification [309], plagiarism detection [397], word sense disambiguation [398] and fake news detection on the health domain [396]. However, the use of neural language models, such as BERT [116] and RoBERTa [265] in the media bias domain is still incipient [17, 18]. Even more, strategies to improve model performance even more, such as Multi-Task-Learning (MTL) [89, 413] or Distant Supervision (DS) [196] are equally not introduced and evaluated within the media bias domain.

> **Problem E:** Existing automated bias classification systems lack performance and new technological advancements.

The implications of selective exposure theory intensify the severity of biased news coverage: Researchers observed long ago that people prefer to consume information that fits their worldview and avoid information that challenges these beliefs [239]. By selecting only confirmatory information, one's opinion is reaffirmed, and there is no need to re-evaluate existing stances [217]. In this way, the unpleasant feeling of cognitive dissonance is avoided [144]. Isolation in one's own filter bubble or echo chamber confirms internal biases and might lead to a general decrease in the diversity of news consumption [377]. This decrease is further exacerbated by recent technological developments like personalized overview features of, e.g., personalized news aggregators [10]. At the same time, news consumers often engage with distorted media but exhibit a lack of media bias awareness [343]. To address this issue, revealing the existence and nature of media can be essential to attain media bias awareness and promote informed and reflective news consumption [10]. For instance, visualizations may generally help raise media bias awareness and lead to a more balanced news intake by warning people of potential biases [14], highlighting individual instances of bias [10], or facilitating the comparison of contents [296]. Although knowledge of how to communicate media bias effectively is crucial, visualizations and enhanced perception of media bias have only played a minor role in existing research, and several approaches yet need to be investigated. Still, to make the benefits of automated media bias detection accessible to more readers, evaluating how effectively different strategies promote media bias awareness is required. Theoretical foundations of bias messages and visualizations are yet scarce, and neither in visualization theory nor in bias theory, suitable strategies in the domain have been extensively tested.

Problem F: Visualizations of media bias have not been tested, and research on the perception of media bias is still in an early stage.

1.2 Research Gap

In total, I can sum up the following main problems within the domain. All problems are open gaps within media bias research.

1.2 Research Gap

A. General: Media bias impacts decision-making but can be both complex and subtle, making it often hard to identify.
B. Conceptualization: No full overview of media bias concepts as well as media bias detection methods exists, resolving in reduced efficiency and success of media bias projects.
C. Evaluation: No standardized evaluation of questions to access media bias perception exists, making it difficult to evaluate survey, dataset, and classification quality in detail.
D. Datasets: No full overview of media bias datasets exists. Also, available datasets do not offer sufficient quality by often not containing a reliable inter-annotator agreement and not checking the personal background of annotators.
E. Classification: Existing automated bias classification systems lack performance and new technological advancements.
F. Visualization: Visualizations of media bias have not been tested, and research on the perception of media bias is still in an early stage.

Overall, to solve the computer scientific challenges in the field, interdisciplinary research is required, and a good overview of the research domain is essential. In my first experiments[13], I just proceeded to build classifiers for linguistic bias, but as the projects progressed, I understood that a real step forward within this research domain can only be achieved by making sure reliable and valid forms of bias are detected, and that the datasets serving as a basis for each classifier are as reliable. Even more, during projects within my first year of being a doctoral researcher, I found out how important a complete overview of concepts and methods in the area is to make an educated choice about future system and algorithm design choices. In the course of my thesis work, I collaborated extensively with researchers from various disciplines to address the aforementioned issues. Our collective efforts aimed to deliver a system that provides a reliable solution, or at the very least, a significant advancement toward resolving Problem E. Identifying media bias, understanding the concepts, and showing humans all around the world what bias is and how critical reading works (which both very much relate to problem F), is a lifetime challenge and project, independent of all the efforts that already went into my work. During all descriptions and explanations within my thesis, especially in Chap. 8, I will give an outlook on what is to come.

---

[13] Mentioned in **Sect.** 1.6

1.3 Research Objective

This doctoral thesis aims to:

> **Research Objective**
> Develop and evaluate an automated classification system that reliably identifies occurrences of linguistic bias.

Further specifics about linguistic bias will be detailed in subsequent sections of the thesis, particularly in Chap. 2. To accomplish the research objective, I have delineated the following five research tasks. Each task corresponds to each problem identified in the previous section, starting with problem B, considering problem A outlines an overarching issue in the area that partially pertains to all other problems.

> **Research Tasks**
>
> I Create a full comprehensive overview of concepts and definitions, as well as computational methods, existing in the domain.
> II Develop a scale that can be used as a reliable standard to evaluate the perception of media bias.
> III Create media bias datasets that tackle the problems in existing datasets.
> IV Implement a reliable automated media bias classification system using technological advancements in language models.
> V Study how bias is perceived and how visualizations can improve a reader's bias awareness.

1.4 Thesis Outline

Chapter 1 generally introduces media bias, the problems/research gaps in the domain, and defines the research objectives and tasks this thesis addresses. Finally, it outlines the structure of the thesis and briefly summarizes the main publications.

1.4 Thesis Outline

Chapter 2 proceeds with a comprehensive overview of media bias, tailored to **Research Task I**. The chapter shows the results of a systematic literature review, which identified relevant research and was later used to outline a first media bias framework, connecting concepts and definitions within the research area. Additionally, the chapter gives an overview of the status of recent computer scientific work focusing on identifying various types of bias instances and on existing media bias datasets.

Chapter 3 first summarizes all research that includes questions about the perception of media bias, relating to **Research Task II**. Then, it shows how the questions were semantically merged and evaluated in a study to finally present and publish a scale that can be used as a reliable standard to evaluate the perception of media bias.

Chapter 4 introduces two major ways of gathering media bias datasets while tackling issues persistent in existing datasets. It shows the conceptualization of the new datasets, summarizes their creation process, and presents the two final datasets called MBIC and BABE. It focuses on **Research Task III**.

Chapter 5 is the first of two chapters that focus on automated media bias detection methods, as entailed by **Research Task IV**. It mainly describes the advantages of feature-based classification systems in the domain and introduces a new and improved feature-based classifier.

Chapter 6 is the second chapter focusing on automated classification within **Research Task IV**, and it evaluates the possibilities and advantages of transformer-based language models when identifying media bias. It mainly introduces multiple major systems that were implemented within the course of this thesis.

Chapter 7 presents research on the perception of media bias, depicted by **Research Task V**. It shows research on the effects of bias visualizations as well as a study connecting bias in news articles to their perception.

Chapter 8 concludes the thesis by summarizing contributions and their impact on the media bias domain. It further provides a brief overview of the remaining issues and future work.

Appendix E.2 provides additional information about certain aspects of this thesis, including extended tables of the literature review, links to repositories holding all related code and further information, and illustrations of future work projects.

1.5 Prior Publications

The publications included in this thesis have all been featured in international, peer-reviewed conferences and journals. Table 1.1 provides a summary of the publications that were used in the thesis, including the chapter they contributed to and the venue ranking. Rankings were obtained from the Core ranking[14] for conferences and the Scimago Journal Rank[15] for journal articles, using the year of publication or submission as reference. Table 1.2 includes publications that played a partial role in the thesis but were not featured in a specific chapter. Two of these publications [11, 12] were previously a part of the author's Master's thesis and served as a precursor for the doctoral thesis. The venue acronyms found in both tables are detailed in the glossary. The author's personal publications, speeches, and submissions are separated from the main bibliography in the back matter and can be found on Appendix **E.2**.

1.6 Research Path

In this section, I will delve into the details of my research journey that culminated in the creation of this thesis. Specifically, I will highlight the key publications and the underlying motivations for each, all marked with corresponding chapters and references. To aid in understanding, I have divided this research path into three distinct sections (ordered logically, not chronologically): Preliminary work, core publications concerning the automated detection of media bias, and research focusing on perception and visualization. In the subsequent parts of this thesis, I will use 'we' rather than 'I' since none of the presented contributions would have been possible without the tremendous and fruitful discussions and help from advisors, colleagues, students, and friends. I also want you / the reader to explore the topic with me. I will only refer to myself in case of specific relations to my past or personal decisions. Also, every paper is marked with the respective chapter where its content is shown in greater detail.

---

[14] http://portal.core.edu.au/conf-ranks/ with the ranks: A*—flagship conference (top 7%), A—excellent conference (top 16%), B—good conference (top 36%), and C—remaining conferences [accessed 2023-01-15].

[15] https://www.scimagojr.com/, with the ranks Q1–Q4 where Q1 refers to the best 25% of journals in the field, Q2 to the second best quarter, etc. [accessed 2023-01-15].

1.6.1 Preliminary Work

My first contact with the topic happened during my undergraduate studies. After one year of studying media and communications, I was looking for more of a challenge and searched for other study programs. I ended up pursuing two bachelor programs, media and communications and internet computing, and combined both issues within my bachelor thesis [9]. Briefly after, I heard a lecture by Christina Elmer, at the time working as a data journalist at the German magazine SPIEGEL, and became interested in combining computer science and journalism even more. Therefore, I studied data science during my master's studies and finally integrated both topics for the first time within my master thesis [24]. During the first half year of work on the issue, I understood how complex and difficult media bias can be. I became more intrigued to investigate opportunities in this area. I started my Ph.D., identified suitable partners to support my project, and started working on the issue.

Table 1.1 Overview of the primary publications in this thesis

Ch.	Venue	Year	Type	Length	Author Position	Venue Rating	Ref.
2	CSUR	2023	Journal	Full	1 of 7	SJR Q1	[13]
2	ICDM[a]	2021	Conference	Full	1 of 1	Core A*	[8]
3	JCDL	2021	Conference	Full	1 of 6	Core A*[c]	[15]
4	JCDL	2021	Conference	Poster	1 of 4	Core A*[c]	[16]
4	EMNLP[b]	2021	Conference	Full	1 of 6	Core A	[18]
4	iConference	2021	Conference	Short	1 of 6	n/a	[21]
4	iConference	2021	Conference	Short	1 of 4	n/a	[23]
5	IPM	2021	Journal	Full	1 of 6	SJR Q1	[22]
6	iConference	2021	Conference	Full	1 of 7	n/a	[17]
6	JCDL	2022	Conference	Full	2 of 5	Core A*[c]	[6]
7	JCDL	2020	Conference	Short	1 of 5	Core AA*[c]	[10]
7	PLOS ONE	2022	Journal	Full	1 of 5	SJR Q1	[14]
7	Online Social Networks and Media	2023	Journal	Full	1 of 4	SJR Q1	[19]

[a] Parts of this paper have been used within all other chapters.
[b] This paper contains both one of the major datasets as well as one of the main classification methodologies. It was used within chap. 4 and chap. 6.
[c] The JCDL was not rated again since 2018, but was A* before.

As I will detail below, my first year was signed by starting experiments to find my way into the research domain. Afterward, the experiments became more detailed and structured, and finally, within the fourth year, resulted in the current systems and status. I will continue my work on the topic and have started a small research network focusing on media bias. Future updates can therefore be found on https://media-bias-research.org/.

The first research I published on media bias directly related to the results and experiments I conducted in my master's thesis. Consequently, the following paper is my first publication:

Table 1.2 Overview of the secondary publications in this thesis

Year	Venue	Type	Length	Author Position	Venue Rating	Ref.
2020	JCDL	Conference	Poster	1 of 3	Core A*	[11]
2020	INRA	Workshop	Short	1 of 3	n/a	[12]
2021	ISI	Conference	Full	2 of 4	n/a	[1]
2021	iConference	Conference	Short	1 of 4	n/a	[20]
2021	INRA	Conference	Short	2 of 6	n/a	[12]
2023	SIGIR	Conference	Full	6 of 6	Core A*	[25]
2023	iConference	Conference	Short	3 of 5	n/a	[7]
2024	LREC	Conference	Full	9 of 9	Core B	[5]
2024	ICWSM	Conference	Full	6 of 6	Core A	[4]
2024	CHI PLAY	Conference	Full	2 of 5	n/a	[3]

[a] The JCDL was not rated again since 2018, but was A* before.

"An Integrated Approach to Detect Media Bias in German News Articles" by **Timo Spinde**, Felix Hamborg, and Bela Gipp. **In:** *Joint Conference on Digital Libraries* (JCDL), 2020.

Not used in this thesis—[12]

The poster proposes a work-in-progress approach to identify biased words in German news texts. We implemented three components and tested them in different combinations: an IDF-based component selecting terms based on their frequency, a dictionary-based component merging multiple sources of emotional and linguistic terms, and a bias word dictionary created using word embeddings. The second and third components combined yielded the best results with F_1 scores of 0.31 and 0.41 when only considering adjectives.

1.6 Research Path

Own contribution: I proposed the initial project idea, designed the methodology, conducted the experiments, and implemented all components. I analyzed the data, evaluated the performance of different component combinations, and achieved the reported F_1 scores. I also wrote the manuscript and prepared the poster presentation. All co-authors were involved only in editing and proofreading the final document.

With additional evaluations, we extended the poster into a short paper with the same focus, published a few months later:

> *"Media Bias in German News Articles: A Combined Approach"* by **Timo Spinde**, Felix Hamborg, and Bela Gipp. **In:** *Proceedings of the 8th International Workshop on News Recommendation and Analytics* (INRA), 2020.
> Not used in this thesis—[11]

These early-stage works are the only publications mentioned in this dissertation that do not focus on English texts. While they represent the first German media bias dataset, the collected dataset was too small (46 raters on three to nine news articles) and had additional issues, which we will detail in Chap. 4.

Own contribution: I extended the initial poster to a short paper with further evaluations, conducted additional experiments to validate the findings, and refined the methods. All co-authors were involved only in editing and proofreading the final document.

Besides early-stage media bias detection approaches, two different attempts to identify media bias are detailed below. Like the previous works, they do not play a significant role in this thesis but represent the foundational research for later projects.

> *"Omission of Information: Identifying Political Slant via an Analysis of Co-occurring Entities"* by Jonas Ehrhardt, **Timo Spinde**, Ali Vardasbi, and Felix Hamborg. **In:** *Information between Data and Knowledge* (ISI), 2021.
> Not used in this thesis—[1]

We present an approach that analyzes co-occurrences of entities across articles from different news outlets to detect bias by omission of information. We evaluate different methods of identifying entity co-occurrences and use the best-performing method, reference entity detection, to analyze the coverage of nine major US news outlets over one year. Our approach yields an F_1 score of 0.51 compared to 0.20 for the TF-IDF baseline.

Own contribution: I proposed the project idea, designed the methodology for analyzing co-occurrences of entities, supervised the reference entity detection method, and evaluated its performance against the TF-IDF baseline. I also supervised the data collection and co-authored the manuscript.

> *"Identification of Biased Terms in News Articles by Comparison of Outlet-specific Word Embeddings"* by **Timo Spinde**, Lada Rudnitckaia, Felix Hamborg, and Bela Gipp. **In:** *iConference* (iConf), 2021.
>
> Not used in this thesis—[20]

This paper presents an exploratory approach comparing the context of related words. We train two word embedding models, one on texts from left-wing and the other from right-wing news outlets. Our hypothesis is that a word's representations in both embedding spaces are more similar for non-biased words than for biased words. Although we did not find statistical significance to accept the hypothesis, the results show the approach's effectiveness. For example, after linear mapping of both word embedding spaces, 31.

Own contribution: I proposed the exploratory approach, trained the word embedding models with Lada Rudnitckaia, developed the methodology for linear mapping of embedding spaces, analyzed the approach's effectiveness, and co-authored the manuscript.

Lastly, four papers were created around the thesis but play a minor role in this work.

> *"A Benchmark of PDF Information Extraction Tools Using a Multi-task and Multi-domain Evaluation Framework for Academic Documents"* by Norman Meuschke, Apurva Jagdale, **Timo Spinde**, Lada Rudnitckaia, Jelena Mitrović, and Bela Gipp. **In:** *iConference* (iConf), 2023.
>
> Not used in this thesis—[7]

While working on this thesis, information retrieval from PDF documents was needed at multiple points. This paper presents a comprehensive evaluation framework for

1.6 Research Path

assessing different tools in extracting information from academic PDF documents. The framework builds on DocBank, enabling the testing of tools on various content extraction tasks. GROBID showed superior performance in metadata and reference extraction, while Adobe Extract excelled in table extraction. However, all tools struggled with lists, footers, and equations, suggesting further research is needed to improve and combine tools.

Own contribution: I proposed and developed the methodology, implemented the experiments with Apurva Jagdale, and edited the final manuscript.

> *"How to Effectively Identify and Communicate Person-Targeting Media Bias in Daily News Consumption?"* by Felix Hamborg, **Timo Spinde**, Kim Heinser, Karsten Donnay, and Bela Gipp. **In:** *9th International Workshop on News Recommendation and Analytics* (INRA), 2023.
>
> Not used in this thesis—[2]

This paper presents a novel system for automatically identifying and communicating person-targeting media bias in news coverage. By leveraging a large-scale user study and conjoint design, the system demonstrates a significant increase in bias awareness among respondents. Unlike previous works, this method uncovers biases embedded in news articles' content rather than through comparisons of different media outlets.

Own contribution: I contributed to the user study design, conjoint analysis, co-implementation of the system, and co-authored the manuscript.

> *"NewsUnravel: Creating a News-Reading Application That Indicates Linguistic Media Bias and Collects Feedback"* by Smi Hinterreiter, Martin Wessel, Fabian Schliski, Isao Echizen, Marc Latoschik, and **Timo Spinde**. **In:** *International Conference on Web and Social Media* (ICWSM) [in review], 2024.
>
> Not used in this thesis—[4]

In this paper, we introduce and test feedback mechanisms for the media bias domain and present NewsUnravel, a news-reading web application to collect reader feedback on machine-generated bias highlights within online news articles. Our approach significantly increases inter-annotator agreement by 26.31

Own contribution: I proposed the idea, co-developed the methodology with Smi Hinterreiter, supervised the project, edited the manuscript, and supported the experiment with funding.

> *"News Ninja: Gamified Annotation Of Linguistic Bias In Online News"* by Smi Hinterreiter, **Timo Spinde**, Sebastian Oberdörfer, Isao Echizen, and Marc Latoschik. **In:** *Annual Symposium on Computer-Human Interaction in Play* (CHI PLAY) [in review], 2024.
>
> Not used in this thesis—[3]

We present News Ninja, a game employing data-collecting game mechanics to generate a crowdsourced dataset for media bias. Before annotating sentences, players are educated on media bias via a tutorial. Our findings show that datasets gathered with crowdsourced workers trained on News Ninja achieve significantly higher inter-annotator agreements than expert and other crowdsourced datasets with similar data quality.

Own contribution: I proposed the idea and co-developed the methodology with Smi Hinterreiter, supervised the project, edited the manuscript, and supported the experiment with funding.

Finally, apart from these early and less related works, I condensed my impressions of the field of media bias into my dissertation research proposal, shown below:

> *"An Interdisciplinary Approach for the Automated Detection and Visualization of Media Bias in News Articles"* by **Timo Spinde**. **In:** *IEEE International Conference on Data Mining* (ICDM), 2021.
>
> All chapters—[8]

Own contribution: All contents of this paper were proposed, executed, written, and presented by me.

In my proposal, I outlined the research described in this book and touched on all the publications mentioned in the following section.

1.6.2 Media Bias Detection—Core Work

As mentioned in **Sect.** 2.1, a major issue at the beginning of our work was the general confusion about definitions and terms used within the domain of media bias. To resolve this problem, we published the following work:

> *"The Media Bias Taxonomy: A Systematic Literature Review on the Forms and Automated Detection of Media Bias"* by **Timo Spinde**, Smi Hinterreiter, Fabian Haak, Terry Ruas, Helge Giese, Norman Meuschke, and Bela Gipp. **In:** *ACM Computing Surveys* (CSUR) [in review], 2023.
>
> Chapter 2—[13]

To structure the domain and support a common understanding of bias across research fields, we introduce the media bias framework, a comprehensive overview of current research on media bias from different perspectives. We show that media bias detection is a highly active research field. Notably, transformer-based classification approaches have led to significant improvements in classification accuracy and fine-granular detection of various bias types. Despite advances in other fields, such as psychology, we identify a lack of interdisciplinarity in existing projects. This insight is integrated into many of the projects below. Without sufficient awareness of media bias types, methodologically thorough evaluations of media bias detection systems are limited. We conclude that integrating recent machine learning advancements with reliable and diverse bias assessment strategies from other research areas is the most promising direction for future research in this domain.

Own contribution: I proposed the idea, structured the Media Bias Taxonomy, conducted the initial literature review, and designed the taxonomy. Together with Fabian Haak and Smi Hinterreiter, I conducted the systematic literature review, analyzed the results with Fabian Haak, and wrote all sections of the paper except those on the systematic literature review, which were co-authored by Fabian Haak and Smi Hinterreiter. The psychological section was written by Helge Giese and edited by me.

One of our first implementations of these strategies for automatically identifying media bias is published in the paper below:

> *"Automated identification of bias-inducing words in news articles using linguistic and context-oriented features Journal Article"* by **Timo Spinde**, Lada Rudnitckaia, Jelena Mitrović, Felix Hamborg, Michael Granitzer, Bela Gipp, and Karsten Donnay. **In:** *Information Processing & Management* (IPM), 2021.
>
> Chapter 5—[22]

This paper presents a method to automatically detect bias-inducing words in news articles. Our feature-oriented approach provides strong descriptive and explanatory power compared to deep learning techniques. We identify and engineer various linguistic, lexical, and syntactic features as potential media bias indicators. To the best of our knowledge, our resource collection is the most comprehensive within the media bias research area. We evaluate all features in various combinations and determine their importance for future research and the task in general. Our approach achieves an F_1 score of 0.43, a precision of 0.29, a recall of 0.77, and a ROC AUC of 0.79, outperforming current media bias detection methods based on features. We propose future improvements, discuss the perspectives of the feature-based approach, and the perspectives of neural classification systems, which we approached in subsequent experiments. The dataset used in [22] is also separately presented in the following paper.

Own contribution: I proposed the idea, developed the methodology, engineered the features, and evaluated their importance. The experiments were implemented together with Lada Rudnitckaia. I supervised the data collection, wrote the initial draft, and co-edited it with the remaining authors.

> *"MBIC—A Media Bias Annotation Dataset Including Annotator Characteristics"* by **Timo Spinde**, Lada Rudnitckaia, Kanishka Sinha, Felix Hamborg, Bela Gipp, and Karsten Donnay. **In:** *iConference* (iConf), 2021.
>
> Chapter 4—[21]

We present the dataset used within our feature-based classification system [22]. The dataset, called MBIC (Media Bias Including Characteristics), is a prototypical yet robust and diverse dataset for media bias research. It consists of 1,700 statements representing various media bias instances and contains labels for media bias identification on the word and sentence levels. The statements are reviewed by ten annotators each and include labels for media bias identification. Unlike existing research, our data incorporate background information on the participants' demographics, political ideology, and their opinion about media in general. MBIC was gathered using our own survey platform since existing systems did not offer sufficient options for text annotations. The survey platform is publicly available within the following paper.

Own contribution: I proposed the idea, developed the methodology, organized funding, designed and implemented the survey platform together with Kanishka Sinha, co-authored the manuscript, supervised the project, and presented the final paper.

> *"TASSY—A Text Annotation Survey System"* by **Timo Spinde**, Kanishka Sinha, Norman Meuschke, and Bela Gipp. **In:** *Joint Conference on Digital Libraries* (JCDL), 2021.
>
> Chapter 4—[23]

We present TASSY (Text Annotation Survey System), a free and open-source tool for creating web-based surveys that include text annotation tasks. Existing tools offer either text annotation or survey functionality but not both. Combining the two input types is particularly relevant for investigating a reader's perception of a text, which depends on the reader's background, such as age, gender, and education.

Own contribution: I proposed the idea, developed the methodology, designed the system to meet media bias research requirements, wrote the initial draft of the paper, and co-edited it with the other authors.

Based on insights from creating MBIC, Tassy, and our feature-based classification system, we concluded that a dataset with higher inter-annotator agreement was needed. The progress of creating that dataset was long, and the idea was published in an early-stage poster:

> *"Towards A Reliable Ground-Truth For Biased Language Detection"* by **Timo Spinde**, Jan-David Krieger, Manuel Plank, and Bela Gipp. **In:** *Joint Conference on Digital Libraries* (JCDL), 2021.
>
> Chapter 4—[16]

We discuss how existing methods to detect bias mostly rely on annotated data to train machine learning models. However, low annotator agreement and comparability are substantial drawbacks in available media bias corpora. To evaluate data collection options, we collected and compared labels obtained from two popular crowdsourcing platforms. Our results demonstrate the lack of data quality in existing crowdsourcing approaches, underlining the need for a trained expert framework to gather a more reliable dataset. Finally, we published the dataset in the following publication.

Own contribution: This poster was published about the work in [18]. I wrote the initial draft with Manuel Plank and Jan-David Krieger, edited and presented the manuscript, designed the methodology, and performed the data analysis with Manuel Plank and Jan-David Krieger.

> *"Neural Media Bias Detection Using Distant Supervision With BABE—Bias Annotations By Experts"* by **Timo Spinde**, Manuel Plank, Jan-David Krieger, Terry Ruas, Bela Gipp, and Akiko Aizawa. **In:** *Findings of the Association for Computational Linguistics: EMNLP 2021* (EMNLP), 2021.
>
> Chapter 4 and 6—[18]

This paper presents BABE, a robust and diverse dataset created by trained experts for media bias research. We analyze why expert labeling is essential in this domain. Our dataset offers better annotation quality and higher inter-annotator agreement than existing work. It consists of 3,700 sentences balanced among topics and outlets, containing media bias labels on the word and sentence levels. Based on our data, we introduce a way to automatically detect bias-inducing sentences in news articles. Our best-performing BERT-based model, pre-trained on a larger corpus of distant labels, achieves a macro F_1-score of 0.804, outperforming existing methods.

Own contribution: I proposed the idea, developed the methodology, funded the project, co-implemented and supervised the experiments, performed data collection with Manuel Plank and Jan-David Krieger, wrote the initial draft, and edited and presented the paper.

1.6 Research Path

Two attempts to improve the model presented in [18] have also been published:

> *"A Domain-adaptive Pre-training Approach for Language Bias Detection in News"* by David Krieger, **Timo Spinde**, Terry Ruas, Juhi Kulshrestha, and Bela Gipp. **In:** *Joint Conference on Digital Libraries* (JCDL), 2022.
>
> Chapter 6—[6]

We present DA-RoBERTa, a state-of-the-art transformer-based model adapted to the media bias domain, identifying sentence-level bias with an F_1 score of 0.814. We also train DA-BERT and DA-BART, two more transformer models adapted to the bias domain. Our domain-adapted models outperform prior bias detection approaches. We will discuss the differences and experiments more in Chap. 6.

Own contribution: I proposed and supervised the experiment, co-authored the first draft, and edited the paper.

> *"Exploiting Transformer-based Multitask Learning for the Detection of Media Bias in News Articles"* by **Timo Spinde**, Jan-David Krieger, Terry Ruas, Jelena Mitrović, Franz Götz-Hahn, Akiko Aizawa, and Bela Gipp. **In:** *iConference* (iConf), 2022.
>
> Chapter 6—[17]

In another work, we introduce the idea of using Multi-Task Learning (MTL) within the media bias research domain for the first time. We propose a Transformer-based deep learning architecture trained via Multi-Task Learning using six bias-related datasets to tackle the media bias detection problem. Our best-performing implementation achieves a macro F_1 of 0.776, a performance boost of 3.

Own contribution: I proposed the idea, developed the methodology, funded the project, co-implemented and supervised the experiments, collected the data with Jan-David Krieger, wrote the initial draft, and edited and presented the paper.

> *"MAGPIE: Multi-Task Media-Bias Analysis of Generalization of Pre-Trained Identification of Expressions"* by Tomáš Horych, Martin Wessel, Jan Philipp Wahle, Terry Ruas, Jerome Waßmuth, André Greiner-Petter, Akiko Aizawa, Bela Gipp, and **Timo Spinde**. In: *Joint International Conference on Computational Linguistics, Language Resources and Evaluation: LREC-COLING 2024* (LREC-COLING), 2024.
>
> Chapter 6—[5]

To build on the prior study, we introduce MAGPIE as an advanced approach to detect media bias through multi-task learning (MTL), significantly enhancing performance across various bias detection tasks. We first build the Large Bias Mixture (LBM) framework, consisting of 59 diverse bias-related tasks, central to MAGPIE's methodology. LBM facilitates the comprehensive training of a new MTL model, employing a RoBERTa-based encoder. The results demonstrate significant improvement, particularly a 3.3.

Own contribution: I proposed the idea, supervised its development, contributed to building the Large Bias Mixture (LBM) framework, and co-authored the manuscript.

> *"Introducing MBIB—the first Media Bias Benchmark Task and Dataset Collection"* by Martin Wessel, Tomáš Horych, Terry Ruas, Akiko Aizawa, Bela Gipp, and **Timo Spinde**. In: *Conference on Research and Development in Information Retrieval* (SIGIR), 2023.
>
> Chapter 4—[25]

In the above publication, we address the problem of the lack of a unified benchmark for evaluating media bias detection techniques. We introduce the first Media Bias Identification Benchmark Task and Dataset Collection (MBIB), a comprehensive benchmark grouping different types of media bias (e.g., linguistic, cognitive, political) under a common framework. After reviewing 115 datasets, we select nine tasks and propose 22 associated datasets for evaluating media bias detection techniques. We evaluate MBIB using state-of-the-art Transformer techniques (e.g., T5, BART). Our results suggest that while hate speech, racial bias, and gender bias are easier to detect, models struggle with certain bias types, e.g., cognitive and political bias. No single technique outperforms all others significantly. We find an uneven distribution of research interest and resource allocation among tasks in media bias. A unified benchmark encourages the development of robust systems and shifts the evaluation paradigm towards solutions that tackle multiple media bias types simultaneously. MBIB is not used within the chapters and projects presented in this thesis but is a logical step based on our work and experiences.

Own contribution: I proposed and supervised the development of the MBIB benchmark, conducted the comprehensive review of existing datasets with Martin Wessel, and co-authored the manuscript.

1.6.3 Perception and Visualization

Regarding our work on the perception and visualization of media bias, four major publications were developed during the time of my dissertation:

> *"Enabling News Consumers to View and Understand Biased News Coverage: A Study on the Perception and Visualization of Media Bias"* by **Timo Spinde**, Felix Hamborg, Karsten Donnay, Angelia Becerra, and Bela Gipp. **In:** *Joint Conference on Digital Libraries* (JCDL), 2020.
>
> Chapter 7—[10]

In the first publication on media bias perception, we describe how many researchers focus on automatically detecting and identifying media bias in the news. However, very few studies systematically analyze how these biases can be best visualized and communicated. We create three manually annotated datasets and test various visualization strategies. The results show no strong effects on bias awareness of the treatment groups compared to the control group, although a visualization of hand-annotated bias communicated bias instances more effectively than a framing visualization. Showing participants an overview page that opposes different viewpoints on the same topic does not yield differences in respondents' bias perception. Using a multi-level model, we find that perceived journalist bias is significantly related to the article's perceived political extremeness and impartiality. Our study employs a conjoint analysis [179] to test how visualizations can improve users' understanding or awareness of media bias in news articles. We show the visualizations and more details in Chap. 7; however, we conducted a second experiment with the same focus, as shown in the following paper.

Own contribution: I proposed the project, designed the study, created manually annotated datasets, tested various visualization strategies, conducted the experiments, analyzed the results with Angelica Becerra, and co-authored the manuscript.

> *"How do we raise media bias awareness effectively? Effects of visualizations to communicate bias"* by **Timo Spinde**, Christin Jeggle, Magdalena Haupt, Wolfgang Gaissmaier, and Helge Giese. **In:** *PLOS ONE*, 2022.
>
> Chapter 7—[14]

In this article, we build on our previous experiment and analyze how to facilitate the detection of media bias with visual and textual aids in the form of (a) a forewarning message, (b) text annotations, and (c) political classifiers. We increased the quality of the visualizations, selected different elements for highlighting, and vastly increased the study size. In an online experiment, we randomized 985 participants to receive a biased liberal or conservative news article in any combination of the three aids. Their subjective perception of media bias in the article, attitude change, and political ideology were assessed. Unlike before [10], both the forewarning message and the annotations significantly increased media bias awareness, whereas the political classification showed no effect. Incongruence between an article's political position and individual political orientation also increased media bias awareness. Visual aids did not mitigate this effect. Likewise, attitudes remained unaltered.

Throughout our experiments, especially in earlier works [10–12], we concluded that the perception of bias varies largely depending on a reader's personal background. Media bias is a complex construct to identify and analyze. Although media bias has been the subject of many studies, previous assessment strategies are oversimplified and lack overlap and empirical evaluation. Thus, a common standard to ask for bias was needed, published in the following publication:

Own contribution: I proposed the project, designed the study, performed the data analysis, conducted the experiments with Christin Jeggle and Magdalena Haupt (whom I supervised), and co-authored the manuscript.

> *"Do You Think It's Biased? How To Ask For The Perception Of Media Bias"* by **Timo Spinde**, Christina Kreuter, Wolfgang Gaissmaier, Felix Hamborg, Bela Gipp, and Helge Giese. **In:** *Joint Conference on Digital Libraries* (JCDL), 2021.
>
> Chapter 3—[15]

Our study aims to develop a scale that can be used as a reliable standard to evaluate article bias. For example, when measuring bias in a news article, should we ask,

1.6 Research Path

"How biased is the article?" or "How did the article treat the American president?". We conducted a literature search to find 824 relevant questions about text perception in previous research on the topic. In a multi-iterative process, we summarized and condensed these questions semantically to conclude a complete and representative set of possible question types about bias. The final set consisted of 25 questions with varying answering formats, 17 using semantic differentials, and six ratings of feelings. We tested each question on 190 articles with 663 participants to identify how well the questions measure an article's perceived bias. Our results show that 21 final items are suitable and reliable for measuring the perception of media bias.

Own contribution: I proposed the project, designed the study, supervised the creation and collection of the survey material, conducted the experiments and data analysis with Christina Kreuter, wrote the initial draft, and edited it with Helge Giese.

> *"What do Twitter Comments Tell About News Article Bias? Assessing the Impact of News Article Bias on its Perception on Twitter"* by **Timo Spinde**, Elisabeth Richter, Martin Wessel, Juhi Kulshreshta, and Karsten Donnay. **In:** *Online Social Networks and Media* (OSNEM), 2023.
>
> Chapter 7—[19]

Lastly, one of the experiments partially analyzes the general impact news bias can have, examining whether Twitter comments on articles can serve as bias indicators. Given the nature of social media, news is no longer just news; it is embedded in user conversations. This is particularly relevant for biased information because user interaction affects whether information gets uncritically disseminated. Biased coverage has been shown to affect personal decision-making. However, it remains an open question whether users are aware of the biased reporting they encounter and how they react to it. In the above paper, we examine whether Twitter comments on articles are indicative of the actual level of bias in a given article. We present the BAT (Bias And Twitter) dataset, connecting reliable human-made media bias classifications of news articles with the reactions these articles had upon publication on Twitter. BAT covers 2,800 bias-rated news articles from 255 different English-speaking news outlets and includes 175,807 comments and retweets.

Based on BAT, we conduct a multi-feature analysis to identify comment characteristics and analyze whether Twitter reactions correlate with an article's bias.

We fine-tune and apply two XLNet-based classifiers for hate speech detection and sentiment analysis. We then relate the classifier results to the article bias annotations within a multi-level regression. The results show that the comments made on an article are indeed an indicator of its bias, and vice-versa. With a regression coefficient of 0.703 ($p < 0.01$), we present evidence that Twitter reactions to biased articles are significantly more hateful. Additionally, our analysis shows that the news outlet's individual stance reinforces the hate-bias relationship.

Own contribution: I proposed the project, designed the study, supervised the creation and collection of the survey material, conducted the experiments and data analysis with Elisabeth Richter, wrote the initial draft, and edited it with Martin Wessel and Elisabeth Richter.

Open Access This chapter is licensed under the terms of the Creative Commons Attribution 4.0 International License (http://creativecommons.org/licenses/by/4.0/), which permits use, sharing, adaptation, distribution and reproduction in any medium or format, as long as you give appropriate credit to the original author(s) and the source, provide a link to the Creative Commons license and indicate if changes were made.

The images or other third party material in this chapter are included in the chapter's Creative Commons license, unless indicated otherwise in a credit line to the material. If material is not included in the chapter's Creative Commons license and your intended use is not permitted by statutory regulation or exceeds the permitted use, you will need to obtain permission directly from the copyright holder.

Media Bias 2

A frog in the well knows nothing of the great ocean.

Japanese Saying

2.1 Introduction

As portrayed in Chap. 1, media bias is a complex concept to identify and analyze. To construct a coherent framework to cover different bias types and to understand the state of the art in computer science when dealing with the domain of media bias is crucial to contribute meaningful research. To do so, in this chapter, we give a more detailed overview about media bias theory, as well as provide the results of an extensive literature review on automated media bias detection methods [13]. To start the journey into this thesis here from a common ground zero, we will briefly summarize the general background of bias first.

> **Research Objective**
> Review which types of bias exist and how they are classified in computer science to date.

Supplementary Information The online version contains supplementary material available at https://doi.org/10.1007/978-3-658-47798-1_2.

Online news articles have become a crucial source of information, replacing traditional media like television, radio broadcasts, and print media (e.g., newspapers, magazines) [108]. However, news outlets often are biased [412]. The primary reason for this bias is that opinionated, entertaining, and sensationalist content is more likely to attract a larger audience while being less expensive to produce [39].

Media bias is widely recognized as having a strong impact on the public's perception of reported topics [108, 181, 257]. Media bias aggravates the problem known as filter bubbles or echo chambers [14], where readers consume only news corresponding to their beliefs, views, or personal liking [257]. The behavior likely leads to poor awareness of particular issues, a narrow and one-sided perspective [11], and can influence voting behavior [124, 395].

Highlighting media bias instances has positive implications and can mitigate the effects of such biases [55]. While completely eliminating bias may be an unrealistic goal, drawing attention to its existence by informing readers that content is biased allows them to compare content easily. It can also enable journalists and publishers to assess their work objectively [108]. In the following, we list systems designed to help readers mitigate the effects of media bias on their decision-making. Most of these systems focus on aggregating articles about the same event from various news sources to provide different perspectives [257]. For example, news aggregators like Allsides[1] and Ground News[2] allow readers to compare articles on the same topic from media outlets known to have different political views. Media bias charts, such as the AllSides media bias chart[3] or the Ad Fontes media bias chart[4] provide up-to-date information on media outlets' political slants. However, it is uncertain whether readers have the possibility and, more importantly, the desire to read several articles on the same topic and compare them.

Media bias has become the subject of increasing interdisciplinary research, particularly in automated methods to identify bias. However, the concept of media bias remains loosely defined in the literature [181]. Existing work uses different subcategories and types of bias [21, 341], but authors tend to focus on only one media bias subcategory while disregarding similar kinds of bias concepts. publications on media bias often work on similar concepts but assign different names to them, leading to confusion and imprecise use of terms. For example, some authors refer to word-based bias as linguistic bias [341], while others call it bias by word choice [22], but the exact difference or overlap between these terms is undefined. The lack

---

[1] https://www.allsides.com
[2] https://ground.news
[3] https://www.allsides.com/media-bias/media-bias-chart
[4] https://www.adfontesmedia.com/

2.1 Introduction

of clarity surrounding media bias can have negative effects on measuring media bias perception [15]. Additionally, recent advances in Deep Learning have shown how awareness of tasks within complex domains, such as media bias, could potentially lead to large performance increases [37]. However, these advancements have yet to be incorporated into media bias research [17].

The literature review presented here seeks to create awareness of media bias detection as a task and to provide a summary of existing conceptual work on media bias and automated systems to detect it. To achieve this, we compare and contrast computer science research while also incorporating media bias-related concepts from non-technical disciplines such as framing effects [133], hate speech [110], and racial bias [118].

We propose a unified taxonomy for the media bias domain to mitigate ambiguity around its various concepts and names in prior work. In addition, we classify and summarize computer science contributions to media bias detection in six categories[5]: (1) traditional natural language processing (tNLP) methods [304], (2) simple non-neural ML techniques [370], (3) transformer-based (tbML) [372] and (4) non-transformer-based (ntbML) [138] machine learning. We also include (5) non-neural network (nNN)-based (**Sect.** 2.5.2.3) [337] as well as graph-based [170] approaches. Lastly, we provide an overview of available datasets. Our aim is to provide an overview of the current state-of-the-art in media bias and increase awareness of promising methods. We show how computer science methods can benefit from incorporating user and perception-related variables in different datasets to improve accuracy. To facilitate the usage of such variables, we give an overview of recent findings about cognitive processes behind media bias. We believe that a systematic overview of the media bias domain is overdue given the numerous papers covering related issues. Such an overview can benefit future work in computer science and other areas, such as Psychology, Social Science, or Linguistics, which all cover media bias. As we show in detail in **Sect.** 2.3, existing literature reviews on media bias [181, 298, 334] do not cover crucial aspects. They do not give a systematic overview of related concepts, instead presenting how media bias can develop. Aside from the major developments within the media bias domain since 2021, they lack details on computer science methods and psychological and social science research.

---

[5] We reason and detail our categories in **Sect.** 2.5.

In summary, our literature review answers the following research questions:

(RQ1) What are the relationships among the various forms of bias covered in the literature?
(RQ2) What are the major developments in the research on automated methods to identify media bias?
(RQ3) What are the most promising computer science methods to automatically identify media bias?
(RQ4) How does social science research approach media bias, and how can social science and computer science research benefit each other?

All resources for our review are publicly available at https://github.com/Media-Bias-Group/Media-Bias-Taxonomy.

2.2 Methodology

The core contribution of this article is a systematic literature review that provides a structured and comprehensive overview of the application of computer science methods for detecting media bias. This review also clarifies and establishes connections among the various concepts employed in the field of media bias. Reviews are susceptible to incomplete data and deficiencies in the selection, structure, and presentation of the content [137], especially when aiming for extensive coverage. To overcome these challenges, we designed our collection and selection processes carefully, with a focus on mitigating common risks associated with literature reviews.

We used automated, keyword-based literature retrieval (described in **Sect.** 2.2.1), followed by a manual selection (**Sect.** 2.2.2), and adhered to established best practices for systematic literature reviews [149, 205, 314]. The number of concepts (and keywords) relevant to media bias is high but hard to define.[6] Reviewing all papers for all related concepts is unfeasible[7]. Therefore, we applied filter criteria to select candidate documents. Moreover, we excluded references from the selected papers as additional candidates since determining an unbiased stopping criterion would be challenging. Our review covers the literature published between January 2019 and May 2022, thus providing a comprehensive overview of the state-of-the-art in the field.

---

[6] For example, the term bias also yields many health-related papers that are irrelevant to our review.

[7] Based on the keywords we searched for, which we detail in **Sect.** 2.2.1, we found over 100.000 publications.

2.2 Methodology

To ensure diversity in the computer science publications included in our review, we retrieved literature from two sources: DBLP (DataBase systems and Logic Programming)[8] and Semantic Scholar[9]. Both sources are reliable and diverse and therefore meet the criteria for suitable sources for literature reviews [76, 226]. DBLP is the most extensive database for computer science publications to date, containing documents from major peer-reviewed computer science journals and proceedings. It is a primary literature platform used in other reviews [120, 300, 423]. Semantic Scholar draws on a considerably larger database than DBLP, going beyond computer science into other research areas. It is also frequently used in literature reviews [184, 400, 415] and allows for applying more filter criteria to searches, particularly filtering by scientific field.

Both platforms are accessible through an API and facilitate the use of an automated retrieval pipeline, which we require to filter our search results efficiently. We retrieved results for a selection of search terms (see **Sect.** 2.2.1). While Semantic Scholar is an extensive general knowledge archive, DBLP focuses on in-depth coverage of computer science. By including both major archives, we aim to retrieve an exhaustive set of candidate documents in computer science.

2.2.1 Retrieving Candidate Documents

We used media bias terms encountered during our initial manual retrieval step (depicted in Fig. 2.1) as search queries to create candidate lists for our literature review.[10] These terms also served as the basis of the media bias categories we consolidated in our Media Bias Taxonomy in **Sect.** 2.4.2. In step 2 (Fig. 2.2), we employed a Python pipeline to retrieve computer science documents from both DBLP and Semantic Scholar, merge and unify the search results, and export them as tabular data.[11] We scraped a list of 1496 publications from DBLP and 1274 publications from Semantic Scholar for the given time frame. We present the complete list and search keywords in our repository. As shown in Fig. 2.1, we obtained a list of 3140

---

[8] https://dblp.org/

[9] https://www.semanticscholar.org/

[10] Initially, we used more general terms such as media bias", hate speech", linguistic bias", and racial bias" which are widely known. We manually identified additional bias concepts in the retrieved publications during our searches depicted in Fig. 2.1 and Fig. 2.2 and added them to our list of search queries. Subsequently, we searched for these newly identified keywords, creating the media bias keyword list presented in Fig. 2.3.

[11] We have made the crawler publicly available for use in other projects. The code and instructions can be found in ourrepository.

candidates for the literature review. After removing 531 duplicates between the Semantic Scholar and DBLP results, the final list contained 2609 publications. All search results were tagged with the relevant search queries and exported as a CSV file for the selection step.

Fig. 2.1 Number of publications at each step of the literature retrieval and review of computer science publications

2.2.2 Candidate Selection

We followed a multi-stage process to select relevant publications, as shown in Fig. 2.1. The figure also shows the number of publications in each step. Three reviewers (Ph.D. students in computer science) filtered the results after the automatic scrape (step 2) and duplicate removal (step 3). In step 4, they filtered for documents that cover media bias, based on the title, abstract, and text, which resulted in 299 documents. In step 5, one reviewer per paper thoroughly inspected every publication to investigate whether computer science methods were used to detect media bias. For each publication, we exported the used methods and datasets (see Sect. 2.5). In step 6, a second reviewer verified the choice of the first reviewer for each publication. In case of disagreement or uncertainty, the third reviewer was consulted. For each publication, at least two of the three reviewers must deem the publication suitable for our review. The detailed selection criteria for each step are available in our repository. In the end, we selected 96 relevant documents. We assigned each paper to its computer science methods category according to Fig. 2.4.

2.2.3 Finding Additional Conceptual Literature for the Media Bias Taxonomy

One goal of our systematic literature review is to develop a taxonomy that organizes the various definitions of media bias into distinct types. However, while conduct-

2.2 Methodology

ing our search, we recognized that most computer science publications focus on methodology rather than defining bias types. Therefore, we expanded our search to other research areas that may have different perspectives on media bias. For this purpose, we conducted a second search, as shown in Fig. 2.2, replacing DBLP with Google Scholar to identify more non-computer science research[12]. We manually selected papers from the first 50 search results for each keyword on Google Scholar and Semantic Scholar[13] and checked the first layer of their references for additional relevant literature.

Overall, the additional search step for non-computer-science publications yielded 867 results, of which 489 were duplicates between Google Scholar and Semantic Scholar. Of the 378 non-duplicate publications, 57 were included in the search for computer science publications. We present the results of our searches in Sect. 2.4.2[14].

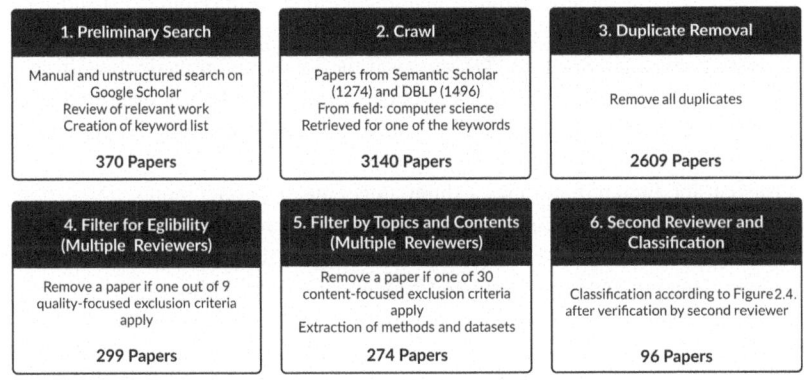

Fig. 2.2 Number of publications at each step of the literature retrieval and review for the Media Bias Taxonomy

---

[12] Google Scholar is also a reliable and diverse database, meeting the criteria recommended in systematic literature review guidelines [76, 226].

[13] In this step, we excluded computer science publications in the Semantic Scholar results.

[14] Due to space restrictions we do not cite all of the filtered works in this article but omit publications focusing on highly similar concepts.

2.3 Related Literature Reviews

Related literature reviews[15] on media bias are scarce. Our literature crawl and search (Sect. 2.2) yielded only three such results [181, 298, 334]. An additional search for the terms "media bias" and "news bias"[16] on Google Scholar did not yield more findings. In their literature review, Hamborg, Donnay, and Gipp [181] defined subcategories of media bias from a social science perspective and showed how they emerge during journalistic work. Further, the authors described the advancements in computer science and indicated that frame analysis exists in both social sciences and computer science.

In the second work, Nakov et al. [298] surveyed media profiling approaches. They summarized computer science methods to analyze factuality (i.e., stance and reliability) and various forms of media bias (selection bias, presentation bias, framing bias, and news slant). The authors separated four prediction bases for media bias: 1) textual content and linguistic features, 2) multimedia content, 3) audience homophily, and 4) infrastructure characteristics.

Lastly, Puglisi and Snyder [334] surveyed the literature on media bias from a sociological perspective and offered an overview of possible bias measurements. They grouped biases into three kinds of measurement: comparing media outlets with other actors, the intensity of media coverage, and tone.

The earlier literature reviews exhibit three major shortcomings. First, both computer science-focused reviews [181, 298] lack a systematic literature search. They only covered selected computer science approaches and datasets. Second, Hamborg, Donnay, and Gipp [181] and Nakov et al. [298] did not cover the psychological perspective on bias, which we argue is essential to create and evaluate detection methods and datasets [15]. Third, no work thus far has provided a detailed overview of the various concepts and subcategories that fall under the umbrella term media bias. Current literature on media bias often addresses related concepts like hate speech, gender bias, and cognitive bias, but uses the umbrella term of media bias without clearly differentiating between overlapping categories and their relationships.

---

[15] We considered a publication a literature review if its main focus is a critical summary and evaluation of research about a topic related to media bias.

[16] We manually examined the first 50 results on Google Scholar.

2.4 Related Work and Theoretical Embedding

To our knowledge, we are the first to offer a large-scale, systematic analysis of the media bias domain. As a result, we provide our Media Bias Taxonomy, which connects the various definitions and concepts in the area. In addition, we briefly summarize the state-of-the-art psychological research on media bias and provide an in-depth overview of all computer science methods currently used to tackle media bias-related issues.

Our review focuses exclusively on media bias and does not include publications on related topics such as fake news. For details on fake news and its detection, we recommend referring to the two literature reviews [130, 384].

2.4 Related Work and Theoretical Embedding

This section will provide an overview of media bias, followed by a presentation and organization of related concepts in our novel Media Bias Taxonomy.

2.4.1 Media Bias

Media bias is a complex concept [10, 15] that has been researched at least since the 1950s [407]. It describes slanted news coverage or other biased media content [181], which can be intentional, i.e., purposefully express a tendency towards a perspective, ideology, or result [408], or unintentional [55, 408]. Different stages of the news production process can introduce various forms of media bias [181].

The lack of a precise and unified definition for media bias, sometimes referred to as editorial slant [124], has contributed to the conceptual fragmentation in the field [15]. For instance, [105] categorized media bias into three primary groups [105]: gatekeeping bias, coverage bias, and statement bias. In contrast, [294] proposed two types of media bias: ideology bias and spin bias [294]. Some scholars referred to media bias as lexical or linguistic bias [60]. Others have proposed less specific definitions. For instance, [22, p. 2] described media bias as "slanted news coverage or internal bias reflected in news articles." [238, p. 1268] defined it as news reporting that "leans towards or against a certain person or opinion by making one-sided misleading or unfair judgments," and Lee et al. [244, p. 1] defined it as reporting "in a prejudiced manner or with a slanted viewpoint." None of these definitions is based on a comprehensive literature review. Therefore, we provide a comprehensive and well-organized description of media bias in **Sect.** 2.4.2, which includes its sub-fields and related computer science methods and discuss the common ground of all media bias concepts in our review in **Sect.** 2.7.

It is worth mentioning that media bias does not only manifest via text but also via pictures or text/news layout [276, 319]. Moreover, biased reporting in one outlet can also cause biased reporting in other outlets by direct citations [169]. Our literature review focuses on text-based media bias and methods only.

2.4.2 The Media Bias Taxonomy

As definitions of media bias often overlap, a clear distinction between the types is challenging. We propose the Media Bias Taxonomy, depicted in Fig. 2.3 to give a comprehensive overview of the media bias domain. Based on a manual selection after the literature search process, described in **Sect.** 2.2.3, we split media bias into four major bias categories: linguistic, cognitive, text-level context, reporting-level, as well as related concepts, which are detailed in the following subsections. We show detailed examples in Appendix **B.2**, available in the electronic supplementary material, for all subtypes of bias[17].

2.4.2.1 Linguistic Bias

Linguistic bias, sometimes called lexical bias [139], refers to a pattern of using certain words that reflects a particular way of thinking about a group or an individual based on their social category. This bias involves a systematic preference for certain words or phrases that may reflect stereotypes or preconceived notions about the group or individual being described [60]. In simpler terms, linguistic bias means using language that reflects a particular attitude or viewpoint towards a particular group or individual.

We identified five bias types within this category: linguistic intergroup bias [367], framing bias [341], epistemological bias [341], bias by semantic properties [167], and connotation bias [338]. Table **B.2** and Table **B.3**, both available in the electronic supplementary material, list examples for each subcategory.

Linguistic Intergroup Bias describes which group members use specific language [367]. The concept is based on the linguistic category model (LCM), which categorizes words into different levels of abstraction (action words, interpretive action words, state verbs, and adjectives) according to their purpose [121, 367]. The

---

[17] Other, overarching concepts exist, such as persuasiveness [166], which we do not cover or organize within this work. In future work, we will address concepts containing multiple forms of bias.

2.4 Related Work and Theoretical Embedding

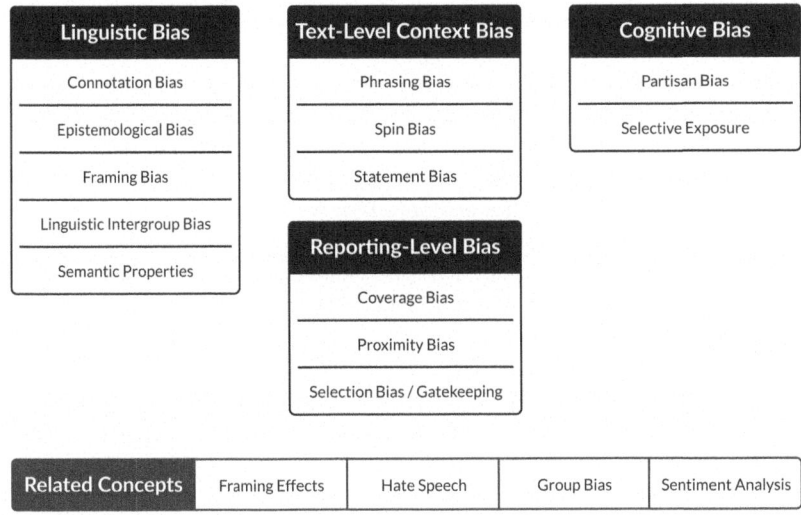

Fig. 2.3 The Media Bias Taxonomy. The four subcategories of media bias consist of different bias types

use of biased language is often subtle and reinforces stereotypes [60, 269]. Maass et al. [269] illustrated linguistic intergroup bias with the following example:

- They considered the hypothetical scenario where "Person A is hitting Person B's arm with his fist" [269, p. 982].
- Describing the scenario using the least abstract form of language, one could say, "A is punching B" [269, p. 982]. This entails no kind of valuation or implication and only describes what happened.
- In contrast, using the most abstract form of language, one could say "A is aggressive" [269, p. 982]. This might or might not be accurate and cannot be judged from the fact that A hit B.

Framing Bias is defined as the use of "subjective words or phrases linked with a particular point of view" [341, p. 1650] to sway the meaning of a statement. The subjective words are often either one-sided terms or subjective intensifiers [341]. One-sided terms are words that "reflect only one of the sides of a contentious issue" [341, p. 1653], while subjective intensifiers are adjectives or adverbs that reinforce the meaning of a sentence.

Epistemological Bias describes the use of linguistic features that subtly focus on the credibility of a statement [341]. Word classes associated with epistemological bias are factive verbs, entailments, assertive verbs, and hedges, see examples in Table **B.2** (available in the electronic supplementary material). Factive verbs indicate truthfulness; entailments are relations where one word implies the truth of another word. Assertive verbs state clearly and definitely that something is true. Hedges are words used to introduce vagueness to a statement. In contrast to framing bias, epistemological bias is rather subtle and implicit [341].

Bias by Semantic Properties describes how word choice affects the framing of content and triggers bias, similar to framing bias and epistemological bias. The difference, however, is that framing and epistemological bias refer to the individual words used, whereas bias by semantic properties refers to how the sentence is structured [167].

Connotation Bias refers to using connotations to introduce bias to a statement [338]. While the denotation of a word expresses its literal meaning, the connotation refers to a secondary meaning besides the denotation. The connotation is usually linked to certain feelings or emotions associated with a point of view [338].

2.4.2.2 Text-level Context Bias

Similar to linguistic bias, text-level context bias refers to the way the context of a text is expressed. Words and statements have the power to alter the article's context, influencing the reader's opinion [201]. The types of bias belonging to this category are statement bias [105], phrasing bias [201], and spin bias [29], which consists of omission bias and informational bias [29]. Table **B.4**, available in the electronic supplementary material, lists examples for each subcategory.

Statement Bias refers to "members of the media interjecting their own opinions into the text" [105, p. 136], which leads to certain news being reported in a way that is more or less favorable towards a particular position [105]. These opinions can be very faint and are expressed "by disproportionately criticizing one side" [79, p. 250] rather than "directly advocating for a preferred [side]" [79, p. 250].

Phrasing Bias is characterized by inflammatory words, i.e., non-neutral language [201]. Depending on the context, a word can change from neutral to inflammatory. Therefore, when analyzing bias, the inter-dependencies between words and phrases must be considered [201].

Spin Bias describes a form of bias introduced either by leaving out necessary information [29, 294] or by adding unnecessary information [139]. The underlying motivation is to tell a simple and memorable story [294]. Spin bias can be divided into omission, and informational bias [29]. Omission bias, also known as simplification, is the act of omitting words from a sentence [29, 294]. Informational bias, or exaggeration, is defined as adding speculative, tangential, or irrelevant information to a news story [139].

2.4.2.3 Reporting-level Context Bias

Reporting-level context bias subsumes all bias types on the reporting level. While text-level context bias observes bias within an article, reporting-level bias observes the general attention for specific topics [79, 105, 150, 354]. Bias types in this category are selection bias, proximity bias, and coverage bias, which are all closely connected. Table **B.1**, available in the electronic supplementary material, lists examples for each subcategory.

Selection Bias (or gatekeeping bias) refers to the selection of content from the body of potential stories by writers and editors [105]. Obviously, not all news events can be reported due to the limited resources of newspapers. However, this decision-making process is prone to bias from personal preferences [105, 294, 354, 407].

Coverage Bias describes situations in which two or more sides of an issue receive imbalanced amounts of attention, such as pro-life vs. pro-choice statements [105].[18] The level of attention can be measured either in absolute numbers (e.g., there are more articles discussing pro-life than pro-choice topics), how much space the topics get in a newspaper (e.g., printed on the front page), or as the length of the article (e.g., pro-life articles are longer and receive more in-depth coverage than pro-choice articles) [105, 354].

Proximity Bias focuses on cultural similarity and geographic proximity as decisive factors. Newspapers tend to report more frequently and more in-depth on events that happened nearby [354]. For instance, the more two countries are culturally similar, the more likely it is that events from one region or country will be reported in the other, and the coverage will be more in-depth [150, 354].

2.4.2.4 Cognitive Bias

The processing of media information may also be biased by the reader of an article and the state the reader is in during reading. In this review, we use the term cognitive bias, defined as "a systematic deviation from rationality in judgment or decision-making" [67, p. 1], to summarize how this processing may be negatively affected. While a failure to detect biased media in a given set of articles may be explained by a lack of ability or motivation (e.g., being inattentive/ disinterested, focusing on identity instead of accuracy motives), biased processing of news by the reader is often attributed to a need for a consistent world view and for overcoming dissonances evoked by discordant information [301]. In this line of reasoning, repeated exposure and increased familiarity with an argument as well as source cues for a reputable, world-view-consistent source, may increase the trust in information quality.

---

[18] Coverage bias refers to a particular event, whereas reporting-level context bias refers to the general attention a topic receives.

Table **B.5**, available in the electronic supplementary material, lists examples for each subcategory, as well as some additional perception bias-related concepts, which we touch upon again in **Sect. 2.6**.

Selective Exposure. Similar to the selection bias of editors and authors, readers also actively select which articles they read [227]. Given this choice, they tend to favor reading information consistent with their views, exacerbating already existent biases through selective exposure to one-sided news reports [302, 391]. Additionally, such selective exposure tends to extend to social tie formation. Topic information is solely exchanged among like-minded individuals, a phenomenon often dubbed echo chamber or filter bubble [247][19], hampering unbiased information processing.

Partisan Bias. Selective attention to world-view-consistent news has led to research on the effects of political identity. There, the evaluation of veracity seems dependent on the fit to the reader's party affiliation, a phenomenon dubbed partisan bias [52, 155]. Similarly, the hostile media phenomenon (HMP) describes the general observation that members of opposing groups rate a news article as biased against their point of view [389].

2.4.2.5 Related Concepts

The last category contains definitions that cannot be exclusively assigned to any other media bias category. Concepts belonging to this category are framing effects [395], hate speech [110], sentiment analysis, and group bias [95], which consists of gender bias [101], and religion bias [271]. Much research focuses on these concepts, so we introduce them only briefly and refer to other sources for more information.

Framing Effects refer to how media discourse is structured into interpretive packages that give meaning to an issue, so-called frames. Frames promote a specific interpretation of the content or highlight certain aspects while overlooking others. In other words, this type subsumes biases resulting from how events and entities are framed in a text [134, 395].

Hate Speech is defined as any language expressing hatred towards a targeted group or intended to be derogatory, humiliate, or insult [110]. Often, hateful language is biased [292]. The consequences of hate speech in media content are severe, as it reinforces tension between all actors involved [27, 292].

Group Bias. We categorize gender bias, racial bias, and religion bias under the umbrella term "group bias," as they all refer to biased views toward certain groups.

Gender Bias is characterized by the dominance of one gender over others in any medium [101], resulting in the under-representation of the less dominant gender and the formation of stereotypes [101, 330]. It is associated with selection bias [38, 211],

---

[19] In case an algorithm was trained to this preference.

2.5 Computer Science Research on Media Bias

coverage bias [80, 241], and context bias at the text level. For instance, women are quoted more frequently than men for "Lifestyle" or "Healthcare" topics, while men are quoted more frequently in "Business" or "Politics" [337]. Linguistic research on gender bias aims to identify gender-specific and gender-neutral words [107] and create lexicons of verbs and adjectives based on gender stereotypes [140].

Racial Bias and **Religion Bias** are other types of group bias. Racial bias refers to the systematic disproportionate representation of ethical groups, often minorities [95], in a specific context [95, 288].

Religion, racial, and gender biases can be observed in word embeddings. For example, "Muslim" is spatially close to "terrorist" in some embeddings [271], which may result from biased texts in the data used to derive these embeddings (as word embeddings depend on their input).

Group biases can manifest in other forms, such as hate speech, which is a subgroup of biases. Although the distinction between racial and gender biases is not always evident, they can exist independently [159, 288].

Sentiment Analysis involves examining text for its emotional content or polarity [132]. In the context of media bias, sentiment analysis can detect biases in statements or articles [180, 200] and help identify other concepts like hate speech, political ideology, or linguistic bias [27, 345].

2.5 Computer Science Research on Media Bias

Computer science research on media bias primarily focuses on methods used to analyze, mitigate, and eliminate bias in texts. Detecting bias is a prerequisite for other applications [340]. Bias detection systems could also be employed to check computer-generated texts for bias. Hereafter, we provide a comprehensive overview of computer science methods used in media bias research in recent years based on a systematic literature review. The methodology of the review is described in **Sect.** 2.2. A systematic overview of computer science methods is essential for capturing the state of media bias research and identifying research trends and gaps. To the best of our knowledge, this is the most comprehensive survey on media bias detection methods so far, as discussed in **Sect.** 2.3.

Table 2.1 organizes the findings of our literature review by the year of publication and category of employed computer science method.[20] We chose the employed methods as the main categorical property to structure the publications since the methods are typically described in more detail than the type of investigated

---

[20] We do not report performance measures for most models, as most approaches work on different datasets and tasks, causing the scores to be incomparable. Instead, we summarize our findings on the most promising approaches at the end of this section.

bias. Our analysis shows that media bias detection methods use approaches ranging from traditional natural language processing (tNLP) methods (e.g., [304]) and simple ML techniques (e.g., [370]) to complex computer science frameworks that combine different advanced classification approaches (e.g., [180]), and graph-learning-based approaches (e.g., [192]). Therefore, we introduce the classification depicted in Fig. 2.4.

Table 2.1 Results of the literature study on computer science methods used for media bias detection

	2019	2020	2021	2022	total
tNLP	[42, 99, 406], [362]*	[12, 26, 111, 143, 284, 304, 312, 420], [240]*	[11, 20, 106, 107, 232, 236, 358], [103]*		21
tbML	[119, 139, 153, 182, 332]	[45, 59, 61, 176, 235, 253, 292, 311, 386], [47, 291]*	[8, 18, 65, 180, 187, 202, 213, 261, 270, 371], [372, 424]*	[6, 17, 245, 266, 340]	33
ntbML	[33, 71, 151, 201, 208]	[92, 102, 145, 199, 209, 273, 403, 414]	[53, 157, 231, 350, 351]	[138, 263]	20
nNN	[34, 46]	[31, 72, 152, 214, 238, 370], [91]*	[21, 22, 337], [307]*		13
graph-based	[252]	[93, 96, 378]	[170, 192, 393, 425]	[175]	9
total	17	38	33	8	96

* We refer to this paper in multiple sections. If a publication covers multiple categories, we assign the most used category. If two categories apply equally, we assign one based on the method performing best.

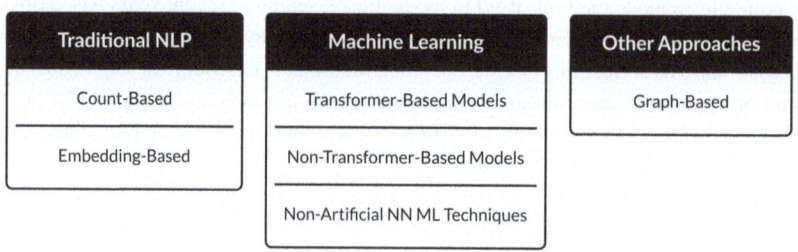

Fig. 2.4 Classification of computer science methods for media bias detection we use in our analysis

2.5 Computer Science Research on Media Bias

Approaches we classify as tNLP (**Sect.** 2.5.1) do not use complex ML techniques and are commonly employed in social sciences (e.g., [232, 284]). We categorize the tNLP publications into two groups: first, count-based techniques supported by lexical resources, and second, more sophisticated embedding-based techniques.

ML-based approaches (**Sect.** 2.5.2) are organized into transformer-based machine learning (tbML), non-transformer-based (ntbML), and non-neural network (nNN)-based (**Sect.** 2.5.2.3) approaches, ordered by the frequency of application in the reviewed literature. Graph-based models represent the third major category presented in **Sect.** 2.5.3.

In the electronic supplementary material, Appendix **B.1** shows the number of publications per year and category according to our search criteria (cf. **Sect.** 2.2). An increasing majority of publications use tbML approaches, while the numbers of nNN- and ntbML-based approaches decrease. Although our review does not fully cover 2022, the numbers suggest that these trends continue.

2.5.1 Traditional Natural Language Processing Techniques

The tNLP category encompasses all publications that identify media bias using techniques not based on ML or graph-based approaches. We include the term "traditional" in the category name to differentiate it from ML and similar techniques. Moreover, techniques similar to what we label as tNLP have already been employed in computational linguistics as early as the sixties and seventies [366]. Frequently, tNLP methods are used as a baseline when introducing new datasets due to their explainability and proven effectiveness (e.g. [107, 240, 358]). Furthermore, social sciences are increasingly adopting them because of their accessibility and ease of use [232]. Although some approaches leverage ML techniques (e.g., [106]), we classify them as tNLP if the main contribution is a non-ML approach. The tNLP methods can be divided into count-based and embedding-based approaches. Count-based approaches quantify words and n-grams in the text to analyze bias, while embedding-based approaches are more sophisticated and serve to represent texts for either facilitating comparisons (e.g., [240, 312]) or analyzing text associations and inherent biases (e.g., [81, 143]).

2.5.1.1 Count-Based Approaches
While recent applications of tNLP techniques primarily employ embedding-based methods, simpler count-based approaches are still in use. Count-based approaches most commonly use word counts and a lexicon as a reference to quantify linguistic characteristics and compare texts.

Niven and Kao [304] measured the alignment of texts to authoritarian state media using a count-based methodology that leveraged the LIWC lexicon [321] for topical categorization. Similarly, Spinde, Hamborg, and Gipp [12] applied various count-based techniques to a custom dataset of German news articles and assessed their effectiveness for media bias detection. They reported precision, recall, and F_1 scores for bias and sentiment lexicons, word embeddings, and general TF-IDF measures, evaluating the identification of human-annotated bias in their dataset. A custom bias lexicon yielded the best performance with a low F_1 score of 0.31.

Sapiro-Gheiler [362] employed Naive Bayes (NB) decision tree, support vector machine (SVM), and lasso-penalty regression models based on bag-of-word representations to classify politicians' ideological positions and trustworthiness. De Arruda, Roman, and Monteiro [111] used a count-based approach within an outlier detection framework to identify selection, statement, and coverage bias in political news. D'Alonzo and Tegmark [106] presented a singular value decomposition (SVD) approach that predicts the newspaper that published an article based on word and n-gram frequencies. Discriminative words and n-grams were derived from a multi-stage (automatic and manual) purging process. The system generates a conditional probability distribution that enables the projection of newspapers and phrases into a left-right bias space.

Zahid et al. [420] used a contingency table showing mention counts and polarity rates for sources (S) and entities (E) within news-related content on Twitter to calculate media bias measures based on definitions for absolute and relative media bias [354]. They investigated coverage, selection, and statement bias towards specific topics and entities, and further quantified and compared the number of positive and negative reports from media outlets on Twitter.

Cuéllar-Hidalgo et al. [103] presented their contribution to the ICON2021 Shared Task on Multilingual Gender Biased and Communal Language Identification [234], where the goal is to classify texts as aggressive, gender biased, or communally charged. They used k-nearest neighbors (KNN) and a mixed approach consisting of NB, SVM, random forest (RF), GBM, Adaboost, and a multi-layer perceptron, for classifying texts.[21]

Dacon and Liu [107] presented a study on gender bias in news abstracts using centering resonance analysis based on specifically filtered attribute words. This technique employs rich linguistic features and graph-based techniques.

---

[21] This work employed both tNLP and NN based methods. However, since the majority of the techniques fall into the tNLP category, we discuss it here.

2.5 Computer Science Research on Media Bias

2.5.1.2 Word Embedding-Based Techniques

A second group of tNLP techniques detects media bias by deriving word associations through word embeddings. We exclude publications that investigate bias in pre-trained word embeddings, e.g., to understand potential biases in systems that use the embeddings, as this analysis does not represent a media bias investigation. However, we include work that uses word embeddings as proxies to help understand biases in texts used for training the embeddings. This is typically done by constructing word embeddings based on a collection of texts and investigating associations in these embeddings (e.g., [143, 240, 312]). We differentiate between sparse and dense embedding-based techniques. Sparse embeddings, primarily based on TF-IDFs, are mostly used to survey the occurrence of certain words [240]. Dense embeddings are employed to examine associations with specific terms [143, 406].

Sparse Word Embeddings. Leavy [240] investigated gender bias in Irish newspapers, examining various discriminative features such as TF-IDFs. Alongside ML techniques, she used count-based tNLP approaches to detect coverage bias towards female politicians. Employing a bag-of-words approach, TF-IDFs, and linguistic labels on word forms, she provided data for classification models and directly detected bias. For instance, she found articles mentioning spouses of female politicians four times more often than male politicians.

Dense Word Embeddings. Most word embedding-based techniques in this section use methods similar to the word embedding association test (WEAT) introduced by Caliskan, Bryson, and Narayanan [81]. WEAT investigates bias in the resulting word embeddings trained on a specific text corpus by measuring the cosine similarity between two sets of tokens (e.g., male and female pronouns) and another two sets of tokens, typically topic or stereotype-based words.

Ferrer et al. [143] explored various aspects of linguistic and gender bias on Reddit using a technique akin to WEAT, while also examining biases through count-based approaches and sentiment analysis. Badjatiya, Gupta, and Varma [42] proposed a debiasing strategy using bias-sensitive words as reference, primarily focusing on replacing bias-sensitive words with less sensitive synonyms to debias text datasets. They identified replacement words using word embeddings with different algorithms such as KNN or a centroid function.

Mendelsohn, Tsvetkov, and Jurafsky [284] primarily employed embedding-based tNLP techniques to investigate the development of dehumanization towards the LGBTQ community in New York Times articles from 1986 to 2015. Wevers [406] conducted a study on gender bias in Dutch newspapers between 1950 and 1990, measuring the distance of "three sets of target words" [406, p. 3] to two gender-representative vectors. These vectors were constructed from the average of lists of "gender words"[406], such as "man," "his," "father," and similar terms for the male vector.

Similarly, Papakyriakopoulos et al. [312] used word embedding associations to compare gender bias in Wikipedia and social media texts. Kroon, Trilling, and Raats [232] analyzed implicit associations with word embeddings to detect racial bias, using the term "ethnically stereotyped bias" in their work. Spinde et al. [20] trained two word embedding models on slanted news corpora: one using left-wing news from HuffPost and another based on right-wing Breitbart news. They employed the Word2Vec Continuous Skip-gram architecture for training and subsequently applied a distance-based technique with their word embeddings to identify strongly biased words, beginning with biased seed words.

Kwak et al. [236] presented a distinct approach to bias detection based on word embeddings. They introduced a method for characterizing documents by identifying the most relevant semantic framing axes ("microframes") that are overrepresented in the text. They then assessed the extent of bias and activity of a given microframe, ultimately providing a more detailed description of the documents. For instance, they might identify that the axis of "depressing" and "cheerful" is central to an article and then analyze the wording that led to this classification [236].

Sales et al. [358] employed a mix of tNLP techniques based on word embeddings to detect subjectivity bias, utilizing methods such as lexicon translation and document similarity measures.

2.5.2 Machine Learning

The following section includes publications that used ML for bias detection. We start by presenting transformer-based models (tbML), which were most frequently applied in the reviewed literature, followed by non-transformer-based models (ntbML), and non-neural network models (nNN). TbML increased in popularity after their introduction in 2017 [390], as shown in Table 2.1 and Appendix **B.1**. Transformers use self-attention to weigh the importance of input data and can be fine-tuned with specific datasets, saving time and resources [390]. Their universal architecture captures dependencies across domains but can over-fit in case of limited training data [258].

2.5.2.1 Transformer-Based Models

Researchers frequently used tbML to detect linguistic bias or political stance with an encoder-only architecture and bias-specific pre-training. Most often they used BERT or models derived from it, e.g, RoBERTa [6, 21, 59, 202, 270, 340, 424],

DistilBERT [17, 65, 340], or ALBERT [213]. Several papers compare the performance of BERT-based models with other transformer models, e.g. T5 [6], BART [187, 245], ELECTRA [18] or XLNet [261]. BERT-based models were also applied to detect media bias in languages other than English, such as Korean ((Kor)BERT) [182], Indian (IndicBERT) [213] or fine-tuning BERT on African American [292]. When researchers used an encoder-decoder architecture model like BART, they used the encoder only for the detection task, while the decoder performed the debiasing task [187, 245]. BERT-based models often outperformed other transformers for most of the tasks and groups we defined for linguistic bias [18, 202, 340, 371], and for political stance detection [119, 372], which typically associates linguistic bias with specific political stances [372].

The prevalent approach in tbML is to create or select bias-specific datasets, fine-tune the most popular models on them, and test the performance of the encoder-only architecture by comparing F_1-scores to baselines of tNLP methods (e.g., [6, 18, 153, 180, 311]). To facilitate the evaluation of using different transformers for identifying various media bias types, we structure our review of tbML by the type of bias used in fine-tuning.

Linguistic Bias. Most tbML applications focus on detecting linguistic bias. Spinde et al. [18] detected bias by word choice following a distant supervision approach with BERT. Based on the BABE dataset, BERT outperformed RoBERTa and other ML classifiers in their application. In contrast, Huguet Cabot et al. [202] achieved the best performance on their Us vs. Them dataset with RoBERTa. Sinha and Dasgupta [371] also fine-tuned BERT with a custom dataset and contextual embeddings. In addition, they parsed sentences using a GCN model with an additional layer of bidirectional long short-term memory (LSTM) to exploit structural information. Raza, Reji, and Ding [340] proposed a four-phase pipeline consisting of detection (DistilBERT), recognition (RoBERTa), bias masking, and debiasing. The system, fine-tuned on the MBIC dataset [21], detected biased words, masked them, and suggested a set of sentences with new words that are bias-free or less biased. Pryzant et al. [332] detected and automatically transformed inappropriate subjective texts into a more neutral version. Using a corpus of sentence pairs from Wikipedia edits, their system used BERT as an encoder to identify subjective words as part of the generation process.

Political Stance Detection. The second most researched classification problem is political stance detection, an umbrella term closely related to partisan bias (cf. **Sect.** 2.4.2) that identifies linguistic biases to identify the political biases of authors. Sinno et al. [372] studied the ideology of specific policies under discussion and presented the first diachronic dataset of news articles annotated at the paragraph level by trained political scientists and linguists. Their fine-tuned BERT model performed best. Dinkov et al. [119] integrated audio, video, metadata, and subtitles in their multimodal dataset. In addition to the text analysis with BERT, their application included metadata and audio data through open SMILE[22], resulting in the highest accuracy. Sinno et al. [372] presented a manually annotated dataset focusing on linguistic bias in news articles. Based on their dataset, in addition to several BERT-based classification approaches, they used a 2-layer bidirectional LSTM for ideology prediction, which was outperformed by all transformer-based systems.

Framing Bias. Mokhberian et al. [291] used BERT with tweet embeddings, fine-tuned on the All The News dataset[23], and an intensity score for moral frames classification based on the moral foundation theory[24]. Kwak, An, and Ahn [235] proposed a similar BERT-based method for conducting sociological frame analysis to detect framing bias. Lee et al. [245] proposed a system for framing bias detection and neutral summary generation from multiple news headlines of varying political leanings to facilitate balanced and unbiased news reading. They performed multi-document summarization, multi-task learning with two tasks, and based their work on BART.

Spin/Informational Bias. Fan et al. [139] investigated lexical and informational bias with BERT on their BASIL dataset, which others also used in their research [59, 266, 371]. Berg and Markert [59] fine-tuned RoBERTa as a context-inclusive model, exploring neighboring sentences, the full article, articles on the same event from other news publishers, and articles from the same domain. Their model is domain-and-task-adapted for informational bias detection on the BASIL corpus. They reported that integrating event context improved classification performance.

Racial/Group Bias. For group bias detection, He, Majumder, and McAuley [187] presented DEPEN, which employs a fine-tuned BERT model to detect biased writing styles. Subsequently, they used BART to debias and rewrite these detected sentences.

Sentiment Analysis. We exclude general sentiment analysis but include publications that leveraged sentiment analysis for linguistic bias detection as a stand-in for political stance detection (cf. Sect. 2.5.2.1). Huguet Cabot et al. [202] investigated populist mindsets, social groups, and related typical emotions using RoBERTa fine-tuned on their populist attitude dataset *Us vs. Them*. Gao et al. [153] utilized BERT in aspect-level sentiment classification, achieving promising performances on three

---

[22] https://www.audeering.com/de/research/opensmile/

[23] https://www.kaggle.com/datasets/snapcrack/all-the-news

[24] Moral foundation theory explains moral differences across cultures. For more information, see the original work by Haidt and Craig [178].

2.5 Computer Science Research on Media Bias

public sentiment datasets[25]. They showed that incorporating target information is crucial for BERT's performance improvement. Hamborg and Donnay [180] applied target-dependent sentiment classification (TSC) with BERT, RoBERTa, XLNET, and a BiGRU. They proposed a classifier, GRU-TSC, that incorporated contextual embeddings of the sentences and representations of external knowledge sources.

Unreliable News Detection. Zhou et al. [424] used RoBERTa to detect unreliable news—a task that overlaps with media bias detection. Further, they proposed ways to minimize selection bias when creating datasets by including a simple model as a difficulty/bias probe. They also suggested that future model development uses a clean non-overlapping site and date split [424].

2.5.2.2 Non-Transformer-Based Models

This section presents publications that use non-transformer-based machine learning for media bias detection, categorized by the type of detected bias. Most commonly, ntbML methods are used to detect media bias at the document level, e.g., hyperpartisanship and political stance. Despite the homogeneity of detected biases, publications using ntbML evaluate numerous aspects of the identification methodology, including training data [273, 372], word embeddings [102, 208, 403], and pseudo-labeling [351].

Linguistic/Text-Level Bias. The detection of hyperpartisanship[26] is the most common application of ntbML. The task's popularity is partly due to the SemEval 2019 hyperpartisan news detection task [220] and the associated dataset, which inspired many publications. Hyperpartisanship is defined as non-neutral news reporting [220], which can be described as a combination of linguistic and text-level biases on a document level. The approach of Jiang et al. [208] performed best in the task. It leveraged a convolutional neural network (CNN) along with batch normalization and ELMo embeddings. In a follow-up study, Jiang et al. [209] incorporated Latent Dirichlet Allocation (LDA) distributions with different approaches to hyperpartisan news detection. They implemented multiple methods, such as a CNN, a recurrent neural network (RNN), a transformer encoder approach, and a hierarchical attention network (HAN) with and without LDA topic modeling. Their results suggested that, in most cases, LDA topic modeling improves the effectiveness of the methods, and hierarchical models outperform non-hierarchical models. Webson et al. [403] presented another study based on the SemEval 2019 hyperpartisan news

---

[25] The datasets include restaurant and laptop reviews, and tweets [153].
[26] Hyperpartisanship is not to be confused with partisan bias as described in **Sect.** 2.4.2. It describes one-sidedness that can manifest in a range of biases [220].

detection task. They focused on decomposing pre-trained embeddings into separate denotation and connotation spaces to identify biased words descriptively. Although their primary goal was to improve the embeddings' reflection of the implied meaning of words, they showed how the discrepancy between the denotation space and the pre-trained embeddings reflects partisanship [403]. Cruz, Rocha, and Cardoso [102] used different ML approaches (e.g., RNN, CNN, bidirectional LSTM/GRU, and the attention-based approaches Attention-based Bidirectional Long Short-term Memory (AttnBL), Hierarchical Attention Network (HAN)) trained on the SemEval 2019 dataset. They evaluated the effects of attention mechanisms and embeddings based on different granularities, tokens, and sentences on the effectiveness of the models. Ruan, Namee, and Dong [351] focused on introducing methods for generating additional data. They presented two approaches for pseudo-labeling (overlap-checking and meta-learning) and introduced a system detecting media bias using sentence representations from averaged word embeddings generated from a pre-trained ELMo model and batch normalization. The same authors also employed an ELMo-based classifier and a data augmentation method using pseudo-labeling [350].

Political Stance Detection. Baly et al. [47] trained two models based on LSTM and BERT for classifying news texts as left-wing, center, or right-wing. Their main contribution is the evaluation of techniques for eliminating the effects of outlet-specific language characteristics (here: political ideology expressed by linguistic bias) from the training process. They used adversarial adaptation and triplet loss pre-training for removing linguistic characteristics from the training data. Further, they incorporated news outlets' Wikipedia articles and the bio of their Twitter followers in the training processes to reduce the effects of outlet-specific language characteristics. While a transformer-based classification outperformed the LSTM model, the techniques for improving training effectiveness improved both models' classification results.[27] As part of their political stance detection approach, Gangula, Duggenpudi, and Mamidi [151] proposed a headline attention network approach to bias detection in Telugu news articles. It leveraged a bidirectional LSTM attention mechanism to identify key parts of the articles based on their headlines, which were then used to detect bias toward political stances. They compared the results of their approach with NB, SVM, and CNN approaches, all of which the headline attention network outperformed. To depolarize political news articles, Fagni and Cresci [138] mapped Italian social media users into a 2D space. Their solution initially leveraged a NN for learning latent user representations. Then, they forwarded these representations to a UMAP [280] model to project and position users in a latent political

---

[27] Since transformers are not the paper's focus, we discuss it here.

2.5 Computer Science Research on Media Bias

ideology space, allowing them to leverage properties of the ideology space to infer the political leaning of every user, via clustering.

Gender/Group Bias. Field and Tsvetkov [145] presented an unsupervised approach for identifying gender bias in Facebook comments. They used a bidirectional LSTM to predict the gender of the addressee of Facebook comments and, in doing so, identify gender biases in these comments. Mathew et al. [273] introduced HateXplain, a dataset on hate speech and gender bias that includes expert labels on the target community towards which the hate speech is aimed. They further included labels of words annotators identified as bias-inducing. They evaluated the effects of including the rationale labels in the training process of a BiRNN and a BERT model on the models' bias detection capabilities. Including the rationale labels increased the bias classification performance for both models.

2.5.2.3 Non-Neural Network Machine Learning Techniques

Besides state-of-the-art approaches using tbML or deep learning techniques for bias detection, other (nNN) ML approaches are still widely used for bias detection. Many employ LDA, SVM, or regression models, but a wide range of models is usually used and compared. These models are particularly common in papers presenting new datasets, as they can be seen as a solid and widely known baseline for the quality of labels within a dataset.

Based on the MBIC dataset [21, 22], we presented a traditional feature-based bias classifier. They evaluated various models (e.g., LDA, logistic regression (LR), glsXGBoost, and others), trained with features such as a bias lexicon, sentiment values, and linguistic word characteristics (such as boosters or attitude markers [22]). Alzhrani [31] contributed a dataset of personalized news. Furthermore, she used a range of classifiers (Ridge classifier, nearest centroid, SVM with SDG, NB) for political affiliation detection. Rao and Taboada [337] investigated coverage and gender bias in their dataset of Canadian news articles. They employed LDA topic modeling to detect biased topic distributions for articles that contain predominantly male or female sources. Kameswari, Sravani, and Mamidi [214] presented a dataset of 200 unbiased and 850 biased articles written in Telugu. They used NB (Bernoulli and multinomial), LR, SVM, RF, and MLP classifiers to evaluate the effectiveness of adding presuppositions as model input. Shahid et al. [370] researched framing effects in news articles using their proposed dataset. They trained an SVM classifier to detect and classify moral framing and compared it to a baseline lexicon-based natural language processing approach, investigating moral framing aspects such as authority, betrayal, care, cheating, etc. Ganguly et al. [152] explored various biases that can occur while constructing a media bias dataset. Part of their work examined the correlation between the political stance of news articles and the political stances of their media outlets. To evaluate this correlation, they compared multinominal NB, SVM, LR, and RF models using ground-truth labels. Several other publications described the application of nNN ML approaches in addition to other ML techniques for data evaluation [238, 240, 291, 307, 424]. We have already mentioned these in **Sect. 2.5.1** and **Sect. 2.5.2.2**.

Baly et al. [46] presented a multi-task ordinal regression framework for simultaneously classifying political stance and trustworthiness at different Likert scales. This approach is based on the assumption that the two phenomena are intertwined. They employed a copula ordinal regression along with a range of features derived from their previous work, including complexity and morality labels, linguistic features, and sentiment scores. Anthonio and Kloppenburg [34] presented an additional[28] model for the SemEval 2019 hyperpartisan news detection task [220]. They used a linear SVM with VADER sentiment scores as a feature, relying exclusively on the intensity of negative sentiment in texts to derive political stances expressed in texts. With a F_1 score of 0.694, their approach failed to match the other competitors in the task. In addition to a FastText classifier, the approach presented by Lazaridou et al. [238] included a manual selection of training data containing examples of media bias. Aside from contributing to a new media bias dataset and evaluating the effect of expert and non-expert annotators, they presented a curriculum learning approach for media bias detection. They concluded that high-quality expert-labeled data improves the performance of the model.

2.5.3 Graph-Based

The research described in this section leverages graph data structures to analyze online social networks through their users and text interactions, which requires a distinctive set of methods for bias analysis. Although most publications used ML, we treat them separately due to the unique characteristics of the analyzed data representations. Graph-based approaches are primarily used to investigate framing bias, echo chambers, and political stances. Therefore, we structure our overview of corresponding publications by the type of bias they investigate.

Framing Bias. The SLAP4SLIP framework [192] detects how concepts are discussed in different parts of a social network with predefined linguistic features, graph NN, and structured sparsity. The authors exploit the network structure of discussion forums on Reddit without explicitly labeled data and minimally supervised features

---

[28] We mention multiple models for the task within **Sect. 2.5.2.2**.

2.5 Computer Science Research on Media Bias

representing ideologically driven agenda setting and framing. Training graph autoencoders, Hofmann et al. [192] modeled agenda setting, and framing for identifying ideological polarization within network structures of online discussion forums. They modeled polarization along the dimensions of salience and framing. Further, they proposed MultiCTX (Multi-level ConTeXt), a model consisting of contrastive learning and sentence graph attention networks to encode different levels of context, i.e., neighborhood context of adjacent sentences, article context, and event context.

Guo and Zhu [175] built on the SLAP4SLIP framework [192] to detect informational bias and ideological radicalization by combining contrastive learning and sentential graph networks. Similarly, Similarly, Tran [386] proposed a framework for identifying bias in news sources. The authors used BERT Base for aspect-based sentiment analysis and assigned a bias score to each source with a graph-based algorithm.

Echo Chambers. Villa, Pasi, and Viviani [393] applied community detection strategies and modeled a COVID-19-related conversation graph to detect echo chambers. Their method considered the relationship between individuals and the semantic aspects of their shared content on Twitter. By partitioning four different representations of a graph (i.e., topology-based, sentiment-based, topic-based, and hybrid) with the METIS algorithm[29], followed up by qualitative methods, they assessed both the relationships connecting individuals and semantic aspects related to the content they share over Twitter. They also analyzed the controversy and homogeneity among the different polarized groups obtained.

Political Stance Detection. Stance detection[30] is a typical application of graph-based classification techniques. Zhou et al. [425] combined network structure learning analysis and NN to predict the political stance of news media outlets. With their semi-supervised network embedding approach, the authors built a training corpus on network information, including macro- and micro-network views. They primarily employed network embedding learning and graph-based label propagation to overcome label sparsity. By integrating graph embeddings as a feature, Stefanov et al. [378] detected the stance and political stance of Twitter users and online media by leveraging their retweet behavior. They used a user-to-hashtag graph and a user-to-mention graph and then ran node2vec. They achieved the best result for

---

[29] As proposed by Karypis and Kumar [216].

[30] We defined stance detection as political bias detection via the identification of linguistic biases, compare **Sect.** 2.5.2.1.

combining BERT with valence scores[31]. Guimarães et al. [170] analyzed news stories and political opinions shared on Brazilian Facebook. They proposed a graph-based semi-supervised learning approach to classify Facebook pages as politically left or right. Utilizing audience interaction information by inferring self-reported political leaning from Facebook pages, Guimarães et al. [170] built an interest graph to determine the stance of media outlets and public figures. The authors achieved the best results for label propagation with a spectral graph transducer. Li and Goldwasser [252] captured social context with a neural architecture for representing relational information with graph-based representations and a graph convolutional network. They showed that using social information, such as Twitter users who have shared the article, can significantly improve performance with distant and direct supervision.

2.5.4 Bias in Language Models

Detecting bias inherent to language models is an important research area due to the models' popularity for many NLP tasks. Researchers have investigated bias in texts and other media generated by language models as well as in classification performed with language models. We did not include publications that address these forms of bias.[32] However, we would like to give some examples to raise awareness of biased language models. Nadeem, Bethke, and Reddy [297] analyzed stereotypical bias with the crowdsourced dataset StereoSet in BERT, GPT-2, ROBERTA, and XLNET, concluding that all models exhibit strong stereotypical bias. Vig et al. [392] used causal mediation analysis to analyze gender bias in language models. Their results showed that gender bias effects exist in specific components of language models. Vig et al. [61] also analyzed gender bias within BERT-layers and concluded that the layers are generally biased. In Liu et al. [262], the authors detected bias in texts generated by GPT-2 and discussed means of mitigating gender bias in language models by using a reinforcement learning framework.

---

[31] A valence score [378] close to zero reflects that an influencer is cited evenly among different groups in a network. Conversely, a score close to −1 or 1 indicates that one group disproportionately cites an influencer compared to another group. In their paper, Stefanov et al. [378] indicated that valence scores are essential in identifying media bias in social networks.

[32] We focus exclusively on detection methods; the field of bias in language models is extensive enough for a dedicated literature review.

2.5.5 Datasets

During our review, we collected both methods and datasets from the publications we selected for inclusion. In total, we found 123 datasets. We categorize the datasets according to the concepts proposed in our Media Bias Taxonomy, similar to the discussion of methodologies as shown in Table 2.2. We added the category General Linguistic Bias as several datasets do not define the subcategory of bias they contain. We did not evaluate the quality of the datasets as they address distinct tasks and objectives but leave this assessment for future work (cf. **Sect.** 2.7).

Only two of the 123 datasets include information on the background of annotators. Moreover, dataset sizes are generally small; only 21 of the 123 datasets contain more than 30,000 annotations. We believe that the use of multiple datasets is promising for future work as we discuss in **Sect.** 2.7. As part of this review, we present the datasets, their statistics, and tasks merely as a starting point for future work, without further assessment. We give a detailed overview of publications, sizes, availability, tasks, type of label, link, and publication summary for each dataset in our repository.

Table 2.2 Overview of datasets found during our literature review

Media Bias Category	Media Bias Type	Amount
Linguistic Bias		45
	General Linguistic Bias	26
	Framing Bias	15
	Epistemological Bias	3
	Bias by Semantic Properties	1
Text-level Context Bias		5
	Statement Bias	2
	Phrasing Bias	3
Reporting-level Context Bias		6
	General Reporting-level Context Bias	2
	Selection Bias	1
	Coverage Bias	2
	Proximity Bias	1
Cognitive Bias		28
	Partisan Bias	28
Related Concepts		
	Hate Speech	14
	Group Bias	20
	Sentiment Analysis	10

2.6 Human-Centered Research on Media Bias

Human-centered research on media bias aims to understand why people perceive media as biased, explore the societal and digital consequences, and develop strategies to overcome biased perception and detect media bias. Debates on all these factors are ongoing and experimental effects tend to be minor. Hereafter, we highlight some of these debates.

2.6.1 Reasons for Biased Media Perception

One explanation for the emergence of cognitive biases in media perception is that information is processed in light of prior expectations, which may be distorted [301]. The veracity of claims is often judged based on familiarity, potentially resulting in illusory truths [147, 154, 229, 374]. Cognitive dissonance theory posits that people experience discomfort when confronted with information inconsistent with their convictions, motivating them to discount it [144].

Extending this notion to groups, Tajfel et al. [383] suggested in their social identity and categorization theory that basic self-esteem is derived from personal affiliation with positively-connotated groups. This results in in-group favoritism, out-group derogation [219, 352], and behavior and information processing in line with group identity. People easily regard reports that negatively affect groups they strongly identify with as a personal threat to their self-esteem and devalue these reports [160, 186]. Furthermore, Turner [388] posited that when people self-categorize with a specific group, they evaluate the validity of arguments by congruence to in-group norms and in-group consensus. This pattern aligns with empirical findings showing that news acceptance depends on group identification and congruent group membership cues of the news source [342, 365].

Generally, prior works expect selective exposure to media to be consistent with previous viewpoints [227], further strengthening prior convictions. Such behaviour can be referred to as confirmation bias [301] through repeated exposure [113]. In the age of social media and the abundance of information available, these cognitive biases may further allow for confrontation only with attitude-consistent information and like-minded individuals in echo chambers [295, 302, 381]. Moreover, algorithms trained on these biases may further limit the available media spectrum in filter bubbles [313].

Consequently, limited exposure to alternative viewpoints may also impact the perception of social norms and the prevalence of opinions. The overestimation of the frequency of one's own position, known as the false consensus effect [349],

2.6 Human-Centered Research on Media Bias

has been widely documented even before the introduction of social media and may be partially due to identity motivations explained earlier [272]. However, when echo chambers are used to gauge the frequency of opinions and social norms, even larger shifts between groups are expected [247]. This feeds into a vicious circle of polarizing group norms, discounting information inconsistent with these shifted norms, and feeling encouraged to voice even more extreme positions (e.g., [123, 275, 365, 388]). These mechanisms lead to expectations that media perception is polarized based on social categories and prior beliefs and that the introduction of social media has exacerbated this phenomenon.

2.6.2 Consequences of Biased Media Perception

Partisan individuals tend to select media that aligns with their prior beliefs and political attitudes, a phenomenon known as the Friendly Media Phenomenon (FMP) [49, 164, 229]. This tendency may be partially due to interpersonal communication among like-minded individuals [190]. People also tend to assess the veracity of information based on its fit with their political convictions, exhibiting partisan bias [155].

Biased media perception can lead to the Hostile Media Phenomenon (HMP), where people perceive media coverage as biased against their side, regardless of the actual political position of the article [185, 326, 389]. This effect increases with the extremity of party affiliation and is primarily due to the derogation of dissenting media [14, 49, 156], making it a cognitive bias rather than a characteristic of the media landscape. Discussions and feedback from like-minded individuals can further amplify the HMP, leading to the perception of general media bias even when primarily exposed to self-selected, like-minded media [83, 228].

Methodologically, the HMP, FMP, and partisan bias complicate the assessment of media bias, as raters' perceptions of bias may reflect more on individual affiliations and idiosyncrasies than the objective properties of the rated article [15]. Subjective bias ratings are relative to their social context; their quality as a scientific measure of media bias depends on the representativeness of raters. Therefore, such ratings should be supplemented by objective bipartisan bias criteria (e.g., language biases).

Socially, the HMP can lead to the mobilization of more extreme positions, distrust in the social system, and, in cases of low efficacy beliefs, political withdrawal [326]. Both the HMP and FMP can contribute to increased political segmentation and polarization, which can negatively impact political communication and interaction, essential for a peaceful and democratic society [156]. Exposure to certain media can also have social consequences, such as altered political participation [228]. For example, Dvir-Gvirsman, Garrett, and Tsfati [128] found that exposure to congruent media is tied to biased perceptions of the opinion climate, influencing how participants communicate their political beliefs and engage in politically meaningful acts, while incongruent exposure has little effect.

The role of the social media environment in this process is somewhat disputed: While selective exposure in social media is widely documented [302, 391], some authors argue that social media is not the main contributor to the variety of media diets globally. For example, Zuiderveen Borgesius et al. [428] deem its general impact negligible and suggest it may expose users to more diverse information compared to traditional media. According to Dubois and Blank [127], people may even cope with this high-choice media environment by developing strategies like verifying news in different outlets, and—even though social networks are polarized—only a subset of the population regards itself as susceptible to echo chambers. After all, the phenomena and underlying cognitive processes were known before the advent of social media. The effects observed in social media may just be more visible to researchers than they were before [428]. In addition, exposure to biased media may not be sufficient to significantly affect attitudes [260]. As such, it is challenging to determine the overall effect of social media on biased media perception and social consequences today, though some feedback loops can be expected [123]. This problem is even more pressing for algorithmic filtering than for personal selections, as the algorithms involved are not transparently disclosed, their application is in flux, and they are not accessible to the user [428]. This fact illustrates that parts of the conclusion on the impact of social media on media bias phenomena are also driven by the selection of media and the assessment method of the effects.

2.6.3 Recipient-Oriented Approaches to Reduce Media Bias

Given that selective media exposure partially explains cognitive media bias phenomena, one intervention approach is to encourage and facilitate a diverse media diet to reduce media bias [127]. This can be achieved by plug-ins that actively diversify the media displayed in a search by identifying the topic and sampling other articles or information related to it [306], or by providing media based on another individual's platform history [62]. In a similar approach, Munson, Lee, and Resnick [295] used a browser widget to provide feedback on the balance of a user's media diet, successfully encouraging these users to explore more media from centrist and opposing viewpoints.

2.6 Human-Centered Research on Media Bias

Other experiments and observations of counter-attitudinal exposure illustrate that the mere presentation and reception of opposing viewpoints do not always decrease the HMP and may even exacerbate the problem. For instance, Weeks et al. [404] found that people who were incidentally exposed to counter-attitudinal information are more likely to subsequently select information that aligns with their attitudes. Other studies found that exposure to incongruent comments increases the perception of bias and decreases the perception of the credibility of a later, neutral news report [156], and that exposure to opposing tweets may backfire and intensify political polarization, particularly for Republicans [43]. These findings are consistent with the notion of motivated reasoning, as the potential threat of backfiring from inconsistent exposure—though rather dependent on the specific materials to which readers are exposed [382]—may be explained by the threat of the presented material to the reader's identity. As a result, diverse exposure with well-crafted materials may help but is not a comprehensive solution for the HMP, FMP, and biased media perception.

As an alternative, some studies have attempted to alter the user's mindset during news processing and shift the attentional focus to aspects of a user's self-identity that are not challenged by the news report. For example, inducing self-affirming thoughts aimed at mitigating the potentially self-threatening aspect of belief-inconsistent arguments has been shown to successfully evoke more unbiased processing of such information [100]. Similarly, focusing readers' attention on a value that may be threatened by information increases their perception of media bias in that article [221]. Likewise, people seem more open to sharing and are better at judging news headlines based on their veracity when nudged to think about their own accuracy instead of their identity motives [325]. Opening the mindset may thus be an effective, albeit situational, approach when tackling phenomena such as the HMP and media bias detection during exposure to attitude-inconsistent materials.

As an additional step, forewarning messages that draw attention to biased media and potential influencing attempts can help "inoculate" against this media by provoking reactance towards manipulations [14, 348, 356]. Exposing individuals to examples of media bias through such messages may teach them to detect and cope with it. In this vein, various forms of training have been tested and generally increase a reader's ability to identify biased media and distinguish it from congruency with one's political stance [10, 14, 260]. This detailed training is necessary, as mere awareness of media bias as part of general news media literacy may not be sufficient for a balanced media diet [387].

Overall, all approaches have yielded relatively small effects on improving media bias detection, and more research on effective interventions is necessary. Regarding partisan bias, there is some indication that interventions are not equally effective in reducing the bias for liberals and conservatives—potentially inadvertently biasing the overall discourse on media towards the less open-minded faction [14, 339]. Thus, further testing of the effectiveness of approaches in reducing partisan media perception and the HMP is warranted.

2.7 Discussion

To address RQ1, we have established a Media Bias Taxonomy that allows to precisely categorize the various sub-concepts related to media bias [15, 21]. We emphasize the complexity of media bias and note that researchers often fail to clearly define the type of media bias they investigate, which leads to confusion when comparing different studies. Furthermore, existing literature reviews on the topic do not address the various media bias concepts [181], making it difficult to understand problems and solutions across different approaches.

Our Media Bias Taxonomy is a crucial first step in establishing a common ground for more clearly defined media bias research. We divide media bias into five major categories: linguistic bias, cognitive bias, text-level context bias, reporting-level bias, and related concepts. We provide subgroups for each of these categories. Throughout the creation of our taxonomy, we engaged in frequent discussions and revised our definitions and structure multiple times, revealing the numerous options available for defining media bias.

While our taxonomy provides a practical foundation and effective starting point for research in the domain, future research should critically re-examine the discussed concepts. We believe that the main common ground among the various types of media bias we identified is smaller than that of existing universal definitions (see **Sect.** 2.4.1) and primarily refers to one-sided media content.

To answer RQ2 and RQ3, we provided an extensive overview of recently published literature on computer science methods and datasets for media bias detection. We manually inspected over 1,528 computer science research papers on the topic published between 2019 to May 2022 after automatically filtering over 100,000 keyword-related publications. Our review reveals valuable insights into best practices and trends in the research field.

In recent years, transformers have quickly become the most frequently used and most reliable method for media bias detection and debiasing [21]. Platforms like Hugging Face facilitate the implementation of the models and their adaption to various tasks [119]. However, as we show in **Section** 2.5, the new models have not yet made their way into all subtypes of bias, leaving room for future experiments. Additionally, available media bias classifiers are largely based on small

2.7 Discussion

in-domain datasets. Recent advancements in natural language processing, especially transformer-based models, demonstrate how accurate results can be achieved by unsupervised or supervised training on massive text corpora [37] and by model pre-training using inter and cross-domain datasets [37].

Although graph-based methods are not as popular as transformers, their application to media bias detection is increasing but mostly limited to analyzing social network content, activities, and structures, and identifying structural political stances within these entities [170, 252, 378, 425]. Transformer-based approaches cannot accomplish such an analysis due to the network properties of the explored data.

Established methods still play a role in media bias detection. Traditional natural language processing approaches, as well as non-transformer-based (deep NN) machine learning models, are simpler and more explainable compared to language-model-based approaches, making them advantageous in applications where transparency of classification decisions is critical (e.g., [22]). Since traditional approaches have been used in many media bias identification tasks, they often serve as a baseline to compare new (transformer-based) approaches. Given their higher explainability and long-term testing, we don't expect language models to completely replace other approaches soon.

Apart from these major trends, including information on spreading behavior, social information [96, 252, 378], metadata [119], and examining the vector spaces of word embeddings [119] also show promise in improving classifier performance to detect media bias.

We addressed RQ4 by reviewing social science research on media bias. One significant takeaway is that media bias datasets largely ignore insights from social science research on the topic, leading to low annotator agreement and less accurate annotations [21]. The perception of bias depends on factors beyond content, such as the reader's background and understanding of the text. Moreover, limited exposure to alternative viewpoints can impact how social norms and opinions are perceived. These insights have never been fully integrated into automated detection methods or datasets. Integrating bias perception research in language models is a promising way to improve annotation-based detection systems [61], which can potentially be achieved by further developing standardized questions within the domain [21].

We see a need to develop further methods to increase news consumers' bias awareness and believe that computer science methods, as described in this review, can be a powerful tool to build such awareness-increasing tools. While some tools already exist, none have been applied on a larger scale in a real-world scenario, which is a promising direction for future research.

Our literature review also exhibits limitations. First, we excluded work from areas other than media bias due to the high number of publications involved, potentially leaving out valuable contributions. Investigating promising concepts from other areas will be necessary for future work. Second, for all computer science methods, we only included literature from 2019 to 2022, excluding valuable earlier research. Analyzing a longer period could yield an even more complete picture of the research domain. Lastly, although we distinguish several categories within our Media Bias Taxonomy, the concepts related to media bias still overlap and appear concurrently. We believe that future work should further discuss and adapt the taxonomy. Although the taxonomy we present is merely a starting point to connect works in the area, we believe it can benefit future approaches by raising awareness of concepts, methods, and datasets in the research domain. During the writing of this literature review, the taxonomy's outline frequently changed in permanent discussions among the authors.

2.8 Conclusion

In 2018, Hamborg, Donnay, and Gipp [181] concluded that (1) powerful computer science methods (such as word embeddings and deep learning) had not yet made their way into the automated detection of media bias and that (2) the interdisciplinarity of media bias research should be improved in the future. The authors suggested (3) that approaches in computer science did not account for bias having many different forms and usually only focused on narrow bias definitions [181].

Our literature review reveals that two of these propositions (1 and 3) have been addressed to some extent, but there is still considerable room for improvement. Transformer and graph-based methods have led to significant increases in the performance of automated methods for detecting media bias, and numerous types of bias have received research attention. However, these concepts are primarily used and analyzed individually, with knowledge overlaps between them remaining unexplored [8]. Recent modeling techniques, such as multi-task learning, enable the use of related datasets to improve classification performance [37].

Regarding (2), datasets and systems still exhibit limited conceptual work, with the cognitive dimension of media bias rarely mentioned in computer science research. Our literature review aims to provide a foundation for increased awareness of bias in media bias datasets (through standardized annotator background assessments), enhanced interdisciplinarity in the research domain (which we believe is particularly relevant since reasonable classifications cannot exist without clear conceptualizations), and future computer science methods.

2.8 Conclusion

We are confident that this review will facilitate entry into media bias research and help experienced researchers identify related works. We hope that our findings will contribute to the development of more effective and efficient media bias detection methods and systems to increase media bias awareness. Finally, we plan to repeat our workflow in three years to reassess the state of the research domain.

Open Access This chapter is licensed under the terms of the Creative Commons Attribution 4.0 International License (http://creativecommons.org/licenses/by/4.0/), which permits use, sharing, adaptation, distribution and reproduction in any medium or format, as long as you give appropriate credit to the original author(s) and the source, provide a link to the Creative Commons license and indicate if changes were made.

The images or other third party material in this chapter are included in the chapter's Creative Commons license, unless indicated otherwise in a credit line to the material. If material is not included in the chapter's Creative Commons license and your intended use is not permitted by statutory regulation or exceeds the permitted use, you will need to obtain permission directly from the copyright holder.

Questionnaire Development 3

To be fixed and finished

German Saying

As we laid out in Chap. 2, media bias is a complex concept to identify and analyze. Constructing a coherent framework to cover different bias types has been an important step in setting a basis for future work. However, not only inconsistent definitions of media bias have called for a unified approach; previous assessment strategies of bias are similarly lacking overlap and empirical evaluation. Current research fails to agree on how study participants or readers react toward bias depending on how they were asked. Most existing studies focus only on specific aspects, for example, the Hostile Media Effect [222, 223, 246]. Some studies asked questions related to particular articles [171], while others chose a more general approach [162]. Some ask about bias directly (e.g., "Regarding the web page that you viewed, would you say the portrayal of the presidential candidates was strictly neutral or biased in favor of one side or the other?" [195]), and some indirectly [10–12]. Some researchers tried experiments [104], while others used surveys [162]. While there is some overlap in questions across multiple studies (for example, questions similar to "Would you say that the content in this article was strictly neutral, or was it biased in favor of one side or the other?" [172] were used in different studies [195, 225, 277]), there is a large variety in methods and definitions used in prior research that limits studies' comparability on media bias perception. Furthermore, a standard of assessing media bias of articles as a general construct is essential to train automated

Supplementary Information The online version contains supplementary material available at https://doi.org/10.1007/978-3-658-47798-1_3.

classifiers or build datasets: Without a clear measurement of the construct, no classifier in the related areas can reach its full potential. Our project, therefore, aims to develop questions that can be used as a reliable standard to perform new analyses or reevaluate past studies independent of the research area. Our primary goal and contribution are to develop a reliable scale to evaluate articles regarding media bias. We, therefore, conducted a literature review to find 824 relevant questions about text perception in previous research on the topic, which we summarized and condensed in a multi-iterative process to a final set of 48 questions. We reduced the number of questions even more and uncovered commonalities between questions empirically using exploratory factor analysis (EFA), a data reduction approach. Given different questions, we assess the perception of bias among various articles with a known bias rating. The scale aims to improve the data collection on media bias. This chapter describes the question-testing process, and summarizes and transparently visualizes the question set. We organize the rest of the chapter as follows: First, in **Sect.** 3.1, we describe existing approaches in querying bias. We describe our methodology in **Sect.** 3.2 followed by our results in **Sect.** 3.3. Finally, in **Sect.** 3.4, we discuss limitations and conclude an outlook for further work in **Sect.** 3.5. We want to mention that we use "question" and "item" interchangeably.

> **Research Objective**
> Develop a scale that can be used as a reliable standard to evaluate the perception of media bias.

3.1 Overview of Approaches

Different platforms try to address media bias in news outlets. For instance, the news aggregator Allsides publishes bias ratings for various news outlets[1]. The bias rating by Allsides represents subjective judgments made by their readers. They are organized into five classes [283]:

$$Left - Lean\,Left - Center - Lean\,Right - Right.$$

---

[1] See https://www.Allsides.com/unbiased-balanced-news, accessed on 2021-01-08.

3.1 Overview of Approaches

Allsides combines different methods to create their ratings. They indicate which outlets and articles have been evaluated with which methods on each source page [283]. Altogether, they use the following methods[2]:

1. *Blind Bias Survey.* Allsides gathers readers "from all parts of the political bias spectrum to read and rate articles and headlines blindly—without telling them the source of the content. (...) To assure that the survey audience reflects the social and political diversity of the US, they then normalize the data" [283].
2. *Editorial Review.* To some extent, the Allsides editorial staff reviewed "the works of any source. The reviews always include diverse individuals covering the full range of political bias from left to right" [283].
3. *Third-Party Analysis.* The third-party "analysis may include academic research, surveys, or analysis from third parties that have a published and transparent system for evaluating the bias of multiple sources" [283].
4. *Independent Review.* An AllSides "editor, or multiple editors, reviewed content from this source and came to a general conclusion on its bias; they also investigated what the media and other sources, both partisan and nonpartisan, reported about the political leanings of this source. This method is frequently used for initial bias ratings before more robust methods can be applied, or ratings for which the bias of an outlet is relatively easy to discern" [283].
5. *Community Feedback.* "For every article posted on Allsides, a user can indicate whether or not he agrees with the ratings. While the ratings are not determined by community votes. they are used to check the performance of the current ratings." [283]

Independent of the research area, all prior research on text perception and particularly bias detection [11, 12, 22, 36, 104, 162, 171, 172, 191, 195, 246, 319, 341, 347, 419] questioned either students, experts, or crowdsource workers about their perception of bias on a word, sentence, article, or image level. However, almost none reported a detailed process description of how they created the respective evaluation surveys or chose the questions that were handed to the participants. Also, especially in the computer science studies, except for the study by Spinde et al. [22], none asked for the participant's personal background. Still, as shown in some of the work from psychology and communication science, the personal background seems to be crucial information needed to understand how to interpret and use the collected feedback annotations. The datasets used in the various computer scientific approaches

---

[2] More about the methods can be found on https://www.allsides.com/media-bias/media-bias-ratingmethods

and projects did not reflect media bias' complexity. Instead, they primarily focused on technical approaches. We believe that bias can only be uncovered in an interdisciplinary approach and that data quality and comparability play a crucial role in training any classifier. Therefore, a common and reliably evaluated question set is necessary even more.

3.2 Literature Collection

To systematically find items relevant to media bias perception, we conducted an extensive search on PsychInfo and Google Scholar. The search term "Perception of Media Bias" was mainly used to identify relevant studies on both literature platforms. We excluded articles in languages other than English and German. We manually screened headlines and keywords for their connection to media, media bias, and media perception. If in doubt, we included articles to avoid missing relevant studies. From an original set of 405 potentially relevant papers, after extensive reading and abstract checking, we excluded all but 107 studies, for which we tried to obtain full texts. We excluded 29 more because the full-text reading showed a non-sufficient connection to the perception of media bias. We excluded another 17 studies because they did not use any items on the perception of media or media bias. Overall, we included 74 studies in our collection to create our questionnaire on media bias perception[3].

3.2.1 Item Collection and Selection

Our paper collection led to a list of media bias and related variables, including the item's source, the response format if mentioned, and other important information. If available, we copied the original items from the supplementary material provided by the authors. If no supplemental materials were available, we extracted items from the articles' method and results sections. When the original wording of the item was named, the original wording was added to the list. If not, we used the provided description to reconstruct the wording as well as possible. This process resulted in a list of 824 items, which we then continued to reduce and filter in three iterations. We illustrate the process in Figure 3.1. It is based on four main criteria, which we will summarize afterward:

---

[3] They are included in the file upload at https://zenodo.org/record/4651186#.YGR5vD9CRxs and in the tree visualization on http://bias-questiontree.gipplab.org/, which we describe both in the remainder of this paper.

3.2 Literature Collection

1. The items relate to media bias.
2. The items cover different aspects of media bias.
3. The items measure media bias on an article level.
4. The items are usable for visual analog scales (VAS[4]).

At first, in the categorization iteration, we organized the questions into general categories (e.g., Political Background, Demographics, Perception of Media Bias, Influence of Media Bias). We only included items categorized into "Perception of Media Bias" and "Influence of Media Bias" to create a list of potential items (419). The other categories were revisited later to find relevant background information items, such as demographics or political background.

A lot of the questions were specific to one particular issue or topic. Since the goal was to create a usable questionnaire in general independently of an issue, we generalized the items. If possible, we replaced the specific part with general expressions like 'author,' 'source,' or others. Whenever these generalizations made the item ambiguous, we added a placeholder to clarify that an issue or a side needed to be added to use this item. We excluded twenty items in this step because they could not be generalized without losing meaning. To further reduce the number of items for assessment, we grouped items into the following bias measurement categories: Cause, Existence, Direction, Strength, and Influence. We then grouped semantically and topically similar items to find a construct that fitted as many items as possible without losing any relevant aspects. To name an example, one of the resulting constructs was: "Would you say that the "person/content/outlet was strictly neutral, biased against, or in favor of "side"? Overall, 42 constructs and 99 general items without constructs were left after this process. Since 141 items were still too many, we grouped the edited items by their content and chose items to cover every aspect of each content in a final iteration. If possible, we selected a construct. We used one of the remaining general items if a construct did not cover an aspect. As a result of this process, we had to exclude some items for the following reasons:

1. We decided on a visual analog scale as the response format for the questionnaire. Most questions could be adapted to fit this format, but we removed questions where this was not possible.
2. Since the questionnaire is supposed to identify bias in an article, some questions were too unspecific or unsuitable for this questionnaire, for example, questions about media outlets.

---

[4] A Visual Analogue Scale (VAS) is a measurement instrument that tries to measure a characteristic or attitude that is believed to range across a continuum of values and cannot easily be directly measured [68].

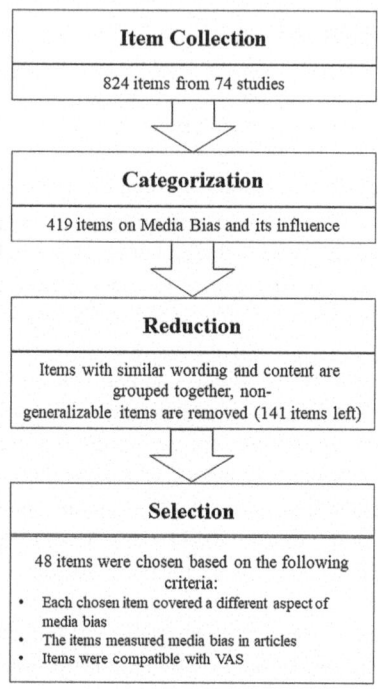

Fig. 3.1 Item reduction process in four main phases

3. Many studies did not include the original wording of their items, and in a few cases, it was not possible to create an adequate item out of the description given in the text.
4. Some items were too specific to the issue of their original study and were unfit to be included in a general questionnaire.
5. Various studies used semantic differentials to ask for respondents' impressions of the articles. In the questionnaire, we only included semantic differentials that at least two different authors used. We applied the same procedure to questions on feelings. We excluded some items because they were only used once.

After this selection, exclusion, and merging process, the final questionnaire consisted of 25 items with varying answering formats, 17 semantic differentials, and six ratings of feelings. To cover third-person perception, we included three items twice, once asking about the article's impact on the participant directly and once about the impact on others. For the question about others, we used the term "another

3.2 Literature Collection

person" to keep the questionnaire as general as possible, as performed likewise in other research [1, 20, 277, 281, 347, 359]. Five items remained with the placeholder that was replaced with article-specific information.

We publish the complete set of final and original questions and all other process information at https://zenodo.org/record/4651186#.YGR5vD9CRxs. We also illustrate which questions were merged and excluded in which way in an interactive tree visualization on http://questions.media-bias-research.org/.

3.2.2 Design

We used the survey platform UniPark[5] for data collection and recruited participants via the recruiting platform Prolific[6]. The study ran on Oct. 20, 2020. Participants were welcomed to the study and given general information on the study's purpose and the data handling. After agreeing to participate, each participant read one of the 190 articles, which was randomly selected. We then asked each participant to rate all 48 items on five pages, separated based on differing anchors, on VAS. All VAS in the study ranged from −10 to 10 and recorded only integer numbers. The order in which the pages and the items on each page were presented was randomized. In addition, an item that asked whether participants read the article was mixed in as an attention check. After rating the article, the participants were asked to answer general media bias questions and give demographic and background information. At the end of the study, we asked them whether their data could be used for scientific purposes, and a chance to comment on the study was given.

3.2.3 Survey Participants

We recruited a sample of 940 American participants, of which 827 participated in the study. We had to exclude 91 because of missing data. We excluded another 18 participants who indicated that their data could not be trusted and a further 55 participants who indicated that they had not read the article (i.e., not the highest quarter of the rating scale of control questions about the articles). The final sample comprised 663 participants (53.5% women, 44.8% men, 1.7% other). The mean age was 33.86 (SD = 13.35), ranging from 18 to 80 years. The highest level of education of participants ranged from some high school education (1.1%), high school graduate

---

[5] https://www.unipark.com/, accessed on 2021-01-08.
[6] https://www.prolific.co/, accessed on 2021-01-08.

(10.9%), vocational or technical school (1.2%), some college education (24.3%), an associate degree (8.6%), and a bachelor's degree (35.7%), to graduate work (18.3%). On average, participants reported spending 2.95 hours per day viewing or reading the news (SD = 3.87). All participants volunteered for the study and gave informed consent. We estimated the duration of this study at 12 minutes. After completing the study, participants received £1.50 as payment. Participants described themselves as tending to be politically interested (M = 2.76, SD = 5.75) and modestly politically involved (M = −0.45, SD = 5.46.). The average self-reported political orientation leaned towards liberalism (M = −2.89, SD = 5.43; −10 = very liberal, 10 = very conservative), and there was no clear agreement to the general existence of media bias (M = −0.51, SD = 4.24).

3.2.4 Article Selection

Regarding the articles each participant read, we followed the article selection process described in [22] to create a sample that balances the number and extremity of both politically left and right articles included. We chose 190 articles from different topics, media outlets, authors, writing styles, and, most importantly, articles that range from unbiased to very biased and politically lean towards different sides. To select such a sample, we obtained the articles for this study from the platform Allsides. Out of the various topics that Allsides covers, we chose ten different topics to cover a broad spectrum based on two parameters: Current issues (e.g., Coronavirus, Elections) versus general topics (e.g., Economy, Racism) and controversial (e.g., Gun Control, Abortion, Immigration) versus less controversial topics (e.g., Arts and Entertainment, Disasters, World News). From each of the ten topics, we chose 17 articles, six articles biased to the left (three left, three lean left), five articles rated center, and six articles biased towards the right (three lean right, three right). Therefore, we overall collected 170 articles for this study from Allsides. To extend our dataset with rather extreme content, we added another 20 articles, ten extremely left, and ten extremely right (two for each topic), directly from alternative news outlets[7]. The extended Allsides ratings of political ideology thus ranged from very liberal (1) to very conservative (7) (M = 4, SD = 1.59; ratings adjusted to include the ten extreme articles of either side). The articles varied among

---

[7] The distribution of outlets can be seen on https://zenodo.org/record/4651186#.YGR5vD9CRxs.

3.2 Literature Collection 75

outlets, were published between Oct. 1, 2019, and Oct. 31, 2020, and are all under 1500 words long. To avoid confounding variables, we showed only plain texts. We present a complete list of articles, their ratings, further information, and their issue statements on https://zenodo.org/record/4651186#.YGR5vD9CRxs. We inspected every article manually and confirmed whether we agreed with the Allsides rating. Still, since the Allsides rating is rather related to a news outlet than a single news article, it might not represent an exact and complete article bias index. We address the possibilities of extending and improving our article set in Chap. 5.

3.2.5 Measures

Perception of Media Bias in articles. Participants were shown 48 items about the perception of media bias. The included items covered cause (e.g., "Do you think that the article includes different points of view regarding the topic in the article?"), direction (e.g., "This article is… liberal/conservative"), existence (e.g., "This article is biased."), influence (e.g., "How much do you think the news article would influence your view of the issue?") and strength of the bias (e.g., "How biased is the article?"). We measured all answers on VAS with a verbal left and a right anchor.

Attention check. To ensure that participants were paying attention, we mixed the item "I read the article" in with the questions on article bias. We anchored the VAS from strongly disagree to strongly agree.

Perception of General Media Bias. Six items measured perception of general media bias on a VAS (-10 = strongly disagree to 10 = strongly agree). The different statements about media in general covered the aspects usually referred to in previous research.

3.2.6 Exploratory Factor Analysis

To empirically reduce the 48 questions even more and derive a final set of questions that is useable in a single study, we used an exploratory factor analysis (EFA) [136]. An EFA is a statistical technique to reduce data to a smaller set of summary variables and explore and uncover response patterns in survey items. It identifies latent constructs (factors) that define the interrelationship among items by accounting for common variance [136]. In computer science, a more widely known special case of an EFA is the Principal Component Analysis (PCA), which uses a linear combination of a set of variables to create one or more index variables. We, however, use the EFA.

The agreement between the survey participants within an EFA can be described in different ways. One of them is the Intraclass Correlation (ICC), which we use in our study. The ICC is a descriptive statistic that describes how strongly units in the same group resemble each other and can be interpreted as the fraction of variance shared by all raters [50].

While our factor analysis results will allow us to reliably reduce the number of questions, the sample size is not large enough to perform cross-validation. We will therefore run a second validation study in the future, which we address in Chap. 5.

3.3 Analysis & Results

All articles were rated between one and five times. On average, each article was rated M = 3.49 times (SD = .76). For the factor analysis, we averaged ratings across participants to obtain a mean article rating per item. We computed the agreement between raters per item as the previously described intraclass correlation (ICC) via REML estimates of random intercept models (Appendix C, available in the electronic supplementary material) [197].

3.3.1 Factor Analysis

The factor analysis used maximum likelihood estimators and oblique promax rotations ($\kappa = 4$). Both KMO (.919) and Bartlett-test ($\chi^2(1128) = 9346.38, p < .001$) indicated that the selected items were suitable for factor analysis. For determining the number of factors, we used the Velicer's MAP criterium [305], which yielded six factors, which could also be viewed as confirmed by the scree-plot (Fig. 3.2). Kaiser criterium yielded seven and parallel test five factors.

As shown in Table C.6 (available in the electronic supplementary material), the first factor has high loadings on items regarding the factuality of information, the second on perceived influence, the third on the agreement to the topic, the fourth on negative emotion, the fifth on the perceived bias, and the sixth on two items on the political affiliation of the text. Both factors, factuality and bias, show large cross-loadings. Thus, they may be regarded as facets of a single construct, which is also reflected in the high correlations between the two scales derived from factors' indicators (Table 3.1). The separate interpretation of the factors bias and factuality is motivated by larger differences in the inter-rater agreement for items in the two factors: While factuality seems to have a clearer interpretation of loadings, the bias factor includes items with considerably larger ICCs. The inter-rater agreement is

3.3 Analysis & Results

Table 3.1 Reliabilities of the final scales built for each factor and their correlations

	Factuality	Influence	Topic Affirmation	Negative Emotions	Bias	Political Ideology	Allsides	Ideology2[0]	Allsides2[0]
Factuality	.966	.155*	.050	−.143*	−.717**	−.273**	−.070	−.493**	−.328**
Influence		.864	−.014	.235**	.098	−.052	−.035	−.064	−.061
Topic Affirmation			.933	−.221**	−.015	.169*	.070	.022	−.081
Negative Emotions				.887	.272**	−.054	−.189**	.203**	.008
Bias					.953	.191**	.070	.520**	.365**
Political Ideology						.929	.445**	.016	.314**
Allsides								.084	.502**
Ideology2[0]									.402**

very low for the factor influence items, indicating that an article's perceived influence is probably widely dependent on a reader-article interaction and, therefore, not an apparent characteristic of an article. Raters seem to agree most on an article's political ideology and whether it affirms a particular topic.

Our basic descriptive analysis of the questions on the perception of media bias in articles showed that most mean values were close to the middle of the scale representing medium item difficulty. Four items showed more extreme values. The articles were generally rated as believable and informative. The articles were rated as not amusing or influential on voting behavior. The limited influence on voting behavior might be related to the study being conducted during the US presidential elections. Nevertheless, the items on influence generally showed less dispersion, raising doubts about their suitability to assess a construct on the article level.

To simplify measurement, we decided to use the mean of the items with factor loadings above .7 as scales for each factor. As the scale for factuality would entail too many items, we decided to use a stricter cut-off of .95 for this factor. Likewise, we had to introduce a more liberal cut-off for the factor bias with .5, as all loadings were considerably lower. Dependent on the different cut-off values, we selected the questions for our final scale and question set. We underlined them in Appendix C, available in the electronic supplementary material. We used five items as indicators for factuality, two for influence, three for topic affirmation, three for negative emotionality, six for bias, and two for political ideology. The respective reliabilities of the final preliminary scales (Cronbach's αs) are presented in the diagonals of Table 2 and were acceptable (.89−.97).

3.3.2 Validation

Besides the rather large correlation between bias and factuality, as seen in Table 3.1, all scales are mostly independent with small to medium-sized correlations. Comparing the factors to the ratings from Allsides, we see a clear picture that the Allsides rating of ideology mainly correlates with the scale of political ideology. As both the Allsides rating and the scale of political ideology were coded to have lower values for left articles, we also centered and squared both scales to obtain a measure of political extremity with the lowest values for politically neutral articles and highest values for both very left and right articles. These computed measures of political extremity yielded medium correlations with both bias and factuality scales. In sum, there is the first indication of the validity of our article-specific scales of bias, factuality, and political ideology.

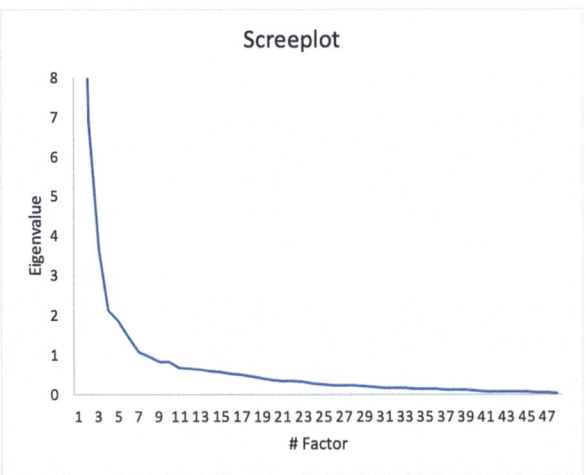

Fig. 3.2 Screeplot showing the number of factors

3.4 Discussion

Our work's main goal was to develop a reliable scale to further evaluate media bias in news articles and improve existing datasets and questionnaires. Our search for items resulted in a list of 419 items from 74 different papers on media bias perception. To the best of our knowledge, such a collection of items is the most sophisticated on the issue to date and even the first of its kind. The items chosen for the questionnaire evaluated in this study covered the different areas and nuances within the different items while limiting the number to a testable amount of 48 questions. The exploratory factor analysis resulted in a structure with six interpretable factors: factuality, influence, topic affirmation, negative emotion, bias, and political ideology. While most of them were independent of each other, marked by low correlations, the factors of bias and factuality were highly interrelated. They thus may also be regarded as sub-facets of one construct in future cross-validation attempts.

For a benchmark for automatic classifiers, the factors of bias and political ideology (potentially squared) appear particularly beneficial, as they primarily align with our concept of bias. Using the political ideology factor may be most efficient, as raters seem to agree more on this dimension than on the bias factor. Both the factuality factor and the negative emotions factor could further contextualize the ratings of the articles.

Conversely, the scale of influence was quite dependent on the rater and therefore seemed less suitable for generating generalized ratings on the article level. Similarly, the topic affirmation factor is somewhat context-dependent, as one has to decide how to define each article's topic separately. However, the high inter-rater agreement could support the inclusion of this factor in bias assessment.

The medium correlations with political ideology and the external Allsides rating may be seen as a validation for the rated items. It also suits our concept of perceived media bias that the extremity of the political ideology was considerably correlated with both the bias and the factuality factors. Please note that the correlations with the Allsides ratings are also deflated, as Allsides provides a rating only for the media outlet but not the actual article. While we believe that the ratings and our manual article inspection offer reasonable ground to measure rater agreement, we will further improve our dataset in the future.

When interpreting the results of our study, a few limitations have to be taken into consideration. At first, the item collection, categorization, and reduction process were only performed by one person, potentially leading to an implicit bias in item selection. To counteract this problem, the entire process was meticulously documented and is transparently visualized on http://bias-question-tree.gipplab.org/. Furthermore, the factors identified were a result of an exploratory factor analysis. In the future, the factor structure should thus be validated with a different set of articles, potentially using additional external validation criteria. Likewise, the suggested six scales with 21 items derived from the factor analysis are preliminary and subject to further testing and validation. Finally, our questionnaire is designed to detect media bias in articles. In today's world, many people get their news from video and audio clips. While we believe it is reasonable to assume that many questions from this questionnaire could also be used in a study on different formats, some aspects could still be medium-specific.

Despite the limitations, our study is an important step towards an improved understanding of media bias and its perception. Our results suggest that the selected items are a good foundation for creating a final questionnaire on media bias, which will be our main focus for future work. Different factors influencing media bias perception can be studied more easily by asking participants additional and reliable questions. This study can help researchers from different fields by providing a good tool for measuring media bias. For example, our questionnaire could be used to compare and validate an automated bias classifier with human assessments (and vice versa) on a more reliable level than before. Since perception is subjective [104], comparing the results of this questionnaire to automated ratings could be a valuable insight into the dimensions of this subjectivity. Overall, we believe that standardized and evaluated questions will be an essential step for researching media bias and related areas of interest.

3.5 Conclusion

The perception of media bias is an important research area because of its strong relation to collective decision-making and communication processes. Our study summarizes and evaluates prior research to create a scale and standard questionnaire on media bias for future applications. The results show that the perception of media bias is a multi-faceted construct influenced by factors like political orientation. The basic analysis of the items we selected and their comparison to the AllSides bias ratings suggest that the items chosen are adequate for measuring media bias perception with an acceptable amount of agreement among raters. The scales constructed and analyzed in this study thus provide a basis to create a standard tool for measuring media bias. We also utilize the question set to evaluate projects in other sections of this thesis, such as for the dataset creation of MBIC (detailed in **Sect.** 4.2), and the two evaluation studies presented in Chap. 7. All questions used in our studies are outlined in Appendix **D**, available in the electronic supplementary material. However, due to the parallel execution of the projects, the questions used in the studies and those from the final questionnaire (as presented in this chapter) do not entirely overlap, even though they were created concurrently and are closely related. Some questions were refined only after the completion of the studies.

Open Access This chapter is licensed under the terms of the Creative Commons Attribution 4.0 International License (http://creativecommons.org/licenses/by/4.0/), which permits use, sharing, adaptation, distribution and reproduction in any medium or format, as long as you give appropriate credit to the original author(s) and the source, provide a link to the Creative Commons license and indicate if changes were made.

The images or other third party material in this chapter are included in the chapter's Creative Commons license, unless indicated otherwise in a credit line to the material. If material is not included in the chapter's Creative Commons license and your intended use is not permitted by statutory regulation or exceeds the permitted use, you will need to obtain permission directly from the copyright holder.

Dataset Creation 4

> *Beth will come back and coach Gretchen and Kailey on how to say the right things. I don't know if anyone is coaching the boys, but it seems unfair. Why do Gretchen and Kailey have to learn how to be the right kind of victims?*
>
> T.E. Carter—*I Stop Somewhere*

At this juncture, we have provided an overview of the media bias domain in Chap. 2, and we have explored how to query the perception of bias in Chap. 3. Nevertheless, we also witnessed the vast array of methods for measuring media bias. This naturally results in an extensive assortment of datasets within the domain. However, many of these datasets focus on concepts related to media (such as the ones demonstrated in Chap. 2), rather than on linguistic bias, which is the primary focus of this thesis. A solid understanding of bias is crucial for constructing a reliable system for automatic media bias detection. More specifically, datasets are indispensable as they form the foundation of our later work. In this section, we delve into the existing datasets and focus mainly on the ones developed during our work. We introduce two primary datasets, named MBIC and BABE, and will discuss their details subsequently[1].

---

[1] Upon the conclusion of this dissertation, we developed a logical sequel: a collection of all existing datasets to be used as a benchmark for media bias classification tasks. However, as outlined in Chap. 1, the so-called MBIB benchmark is no longer a central part of the thesis. Nonetheless, we refer to [25] for further information on projects advancing the need for dataset creation and overview in the media bias domain.

Supplementary Information The online version contains supplementary material available at https://doi.org/10.1007/978-3-658-47798-1_4.

> **Research Objective**
> Create media bias datasets that tackle the problems in existing datasets.

4.1 Overview

As mentioned, a significant challenge in the automated detection of media bias is the lack of a gold standard large-scale dataset with labeled media bias instances [21]. In particular, existing datasets do not control for the individual background of annotators, which may affect their assessment and, thus, represents critical information for contextualizing their annotations [21]. Our work includes a broad range of datasets, and we provide a few examples here to illustrate the types of resources available.

For example, Lim, Jatowt, and Yoshikawa [257] present 1,235 sentences labeled for word and sentence level bias by crowdsourced workers. All the sentences in their dataset focus on one event. Another dataset focusing on just one event is presented by Lim et al. [256]. It consists of 2,057 sentences from 90 news articles, annotated with bias labels on article and sentence levels, and contains labels such as overall bias, hidden assumption, and framing. The annotators agree with a Krippendorff's $\alpha = -0.05$. Lim et al. [256] also provide a second dataset with 966 sentences labeled on the sentence level. However, in the second datatset, the reported interrater-agreement (IRR) of Fleiss' Kappa on different topics averages at zero.

Baumer et al. [55] classify framing in political news. Using crowdsourcing, they label 74 news articles sourced from eight US news outlets, collected from politics-specific RSS feeds on two separate days. Chen et al. [92] create a dataset of 6,964 articles containing political bias, unfairness, and non-objectivity labels at the article level. They present 11 different topics such as "presidential election", "politics", and "white house".

Fan et al. [139] introduce a dataset of 300 news articles containing annotations for lexical and informational bias created by two experts. They define lexical bias as bias stemming from specific word choice, and informational bias as sentences conveying tangential or speculative information to sway readers' opinions towards certain entities [139]. Their dataset, BASIL, allows for analysis at the token level and relative to the target, but only 448 sentences are available for lexical bias.

Even though the referenced datasets contribute valuable resources to the media bias investigation, they still have significant drawbacks, such as (1) a small number of topics [256, 257], (2) no annotations on the word level [257], (3) low

4.2 MBIC

inter-annotator agreement [55, 256, 257], and (4) no background check for participants (All datasets mentioned here). Also, some related papers focus on framing rather than bias [55, 139], and results are only partially transferable.

To address the existing drawbacks, our datasets cover a greater topic variety and incorporate background information on the participants' demographics, political ideology, and their opinion about media in general. As the participants' individual background may affect their assessment, it represents critical information for contextualizing their annotations. Since it is still unclear whether annotations should be gathered on the word or sentence level [18], we collect both levels in our datasets[2].

The first dataset we built was MBIC (**M**edia **B**ias **I**ncluding **C**haracteristics). In MBIC, 1,700 statements were reviewed by ten crowdsourced annotators each for media bias identification both on the word and sentence level. MBIC offers a balanced content selection. Also, to the best of our knowledge, our dataset is the first in the research area to collect detailed background demographic information about the annotators, such as gender, age, education, and English proficiency, but also information on political affiliation and news consumption. Our second dataset BABE (**B**ias **A**nnotations **B**y **E**xperts) builds upon MBIC. Therefore, we will detail MBIC first.

4.2 MBIC

Research Objective
Create a media bias dataset that includes annotator background of crowdsource workers to assess better who made the annotations and lead to a stronger balance in the annotations.

4.2.1 Dataset Creation

In order to cover all of the United States' political and ideological spectrum, we used articles from three left-wing media outlets: HuffPost, MSNBC, and AlterNet, three right-wing media outlets: The Federalist, Fox News, Breitbart, and two outlets from the center: USA Today and Reuters. When selecting the media outlets, we relied

---

[2] Generally, sentences are considered more important, but some works report words additionally [139].

on media bias charts provided by Allsides and Ad Fontes Media to ascertain the overall partisan leanings of each outlet [20].

Our dataset contains 14 topics that describe different events and issues that happened and were discussed in news articles from January 2019 to June 2020. We selected ten topics that are very contentious in the United States and are more likely to be described with biased language [201] (abortion, coronavirus, elections 2020, environment, gender, gun control, immigration, Donald Trump's presidency, vaccines, white nationalism). We also introduced four less contentious topics (student debt, international politics, world news, middle class, sports) for comparison.

The collection process was as follows: We specified the keywords characterizing the selected topics, the chosen media outlets, and the Media Cloud time frame, an open-source platform for media analysis, to retrieve all the available links to the relevant news articles. Using the available metadata, we then manually collected the sentences with examples of media bias across the articles. Note that we tried to include only sentences from the news section and avoid sentences from the commentary section of the selected news outlets. The ultimate goal of media bias identification systems is to recognize subtle bias arising in factual reporting—the section where, ideally, there should be no or little bias.

4.2.2 System Setup

To gather the annotations for MBIC, we needed to decide on a survey platform to execute our study. Since no platform fits our needs, we decided to build our own. In the following, we will briefly overview existing survey platforms and present our solution.

In the field of Natural Language Processing (NLP), numerous text annotation tasks require the labeling of certain parts or properties of a text for which there exists an objective truth. This is not confined to the study of media bias. Tasks of this nature include tagging parts of speech or resolving coreferences. Notably, the characteristics of the annotators are generally irrelevant for such tasks. Many tools support text annotation tasks, i.e., aiding human coders in finding relevant parts of a text and assigning labels. Likewise, numerous, typically web-based tools allow the creation of customized surveys, which typically offer templates for common tasks like labeling named entities. The templates propose a workflow, GUI layout, and labels annotators should use. The focus is on minimizing the time for creating annotation tasks and maximizing annotator efficiency. To this end, the tools offer search and navigation functions that help users to find relevant text parts. Text annotation tools commonly allow customizing task-specific templates or creating new templates from scratch to support other annotation tasks. However, none of the tools offers ready-to-use functionality to create survey questions.

The ability to create, distribute, and analyze large-scale surveys characterizes another class of tools. Survey tools are predominantly web platforms that allow users to create surveys by customizing question templates and configuring the survey logic, e.g., specifying follow-up questions that depend on the answer to a previous question. Despite the typically large number of features in survey tools, we could not find a tool that offered a text annotation question type. Table 4.1 summarizes three of the most widely-used text annotation and survey tools to highlight their complementary strengths that triggered the development of our tool, TASSY (**T**ext **A**nnotation **S**urvey **SY**stem).

TASSY addresses a basic yet significant shortcoming of existing tools—none of the ones we are aware of offer a combination of text annotation and survey functionality. In the creation of our dataset, we required several hundred participants to annotate words and phrases they perceived as opinionated within news articles. Additionally, we needed to record each participant's personal background information.

Our platform is a progressive web application implemented using the Python Flask and Vue.js frameworks that supports a MySQL/MariaDB or SQLite database. The tool's appearance and functionality are highly customizable via a Python API. The source code (MIT license) is available at https://github.com/Media-Bias-Group/Teaching-Platform. Figure 4.1 shows a question in TASSY that combines a text annotation task with a single-select input. The order of the questions can be configured to be identical for all participants or chosen randomly. The text that participants should annotate is given in italic font (1)[3]. The question or task description (2) can contain instructions (3). A link to detailed instructions, e.g., a coding book, can be inserted if desired. Clicking the link will open the instructions in a modal window. Participants can select parts of the provided text at will. Ending or pausing the selection for one second triggers the system to store the selected text as an annotation. Annotated text parts are highlighted in yellow and shown below the instructions (4). Participants can reverse any annotation by clicking the x-button associated with each annotation. Administrators can configure lower and upper bounds on the length of the text parts that users may select. In the demo application, the maximum number of words that participants can select for one annotation is set to six. Exceeding the threshold will show an error overlay, informing the user that this selection is invalid. The lower part of the screen shows a single-select survey input (5). Administrators can configure which inputs are mandatory. In the demo application, annotating parts of the text is optional, while completing two

---

[3] Numbers in brackets refer to Fig. 4.1.

Table 4.1 Widely used text annotation and survey tools

Criterion	Text Annotation Tools				Survey Tools		
	Tassy	Prodigy	Tag-tog	Docano	SoGo Survey	Survey Monkey	Lime Survey
Text annotations	✓	✓	✓	✓	✗	✗	✗
Survey questions	✓	✓	✓	✓	✗	✗	✗
Delivery	SWA[a]	SWA	Cloud	SWA	Cloud	Cloud	Cloud/SWA
Costs	Free	$390–$490	$0–$99 p.m.	Free	$0–$99 p.m.	$0–$99 p.m.	$0–$849 p.a.
License	MIT	Commerc-al	Commercial	MIT	Commercial	Commercial	GNU height

[a]SWA—Self-hosted web application

4.2 MBIC

single-select questions is mandatory. Note that Fig. 1 only shows one of the two questions. Providing the required inputs activates the next button at the top of the page that allows proceeding to the next question (6). A configurable section label and progress indicator inform the participants about the progression of the survey (7).

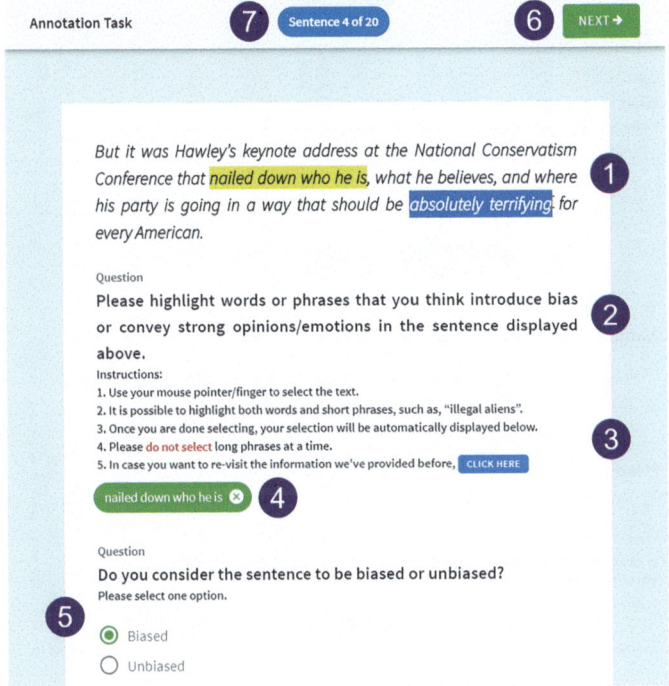

Fig. 4.1 Survey question requiring text annotation

The system includes several other input types that allow creating versatile surveys. Figure 4.2 exemplifies a simple numeric input to record the age of participants. Figure 4.3 shows a slider input that enables participants to indicate their political views on a discretized scale ranging from very liberal to very conservative. TASSY also enables open-ended questions, for which users can input text freely or as an extension to existing answers. Figure 4.4 shows an example of the latter. The user can select one or multiple answers from the provided list and optionally enter additional answers for the shown question. For all input types, administrators can configure the inputs required for a) activating the next button that allows proceeding to the next question and b) the submit button that enables completing a section of the survey (for the example shown in Fig. 4.4, the section on participants' news consumption).

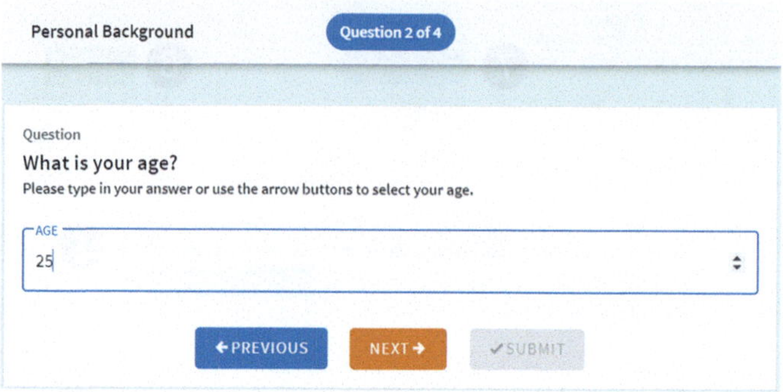

Fig. 4.2 Example of a numeric input in TASSY

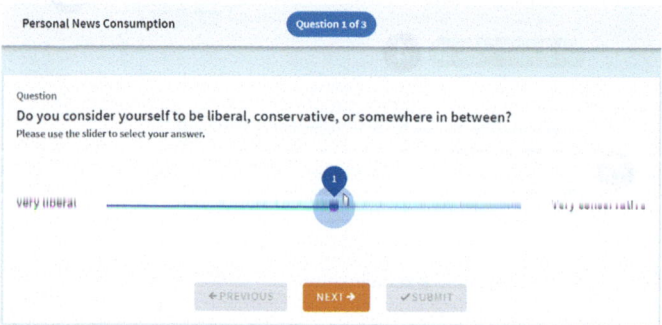

Fig. 4.3 Example of a slider input in TASSY

4.2.3 Study Execution

To recruit study participants for the creation of MBIC (and to send them towards TASSY), we hired participants via Amazon Mechanical Turk to complete

4.2 MBIC

microtasks. Annotation quality ensured by experts is often preferable, but, as mentioned at the beginning of the chapter, we explicitly wanted to collect a large number of annotations from non-experts. Specifically, the objective was to create data that allow insights into the perception of media bias by a broader public. Existing research shows that many complex problems can be resolved successfully through crowdsourcing if the existing crowdsourcing platforms are used in combination with appropriate management techniques and quality control [289, 290].

In total, 784 annotators participated in the survey, all located in the United States. The vast majority (97.1%) of the annotators are native English speakers, 2.8% are near-native speakers. The annotators from diverse age groups participated in the survey; people from 20 to 40 years old prevail over other age groups. The annotators' gender is balanced between females (42.5%) and males (56.5%). The annotators have diverse educational backgrounds; more than half have higher education. The annotators' political orientation is not well balanced: liberal annotators are in the majority as compared to conservative annotators and annotators from the center. The vast majority of the annotators read the news sometimes, more than half one or more times per day. We summarize all background information on the annotators in Fig. E.6, available in the electronic supplementary material.

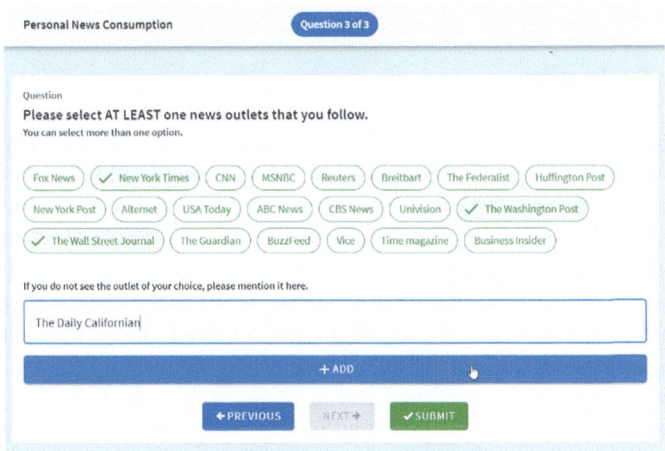

Fig. 4.4 Example of an extensible multi-select input in TASSY

Within our platform[4], we first instruct participants about the general goals of the study. We explain the tasks in detail and ask them to leave aside their personal views. We also give them a few examples of bias and ask a control question to check whether participants understood media bias's general concept. If the control question was not answered correctly, participants had to reread the instructions. Within the annotation task itself, we provide detailed instructions on the workflow. We then ask each annotator to highlight words or phrases that induce bias according to the provided instructions. After that, we ask them to annotate the whole sentence as biased or impartial, and whether they would describe it as opinionated, factual, or mixed.

Overall, our dataset allows performing three different tasks: bias identification on the word level, sentence level, and a classification of the sentence as opinionated, factual or a mixture of both. To avoid question ordering effects or interdependencies, each annotator received 20 randomly reshuffled sentences about various topics and from various outlets. The annotators did not receive any additional information about the sentences apart from the sentences themselves. We showed each sentence to ten annotators. To motivate the workers to look for biased words more attentively and not to select all the words in the sentence, we introduced a small monetary bonus for each word that was selected by at least one other annotator and a small penalty for each selected word that was not selected by anybody else [55].

4.2.4 Evaluation

We assign a biased or impartial label to a sentence if more than half of the respondents annotated a sentence as biased or impartial, respectively. 149 sentences could not be labeled due to a lack of agreement between annotators. Diverse measures for assessing inter-annotator agreement have been used in similar computational linguistics projects. Based on the way in which we organize our crowdsourcing workflow, i.e. having 10 annotators per task, we decide to use Fleiss Kappa [148] to assess the inter-annotator agreement. It represents the task's general difficulty: for example, Hube and Fetahu [200] reported $\alpha = 0.124$ on word-level bias, and Recasens, Danescu-Niculescu-Mizil, and Jurafsky [341] reported a 40.73% agreement when looking at only the most biased word in Wikipedia statements. The value of 0.21 that we achieved can be considered a fair agreement.

---

[4] Our platform including all instructions and questions is public on https://github.com/Media-Bias-Group/Teaching-Platform.

4.2 MBIC

Noteworthy, inter-rater agreement is higher between annotators who reported similar political ideology, especially within liberal annotators, as we show in Fig. 4.5, available in the electronic supplementary material. The annotation results confirm our data sampling strategy: biased and non-biased statements are not balanced in the dataset, and biased statements prevail over non-biased statements. Besides, most media bias instances are taken from liberal and conservative news sources, whereas sources from the center were used mainly to retrieve non-biased statements. Note that this does not imply that liberal and conservative news outlets, in general, experience linguistic bias and labeling and provide opinionated news more often than news outlets from the center. We observe these differences due to our data collection scheme.

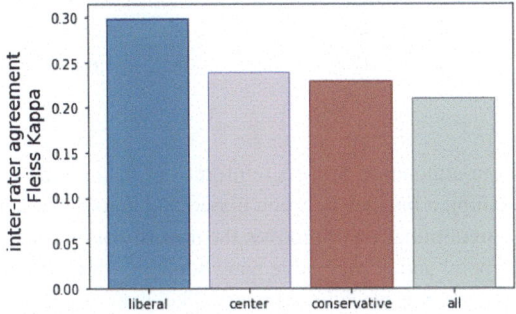

Fig. 4.5 Differences in inter-coder agreement between annotators with different political ideology

We assign an opinionated, factual, or mixed label to a sentence if most respondents annotated a sentence as opinionated, factual, or mixed, respectively. We could not label 174 sentences due to the lack of agreement between annotators. According to our crowdsourced annotations, the dataset contains an almost equal number of factual, opinionated, and mixed statements. The annotation scheme for biased words allowed respondents to highlight not only the words but also short phrases. A word is considered biased if at least four respondents highlight it as biased. On average, a sentence that contains biased words contains two biased words. Out of 31,794 words for training, only 3,018 are biased, which constitutes 9.5% of our current data. The types of words annotated as biased are presented in Table 4.2.

4.2.5 Results

To better understand our dataset's characteristics, we carry out quantitative and qualitative analyses. The results of the sentence classifications are presented in Appendix **E.1**, available in the electronic supplementary material.

Table 4.2 The characteristics of the words annotated as biased

Category	Amount	Percentage
NOUN	1053	34.9%
ADJ	962	31.9%
VERB	784	26.0%
ADV	169	5.6%
PROPN	48	1.6%
Named Entities	47	1.6%

The results of our annotation process reinforce our data sampling strategy: The dataset does not exhibit a balance between biased and non-biased statements, with biased statements predominating. Moreover, the majority of instances of media bias are derived from liberal and conservative news sources, while center sources were mainly used to retrieve non-biased statements. This pattern does not suggest that liberal and conservative news outlets inherently exhibit more linguistic bias or often deliver more opinionated news than centrist outlets. This observation is solely a product of our data collection strategy.

We observe that annotators select not only extreme and emotional words that can be considered biased even without context but also *context-dependent* bias words. For instance, while the word "Chinese" is generally not biased it can be in specific contexts, such as "House Democrats' **Chinese** coronavirus relief package bails out coastal millionaires and billionaires while ensuring big businesses are able to freely hire illegal aliens and visa overstayers over unemployed Americans."[5]

While our instructions emphasized that words related to highly controversial topics or carrying strong negative sentiments are not inherently biased, some such words were nonetheless annotated as biased. For instance, the term "neo-Nazis" in the sentence "For years now, Fox News has been mainstreaming arguments that used to be the province of fringe websites run by **neo-Nazis** and other groups who

---

[5] https://www.alternet.org/2019/07/fox-news-has-gone-so-deep-into-white-nationalism-that-donald-trump-now-believes-its-how-hell-win-in-2020/, accessed on 2020-10-27.

4.2 MBIC

believe the U.S. is meant to be a country of white people and for white people"[6] was annotated as such.

Moreover, we discovered that annotators occasionally overlooked certain words as biased if a sentence contained overtly extreme or emotive language. For example, while the majority of annotators labeled "cray-cray" as biased in the sentence "Over the past few decades, RFK Jr.'s famous name has helped him get in the door to talk to important people, and it probably isn't long before the person who is all jacked up to meet a Kennedy realizes the guy is totally **cray-cray**"[7], they missed marking "totally".

As expected, we find a positive correlation between marking sentences as biased and opinionated, and factual and non-biased. Furthermore, more controversial topics are annotated as non-biased, on average, 7.4 per person less than less controversial topics. Interestingly, in 49.3% of the sentences labeled as non-biased, annotators still labeled some words as biased.

Annotators who estimate themselves as conservative mark 3.76 p.p. more sentences as biased than others who describe themselves as being liberal – except if the sentence stems from a conservative news outlet [417]. Furthermore, annotators who report that they check news at least sometimes, label sentences as biased 6.85 p.p. more than those who report to check news very rarely, and 19.95 p.p. more than those who report that they never check news.

4.2.6 Conclusion

In difference to already existing studies on the topic, MBIC contains detailed background information about the annotators, increasing our results' transparency and reliability. We argue that the research community lacks large labeled datasets for media bias detection methods. We also believe that the data could be interesting for other research areas, especially since they measure the perception of bias by a broad and diverse public audience. The articles in our dataset include a variety of topics, from controversial to non-controversial, and recent as well as general topics. We publish the full dataset at https://zenodo.org/record/4474336#YBHO6xYxmK8.

We perform visual analysis and observe the following findings: Topics that are less controversial are annotated as non-biased slightly more often than very

---

[6] https://www.alternet.org/2019/07/fox-news-has-gone-so-deep-into-white-nationalism-that-donald-trump-now-believes-its-how-hell-win-in-2020/, accessed on 2020-10-27.
[7] https://thefederalist.com/2017/01/12/no-anti-vaxxer-robert-kennedy-jr-wont-trumps-vaccine-czar/, accessed on 2020-10-27.

controversial topics. Conservative annotators perceive statements as biased slightly more often than liberal annotators, but for both, it is only true if the the statement is not from a conservative media outlet. We also find that annotators who read news never or very rarely are less likely to annotate statements as biased. Besides, our annotation results show the connection between bias and opinion.

While using crowdsourcing gave us an insight into the perception of bias by a broad audience, some related issues could not be resolved, e.g., the submission of random words. Furthermore, even honest workers made mistakes because the identification of media bias is generally not a trivial task, especially for non-experts [257, 341]. Considering the relatively low 0.21 inter-rater agreement of MBIC, we decided to follow up on MBIC, and increase both size and quality of the datatset. Therefore, we propose BABE (**B**ias **A**nnotations **B**y **E**xperts), which we introduce in the following.

4.3 Expert Dataset Creation

Research Objective
Create a media bias dataset based on expert ratings to achieve higher inter-annotator agreement and bias label reliability than previous studies.

Different than for MBIC, annotations are performed by a large number of trained experts. Even more, the corpus size is expanded considerably with additional 2,000 sentences. The resulting labels are of higher quality and capture media bias better than labels gathered via crowdsourcing. In sum, BABE consists of 3,700 sentences with gold standard expert annotations on the word and sentence level.[8] To analyze the ideal trade-off between the number of sentences, annotations, and human annotation cost, we divide our gold standard into 1,700 and 2,000 sentences, which are annotated by eight and five experts, respectively.[9] We publish all our code and resources on https://github.com/Media-Bias-Analysis-Group/Neural-Media-Bias-Detection-Using-Distant-Supervision-With-BABE.

---

[8] We also provide another 1,000 yet unlabeled sentences for future work. We have not labeled them to date due to resource restrictions.
[9] With the 1,700 stemming from MBIC [21].

4.3.1 Definition of Experts

High-quality annotations are often obtained if the participants are properly instructed and have sufficient training [22, 139]. We compare our expert annotations with the crowdsourced labels provided by MBIC to further analyze quality differences between the two groups. Our results show that expert annotators render more qualitative bias labels than MBIC's crowdsourcers.

An expert, in our definition, is someone with at least six months of experience in the domain of media bias[10], who has undergone sufficient training to: (1) reliably identify biased wording, (2) distinguish between bias and plain polarizing language[11], and (3) take on a politically neutral viewpoint when annotating.[12]

4.3.2 Dataset Creation

The general data collection and annotation pipeline is outlined in Fig. 4.6. Similar to the filtering strategy proposed in Chap. 5, the sentences should contain more biased than neutral sentences. BABE contains 3,700 sentences, 1,700 from MBIC [21] and an additional 2,000. Like in MBIC, we extracted our sentences from news articles covering 12 predefined controversial topics.[13] The articles were published on 14 US news platforms from January 2017 until June 2020. We focused on the US media since their political scenario became increasingly polarizing over the last years [39].

We selected appropriate left-wing, center, and right-wing news outlets based on the media bias chart provided by Allsides.[14] The sentence collection was performed on the open-source media analysis platform Media Cloud.[15] The collection process was as follows. We defined keywords describing every topic in one word or a short phrase, specified the news outlets, their time frame, and retrieved all available links for the relevant articles.[16] Then, we extracted sentences by manually inspecting the provided list of articles. The sentence selection was based on our media bias

---

[10] As which we here define someone working in or studying journalism, working in media bias research, or someone working or studying in very language-affine areas such as language studies.

[11] For example, quotes can sometimes contain biased wording, but not be biased per se.

[12] Note: We cannot guarantee that a media bias expert is fully neutral, but we assume that an expert is able to leave political viewpoints aside to a substantial extent.

[13] The list of topics is provided at the repository mentioned in **Sect.** 4.3.

[14] https://www.allsides.com/media-bias/media-bias-chart, accessed on 2021-04-13.

[15] https://mediacloud.org/, accessed on 2021-04-13.

[16] The keywords can be found at the repository mentioned in **Section** 4.3.

annotation guidelines comprising diverse examples of biased and neutral text instances (see **Sect.** 4.3).

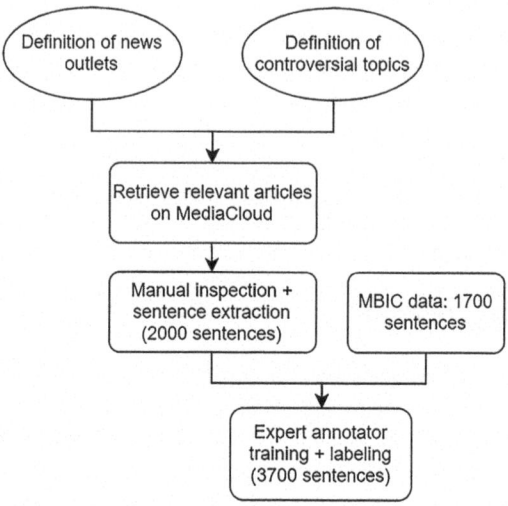

Fig. 4.6 Data collection and annotation pipeline

4.3.3 Training Phase

To cultivate expertise among our raters, we devised detailed instructional guidelines that are provided prior to the annotation task.[17] These instructions are notably more thorough than those typically presented in a crowdsourcing setting. Considering that the annotation of bias on a fine-grained linguistic level is a complex task, and cognitive and language abilities likely have an impact on text perception [218], we hired only master students from programs completely held in English, who were among the top 20% with respect to their grade. Based on an iterative feedback loop between all annotators and us, we refined the guidelines multiple times with richer and clearer details. We discussed and evaluated existing annotations weekly as a group during the first three weeks of each annotator's work. We also always asked each annotator to hand in annotations before the discussion sessions, so they could

---

[17] These guidelines can be found in the repository referred to in **Sect.** 4.3.

4.3 Expert Dataset Creation

not influence each other. The annotators had to provide basic reasoning about their annotation decisions during our discussions. We maintained the labels only if the annotators were able to elaborate on their annotations. Annotations of one annotator were discarded based on this method.

Apart from evaluation and instructions, each annotator rated at least 1,700 sentences.[18] On average, per hour, they were paid 15€ and labeled 40 sentences, costing approximately 10.000€. The sum of money required to obtain a sufficient number of reasonable bias labels can be restrictive for media bias research. Therefore, BABE represents a major contribution that alleviates the lack of high-quality annotations in the domain. The annotators were instructed to label carefully and not as fast as possible, even though this resulted in a higher overall cost.

4.3.4 Study Execution

The general instructions for the annotation task were identical to the approach for MBIC. First, raters were asked to mark words or phrases inducing bias. Then, we asked them to indicate whether the whole sentence was *biased* or *non-biased*. Lastly, the annotators labeled the sentence as *opinionated, factual, or mixed*.

As our resources were limited and the ideal trade-off between the number of sentences and annotators per sentence is not yet determined, we organized BABE into subgroups (SG), as described below:

- **SG1.** 1,700 sentences annotated by eight expert raters each.
- **SG2.** 3,700 sentences annotated by five expert raters each.

For SG1, we hired eight raters to annotate the 1,700 sentences from MBIC on word and sentence levels [21].[19] Therefore, we obtained an expert-labeled ground truth comparable to MBIC's crowdsourcing results. For SG2, five of the previous eight annotators also labeled the 2,000 additionally collected sentences. We explored the ideal number of annotators by sampling. 5 annotators is a compromise between the agreement quality for both the bias and opinion labels, assuming that the annotation quality stays the same. To show the difference to 8 annotators, and as an outlook into future extensions of the dataset, we also release the annotations made by 8 raters[20]. We will also add detailed statistics and results about all data and clearly highlight our

---

[18] The same sentences as in MBIC.

[19] In the MBIC dataset, each sentence was evaluated by ten crowdsource workers [21].

[20] But recommend to use 5-person ratings when using the full dataset.

selection process. As resources and time were limited, we include further annotators and more sentences in future work. All raters were master students with a Data Science, Computer Science, Psychology, or Intercultural Communication background. The groups and their annotators are described in detail in the repository mentioned in **Sect. 4.3**.

4.3.5 Evaluation

The raw labels obtained during the annotation phase were processed as follows. We calculated an aggregated bias/opinion label for every sentence based on a majority vote principle. For instance, if a sentence was labeled as biased by more than four expert annotators in SG1, we assigned the label *biased* to the sentence. Otherwise, the sentence was marked as *non-biased*.[21] The annotators did not agree on a label (no majority vote) in some sentences. Here, we assigned the label *no agreement*.

Our annotation scheme allows respondents to mark biased words. In SG1, a word is marked as biased if at least three annotators label it as such. In SG2, because of the lower number of annotators, the threshold is subsequently reduced to two expert annotators labeling a word as biased[22]. We compute agreement metrics on the sentence level to acquire knowledge about data quality resulting from all annotation approaches. Our agreement metric of choice is Krippendorff's α [230], which is a robust agreement metric for studies including varying numbers of annotators per text instance [35].

We first compared the annotations from MBIC's crowdsourcing approach with our expert-based approach, including eight annotators labeling 1,700 sentences (SG1). Table 4.3 shows the agreement scores for the bias and opinion labels on a sentence level. Considering the bias agreement, SG1 exhibits fair agreement ($\alpha = 0.39$) and outperforms MBIC's agreement score ($\alpha = 0.21$).[23] A similar pattern can be observed regarding the opinion labels (i.e., SG1: $\alpha = 0.46$; MBIC: $\alpha = 0.26$). Furthermore, MBIC's crowdsourcers labeled more words as biased compared to SG1's experts, i.e., 3,283 vs. 1,530 (absolute) and 2.40 vs. 1.95 (average per biased sentence). Even though media bias detection is generally a difficult task, our interannotator agreement is much higher than in existing research in the domain, where α ranges between 0 and 0.20, as shown in **Sect. 4.2**.

---

[21] Note: In SG2, the threshold reduced respectively due to the lower number of expert annotators.

[22] We manually inspected all instances to determine reasonable thresholds.

[23] The scoring interpretations are based on guidelines published by Landis and Koch [237].

4.3 Expert Dataset Creation

Table 4.3 Annotation results for the expert-annotated (SG1) and crowdsourced (MBIC) approach based on 1,700 sentences

Metric	Data	
	SG1	MBIC
Bias Agreement[a]	0.39	0.21
Opinion Agreement[a]	0.46	0.26
Total Biased Words	1530[c]	3283[d]
∅ Biased Words[b]	1.95	2.40

[a] Based on Krippendorff's α.
[b] Biased words per biased sentence.
[c] Out of 56,826 words in total.

Table 4.4 shows the label distribution comparison between SG1 and MBIC.[24] We can observe that our expert annotators (SG1) are more conservative in their annotation than the crowdsourcers (MBIC). In the expert data, 43.88% of the sentences are labeled as biased, whereas the crowdsources annotated 59.88%. The opinion labels' distribution is fairly balanced in both the expert annotator and crowdsourced data. Factual sentences occur slightly more often than opinionated sentences in both datasets.

Table 4.4 Class distribution for SG1's and MBIC's 1700 sentences

Label	Data	
	SG1	MBIC
Biased	43.88%	59.88%
Non-biased	47.05%	31.35%
No agreement	9.05%	8.76%
Opinionated	25.00%	30.65%
Factual	37.59%	33.65%
Mixed	26.64%	25.47%
No agreement	10.76%	10.24%

Next, we evaluate our expert-based annotation approach, including five expert annotators labeling 3,700 sentences (SG2) in comparison to 1,700 (SG1). We compare metrics between both approaches to ascertain whether the reduced number of annotators in SG2 has a substantial impact on the annotator agreement. The finding

---

[24] Absolute numbers for all labels are reported in the code files at the repository mentioned in **Sect.** 4.3.

could yield implications for future research on our extended dataset (SG2). Table 4.5 shows agreement metrics for the bias and opinion labels of both expert-annotated approaches and Table 4.6 represents label distributions. SG2 exhibits moderate agreement ($\alpha = 0.40$) in the bias annotation task, and slightly outperforms SG1 ($\alpha = 0.39$). Regarding the opinion labels, we observe a similar pattern, with SG2 outperforming SG1 substantially (SG2: $\alpha = 0.60$; SG2: $\alpha = 0.46$). The expert annotators of SG1 are more conservative in labeling bias than SG2 (SG1: 43.88% vs. SG2: 49.26% labeled as biased).[25] The opinion labels are distributed marginally skewed in both annotator groups. Factual sentences occur more often than opinionated sentences in both datasets. Further statistics on SG1 and SG2, such as bias/opinion distribution per news outlet and topic, the connection between bias and opinion, and the overall topic distribution, are provided in the repository mentioned in **Sect. 4.3**. Additionally, we show more visual comparisons between BABE and MBIC in Appendix **E.2**, available in the electronic supplementary material.

Table 4.5 Dataset annotation results for the expert-based approaches (left: eight annotators labeling 1,700 sentences (SG1); right: five annotators labeling 3,700 sentences (SG2))

Metric	Data	
	SG1	SG2
Bias Agreement[a]	0.39	0.40
Opinion Agreement[a]	0.46	0.60

[a]Based on Krippendorff's α

Table 4.6 Dataset class distribution for the expert-based approaches (left: eight annotators labeling 1,700 sentences (SG1); right: five annotators labeling 3,700 sentences (SG2))

Label	Data	
	SG1	SG2
Biased	43.88%	49.26%
Non-biased	47.05%	50.70%
No agreement	9.05%	0.00%
Opinionated	25.00%	23.35%
Factual	37.59%	43.54%
Mixed	26.64%	27.21%
No agreement	10.76%	5.88%

---

[25] Due to the uneven number of annotators in SG2, "no agreement" cases do not exist here.

4.3.6 Conclusion

Employing annotators with domain expertise allows us to achieve an inter-annotator agreement of $\alpha = 0.40$, which is higher than existing datasets [21]. We believe domain knowledge and training alleviate the difficulty of identifying bias and are imperative to create a strong benchmark due to the complexity of the task. In addition to the 3,700 labeled sentences, we also include word level annotations in our dataset to encourage solutions focusing on more granular characteristics. We believe that word level bias might convey strong explanatory and structural knowledge[26] and see a detailed word level bias analysis and detection as a promising research direction.

In conclusion, BABE demonstrates that identifying bias without prior training can be challenging, but it is possible to improve in this aspect. While the dataset represents a significant initial step towards future advancements in the domain, its size of just 3,700 sentences limits the depth of insights it can provide. Still, it can serve as an excellent basis for model developments, and we will describe our efforts in this direction in Chap. 6. Looking at MBIC and BABE, we believe it is required to go into multiple directions simultaneously for future media bias dataset developments: While MBIC was created fast and scalable, it lacked agreement and annotation quality. While BABE has a high agreement and annotation quality, developing was expensive and effortful. Since crowdsourcing offers an evaluation of larger-scale data, and expert rating offers high-quality annotations, we believe only both ways together can lead to a fully reliable media bias ground truth. However, the exact design of such a process will need to be experimented with. Consequently, in our future work, we plan to develop a feedback platform for gathering annotations using our classifier, enhance the expert process with better resources (thereby enabling the engagement of more raters and sentences), and create a game to make the training of raters and collection of annotations a more playful and enjoyable experience. Additionally, these approaches will need to be executed across multiple languages and social groups. Particularly in the area of dataset creation, substantial efforts will need to be invested. We will elaborate more on this in **Sect.** 7.4.5.

---

[26] The distinction between the importance of word, sentence or text level bias is yet unclear.

Open Access This chapter is licensed under the terms of the Creative Commons Attribution 4.0 International License (http://creativecommons.org/licenses/by/4.0/), which permits use, sharing, adaptation, distribution and reproduction in any medium or format, as long as you give appropriate credit to the original author(s) and the source, provide a link to the Creative Commons license and indicate if changes were made.

The images or other third party material in this chapter are included in the chapter's Creative Commons license, unless indicated otherwise in a credit line to the material. If material is not included in the chapter's Creative Commons license and your intended use is not permitted by statutory regulation or exceeds the permitted use, you will need to obtain permission directly from the copyright holder.

Feature-based Media Bias Detection 5

> *Curiously enough, the only thing that went through the mind of the bowl of petunias as it fell was Oh no, not again. Many people have speculated that if we knew exactly why the bowl of petunias had thought that we would know a lot more about the nature of the Universe than we do now.*
>
> Douglas Adams—*The Hitchhiker's Guide to the Galaxy*

Thus far, we have presented a comprehensive literature review on media bias in Chap. 2, evaluated reliable measures for understanding media bias perception in Chap. 3, and introduced our two new datasets, MBIC and BABE, in Chap. 4. We now turn our attention to the design and implementation of automated bias classification systems. This chapter centers on a traditional machine-learning approach grounded on linguistic features. In our exploration of feature-based classification, we propose a prototype system for the automated identification of bias-inducing words in news articles. Primarily, we outline how we:

1. analyze and engineer features potentially indicating biased language;
2. train a classifier to detect bias-inducing words and
3. evaluate the performance.

Our study holds both theoretical and practical importance. We consolidate all existing research to provide a comprehensive overview of possible classification features for media bias and demonstrate the relevance of these features. Finally, we train and present a classifier for biased words that surpasses existing feature-based classifiers

---

Supplementary Information The online version contains supplementary material available at https://doi.org/10.1007/978-3-658-47798-1_5.

for bias. Our model serves as a crucial reference point and baseline for the neural models we introduce in the subsequent Chap. 6.

> **Research Objective**
> Implement a reliable automated media bias classification system based on manually selected features.

5.1 Related Work

Despite the challenging nature of the task, several researchers attempted to annotate media bias by word choice automatically. In the following, we will show the most relevant works relating to feature-based approaches[1].

Lim et al. [254] use crowdsourcing to construct a data set consisting of 1,235 sentences from various news articles reporting on the same event, namely, the arrest of a Black man. The data set provides labels on the articles and word level. The authors then train a Support Vector Machine on the Part of Speech (POS) tags and various handcrafted linguistic features to classify bias on the sentence level, achieving the accuracy of 70%.

Additionally, Lim et al. [257] propose another media bias data set consisting of 966 sentences containing labels on the sentence level. The data set covers various news about four events: Donald Trump's statement about protesting athletes, Facebook data misuse, negotiations with North Korea, and a lawmaker's suicide.

Baumer et al. [55] focus on the automated identification of framing in political news and construct a data set of 74 news articles from various US news outlets covering diverse political issues and events. They then train Naïve Bayes on handcrafted features to identify whether a word is related to framing and achieve 61% accuracy, 34% precision, 70% recall, 0.45–0.46 F_1-score.

Fan et al. [139] create the dataset BASIL, annotated by two experts, covering diverse events and containing lexical and informational bias. The data set allows analysis at the token level and relative to the target, but only 448 sentences are available for lexical bias. Then, they employ BERT lexical sequence tagger to identify lexical and informational bias at the token level and achieve an F_1-score of 25.98%.

Chen et al. [92] create a data set of 6,964 articles covering various topics and news outlets containing political bias, unfairness, and non-objectivity labels at the article level. They then train the recurrent neural network to classify articles according to

---

[1] Newer and more powerful models exist, but since these are not feature based, we detail them in the respective Chap. 6.

5.1 Related Work

these labels. Finally, the authors conduct a reverse feature analysis and find that, at the word level, political bias correlates with such LIWC categories [320] as negative emotion, anger, and affect.

Recasens et al. [341] create static bias lexica based on Wikipedia bias-driven edits due to NPOV (Neutral Point of View) violations.[2] The bias lexicon and a set of various linguistic features are then fed into the logistic regression classifier to predict which words in the sentences are bias-inducing. The authors reached 34.35% to 58.70% accuracy for predicting 1 to 3 potential bias-inducing words in a sentence, respectively.

Hube & Fetahu [200] propose the semi-automated approach to extract domain-related bias words lexicon based on the word embeddings properties. The authors then feed obtained bias words and other linguistic features into a random forest classifier to detect language bias in Wikipedia at the sentence level. The authors achieve 73% accuracy, 74% precision, 66% recall, and an F_1-score 0.69 on the newly created ground truth based on Conservapedia[3], and state that the approach is generalizable for Wikipedia with a precision of 66%.

In their later work, Hube & Fetahu [201] train a recurrent neural network on a combination of word embeddings and a few handcrafted features to classify bias in Wikipedia at the sentence level and achieve 81.9% accuracy, 91.7% precision, 66.8% recall, and 0.773 F_1-score.

In our own preliminary work (mentioned in **Sect.** 1.6), we analyze media bias in German news articles [10, 12]. The three components: an IDF component, a combined dictionary-based component, and a component based on a semantically created bias dictionary, are analyzed to identify bias on the word level. The combination of the dictionary component and the topic-dependent bias word dictionary achieves an F_1-score of 0.31, precision of 0.43, and recall of 0.26.

5.1.1 Workflow Overview

The general workflow of our system for the automated identification of bias-inducing words in news articles is presented in Fig. 5.1. Our work starts by collecting the sentences and gathering annotations via a crowdsourcing process (1)[4]. We then obtain various features (3) described in more detail in **Sect.** 5.1.4. One of the features is a bias lexicon built semi-automatically by computing words similar to potential bias words using outlet-specific word embeddings (2). We then train a supervised classifier on our engineered features and annotated labels (4). After the best model is

---

[2] https://en.wikipedia.org/wiki/Wikipedia:Neutral_point_of_view, accessed on 2020-10-31.
[3] https://conservapedia.com/Main_Page, accessed on 2020-10-31.
[4] This is the MBIC dataset, which we described.

selected and optimized, we evaluate the performance of the feature-based approach for detection of media bias. Furthermore, we evaluate all features individually (5).

5.1.2 Biased Words Lexicon Creation

As one of our features, we present a lexicon of biased words, built explicitly for the news domain [200]. Interestingly, although such a lexicon cannot serve as an exhaustive indicator of media bias due to high context-dependence [201], it can potentially serve as a useful feature of a more complex media bias detection system. To extract a biased word lexicon of high quality, we replicate the method proposed by Hube & Fetahu [200]. The authors proposed a semi-automated way to extract biased words from corpora of interest using word embeddings. We present the whole pipeline of the approach in Fig. 5.2.

We first manually create a list of words that describe contentious issues and concepts. Then, we use this list to manually select "seed" biased words in the two separate word embedding spaces trained on news articles potentially containing a high number of biased words. We select seed-biased words among the words that have high cosine similarity to the words describing contentious issues. We publish our list of seed-biased words at https://zenodo.org/record/7564371#.Y8-SLq2ZMQ8.

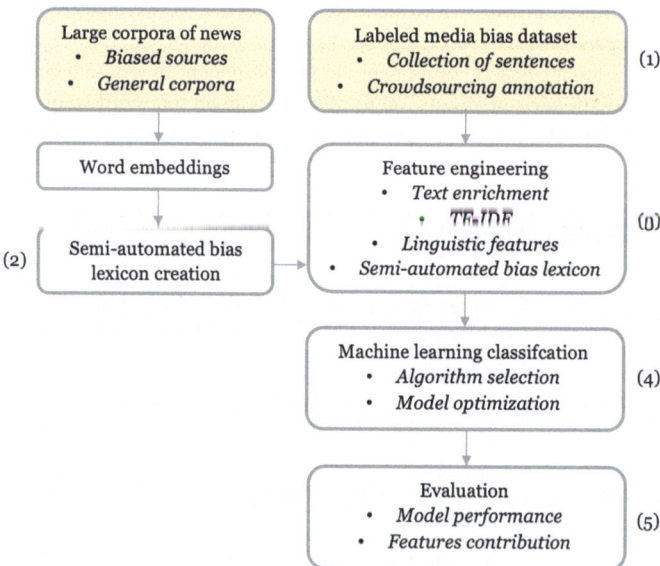

Fig. 5.1 Workflow for the feature based automated identification of bias

5.1 Related Work

We assume that news outlets with presumably stronger political ideology would use bias words when describing contentious issues with a higher likelihood than politically more central media. To capture both liberal and conservative biases, we train word embeddings separately on the corpora of news articles from HuffPost and Breitbart, respectively. In the choice of the outlets, we relied on the information provided by Allsides: both outlets are presented at the media bias chart[5], and for both outlets, the confidence level of the assigned ratings is high[6]. Noteworthy, these two sources are also some of the most popular media sources that left- and right-leaning communities share respectively in Reddit [375]. The articles from both sources, published from 2010 to 2020, are scraped from Common Crawl[7]. We split the initial text into lower-cased tokens, remove punctuation marks and numbers, and train Word2Vec word embeddings [286]. The hyperparameters are summarized in Table 5.1.

Since evaluation of such an unsupervised task as word embeddings creation is quite challenging [44], we choose the hyper-parameters based on the existing research. The number of dimensions is set to 300 and is not increased further due to the scarcity of the training data [286]. The window size is set to 8, also based on existing examples [250]. We increase the number of iterations to 10 since the training data size is small and cannot be increased. In this project's scope, it is important to avoid unstable low-qualitative vectors; therefore, words appearing less than 25 times are excluded. Finally, treating n-grams as single units may lead to better training of a given model [82]. We use the default scoring for n-grams generation and run two passes over training data. The thresholds for n-grams inclusion are based on manual analysis of the generated n-grams. The rest of the hyper-parameters are set to the default values.

As a next step, we divide the set of seed-biased words into random batches consisting of ten words and repeat this process ten times to create batches with various combinations of words. Then, for each batch, the average vector in the word embedding space trained on a 100 billion Google news data set[8]. For each average vector, we extract the top 100 words close to this average vector. Hube and Fetahu [200] do not reshuffle words in batches and extract the top 1000 words. The average cosine similarity of the farthest words among the top 1000 is 0.47, whereas the average cosine similarity of the farthest words among the top 100 is 0.52. Besides,

---

[5] https://www.allsides.com/media-bias/media-bias-chart, accessed on 2020-10-31.
[6] https://www.allsides.com/news-source/huffpost-media-bias, https://www.allsides.com/news-source/breitbart, both accessed on 2020-10-31.
[7] https://commoncrawl.org, accessed on 2020-10-31.
[8] https://code.google.com/archive/p/word2vec/, accessed on 2020-09-04.

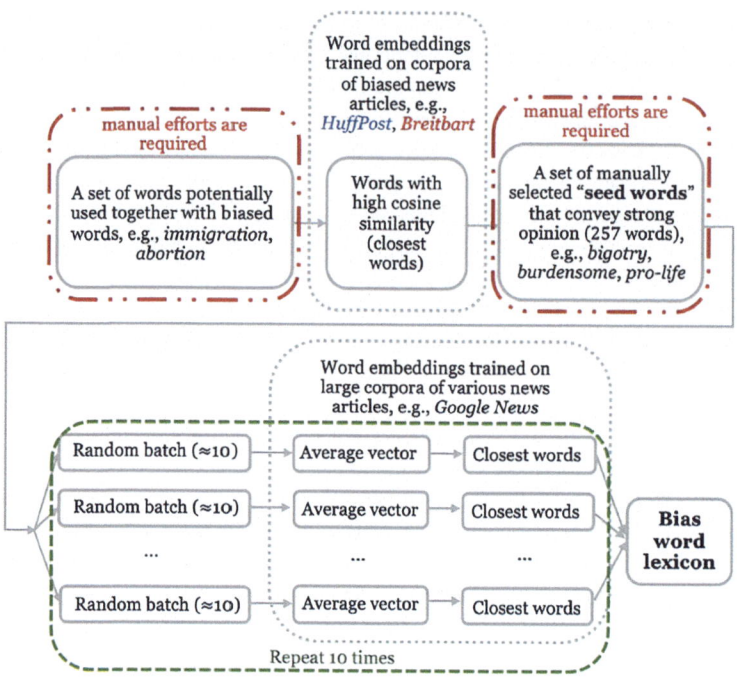

Fig. 5.2 Pipeline for building bias lexicon semi-automatically

extracting the top 1000 words introduces noise. Finally, we add extracted words to the resulting bias word lexicon, and remove duplicates.

5.1.3 Detection Methodology

We define bias-inducing word detection as a binary classification problem with only two mutually exclusive classes: whether a word is biased (class 1) or not (class 0). No exhaustive set of precise media bias characteristics exists with our binary classifier and in the context of media bias by word choice. Therefore, we combine different linguistic features of biased language proposed by Recasens et al. [341] and a variety of other syntactic and lexical features [256]. As the context is crucial when distinguishing between unbiased and biased words, we attempt to capture useful information from context by including collective features adding two previous and two

Table 5.1 Hyper-parameters for training word embeddings on HuffPost and Breitbart

Hyperparameter	Value
Dimensionality	300
Window size	8
# of iterations	10
Maximum token length	28
n-grams threshold	90
Minimum frequency	120
Subsampling rate	10^{-5}

following words into a word's feature vector. We admit that such a way to account for context is not optimal and requires elaboration in future. We compare different combinations of the features, and also train different machine learning classification algorithms, such as logistic regression, linear discriminant analysis (LDA), quadratic discriminant analysis (QDA), complement Naïve bayes (NB), support vector machine (SVM), k-nearest neighbor (KNN), decision tree (DT), random forest (RF), XGBoost and a simple neural network—multilayer perceptron (MLP). To the best of our knowledge, we present the first detailed comparison of classifiers for word-level bias detection. All experiments building our feature-based system are performed on the MBIC dataset [21]. BABE [18] was not yet published at the time.

5.1.4 Feature Engineering

We present our entire feature list in Table 5.2. In continuation, we describe the individual features and the intuition behind using them for our task. For POS tags, syntactic dependencies, named entity types, word vector norms, and linguistic features, we refer to the previous work on these topics as described by Recasens et al. [341] and Hube & Fetahu [200].

Table 5.2 The complete set of features used in our approach for detecting biased words

Feature	Description
POS Tags	POS tag indicating the syntactic role of each word, e.g., noun, adverb, etc. [193].
Syntactic dependencies	Dependencies revealing how words in the text relate to each other, e.g., whether a word is a root, object, or subject [64, 193].
LIWC features	LIWC features based on psychological and psychometric analysis [320].
Named entity types	Named entities, e.g., persons, organizations, locations, etc. [64, 193].
Word Vector Norms	Norms of GloVe word embedding vectors pre-trained on the Common Crawl[9] [193].
TF-IDF	Frequency of the term in a document and in the whole article collection [254, 318].
Linguistic features	Word is a report / implicative / assertive / factive / positive/ negative word, is strongly or weakly subjective, or a hedge [341].
Additional lexica	Classifications as kill verb [167], hyperbolic term [87], boosters, and attitude markers [204].
Semi-automated bias lexicon	Previously described semi-automatically created bias word lexicon [200].

TF-IDF. Lim et al. [254] propose detection of bias using inverse document frequency (IDF) as one of the features to detect media bias, under the assumption that rare occurring terms are more likely to be extreme in any direction and are hence more likely to induce bias. As our data set consists of sentences where the terms are probably rarely repeated within one sentence, we adjusted Lim et al.'s assumption [254] slightly by calculating the TF-IDF statistic based on the whole text of articles the sentences were collected from.

LIWC Features. Linguistic Inquiry and Word Count [320] is a common approach to analyzing various emotional, cognitive, and structural components in language. It identifies linguistic cues related to psychological processes, such as anger, sadness, or social wording. We consider all feature categories from LIWC, as this has shown to be the most effective usage of the resource to identify bias.

---

[9] https://commoncrawl.org, accessed on 2020-10-31.

Additional lexical features. It is not well known which features are the most efficient indicators of media bias [55]. Therefore, we test additional features that have been used by researchers to study similar constructs but have not been applied for the detection of media bias yet. According to Green and Resnik [167], the so-called "kill verbs" together with the relevant grammatical relation (governor or dependent term) cause different sentiment perceptions. In the following example, the second one is perceived as more negative since it implies an intention [417]:

1. Millions of people **starved** under Stalin.
2. Stalin **starved** millions of people.

Chakraborty et al. [87] study click baits in online news and find that click bait headlines usually include hyperbolic words—words with highly positive sentiment. We assume that hyperbolic words used in click bait titles to attract readers' attention can be used to emphasize some concepts and induce bias in news articles. Hyperbolic words are, for example, "absolutely," "brilliant," or "impossibly."

Hyland [204] introduces linguistic features that help authors to express their views on the discussed proposition. One such subcategory are boosters—words that express certainty about a particular position, e.g., "believed,' "always," "no doubt." In some regard, boosters are the opposite to hedges (such as "sometimes' or "seems to"), which, on the contrary, reduce the confidence of a statement. Another subcategory is attitude markers—indicators of the author's expression of affective attitude to statements, e.g., "fortunately," "shockingly," "disappointed," etc.

5.1.5 Evaluation

In MBIC, classes are highly imbalanced (**Sect.** 4.2). Since accuracy does not capture the capability of a model to predict rare class correctly [74], we focus on such evaluation metrics as a confusion matrix, precision, recall, F1-score, and receiver operating characteristic area under the curve (ROC AUC).

We compare the performance of our system to several possible baselines:

- Baseline 1 (B1) – a purely random classifier;
- Baseline 2 (B2) – occurrence of a word in the negative sentiment lexicon;
- Baseline 3 (B3) – occurrence of a word in the negative or positive lexicon;
- Baseline 4 (B4) – occurrence of a word in the semi-automated bias lexicon.

In our final data set, each observation corresponds to one word, its feature vector (including the collective context features), and the label. We perform 10-fold cross-validation when comparing the performance of different classifiers, 5-fold cross-validation when optimizing hyper-parameters of the selected model, and finally, estimate the final performance on a test set of words that did not participate in training and manually investigate correctly and wrongly classified instances.

5.2 Experiments

5.2.1 Lexicon of Biased Words

In this section, we first present the characteristics of the articles we used to train our word embedding models and the performance of the trained word embeddings. We also provide the characteristics of the pre-trained Google News embeddings. We measure semantic word similarity and word analogy [78, 146, 286]. Table 5.4 depicts the results of our measures. Two data sets—WordSim-353 [146] and MEN [78]—allow to estimate the Pearson correlation for the semantic similarity between pairs of words in respective word embeddings and, as estimated by human assessors. The Google analogy test set [286] allows to evaluate accuracy. Even though those evaluation data sets are not perfectly suited for our task, the comparison shows that our data sets are large enough to give comparable results to the full Google News data set. We also manually inspected the embeddings' results and confirmed that they capture bias to a reasonable extent (Table 5.3).

Table 5.3 Characteristics and evaluation results of word embedding models

Corpus	Tokens	Vocab. size	WordSim-353	MEN	Google
HuffPost	68 M	53 K	0.65	0.71	0.50
Breitbart	39 M	36 K	0.57	0.59	0.38
Google News	100 B	3 M	0.62	0.66	0.74

Second, we qualitatively investigate the lexicon of biased words resulting from the semi-automated expansion (**Sect.** 5.1.2). We manually inspected a random sample of 100 words and find that the vast majority (Around 69% in a random sample of 100 words) are negatively connotated, are emotional, and convey strong opinion (Fig. 5.3). Furthermore, the dictionary includes a disproportionate number of relatively uncommon words (e.g., "teapartiers", "obamian", "eggheaded",

5.2 Experiments

"mobocracy"). These words are only interpretable when one is familiar with the context in which they originated. We find only one word ("similarly") that can not directly be related to bias, while we personally would classify all 99 other words as very likely to induce bias. Among 96 words for which POS tag can be identified unambiguously, 41.7% are nouns, 24.0% are verbs, 21.9% are adjectives, and 11.5% are adverbs.

Finally, we compare the method of batches developed by Hube & Fetahu [200] to the naive approach where close words are retrieved for a single seed bias word instead of an average of a batch. We find the employed batched extraction to be superior. Specifically, while both approaches yield a high proportion of biased words, the naive approach also yields many words that are not biased but co-occur with biased words, such as "abortion", "personhood", "immigrants", "mexicans", etc. Table 5.4 contrasts extraction for two methods.

quiddity, transcends, instigate, foolishness, nonracist, overhasty, harangue, similarly, stoically, bigotted, inuendo, gleefully, thoughtless, upbraiding, ahistoric, majoritarianism, bigots, antilabor, nauseating, postmodernists, subterfuge, defeatest, denounces, militarising, marshbaum, disloyalty, pandered, nonrational, mendaciously, blantantly, gutlessness, narrowminded, rawly, necrophiliacs, bsing, oppressive, condescension, dissemblers, brutalises, bureaucratization, scandalizes, solipsistic, delegitimise, hyping, impugns, contumely, totalistic, unwise, bureaucratize, invective, triumphalism, insinuating, mobocracy, bewails, jackassery, rankles, greedy, dishonesties, pathetic, chafes, childish, teapartiers, barbarism, sneery, obamian, resents, immobilism, carped, oppression, vilification, fuzzily, libertines, hogarthian, snub, vapidly, backpedals, incommunicable, particularist, incensed, satans, communitarians, enlightened, yobbishness, naysay, thuggy, credulously, fundamentalism, pffft, demurring, morals, maligns, tactless, scarcely, eggheaded, parvenus, wickedness, bestiality, nutty, smacks, negativists

Fig. 5.3 Random sample of the semi-automatically extended dictionary of biased words

So far, the lexicon seems to be valuable, especially in finding negatively connotated neologisms and words that convey strong opinions even by themselves. Despite being more efficient than the naive approach, the method of batches still cannot avoid some degree of noisy words and words falsely included as biased. Among such words are misspellings, abbreviations, and words that describe a contentious or negative issue or concept, e.g., "xenophobia", "criticize", "anti-Semite", "solipsist".

Table 5.4 Comparing the method of batches and the naive approach

Batch: ghastly, deterred, incitement, pains, hyping, unsettling, colossal, **prolife**, unscrupulous, bluntly	Single word: **prolife**	Batch: doubtful, **illegals**, harassment, instigating, unskilled, oppression, outrages, deceptively, troublemaker	Single word: **illegals**
shameful	antiabortion	splittists	illegals
calumnious	prochoice	oppression	undocumented
hyprocrisy	abortion	harassment	noncitizens
dishonest	antichoice	racist	immigrants
immoralities	personhood	tyrannise	mexicans
demonising	faith2action	islamophobic	hispanics
disconcerts	dfla	racists	illegaly
hypocricy	naral	persecution	otms
grotesque	prolifers	harrassment	immigration
unpatriotism	nrlc	opressed	aliens
gadaon	massresistance	facism	lawbreakers
hyping	grtl	descrimination	wetbacks
sensationalization	bereit	hateful	noncriminals
disgraceful	dannenfelser	bigots	imigration
appalling	mccl	extremisms	guestworker
despicable	evangelical	udbkl	latinos
demonizing	baipa	immiseration	imigrants
hypocritical	paulites	exclusionist	alipac
reprehensible	homosexualist	nonracist	migrants
shameless	lifenews.com	mobocracy	arizonians

5.2.2 Detection of Biased Words

We first train "quick and dirty" models [168] on all available features with default parameters (as implemented in Scikit-Learn [318] and XGBoost [90] libraries) and compare the performance based on scores averaged from ten-fold cross-validation [318]. We compare F_1-score, precision, recall, and ROC AUC. Since data are imbalanced (only $\approx$ 10% are biased), the weighting of classes is employed for all

5.2 Experiments

methods (where possible). Table 5.5 shows that no model yields a high F_1-score. Instead, the best-performing models yield either high precision or high recall. Since the results of our method are, for now, intended to be verified by a user, we prefer recall over precision while still aiming for a moderately high F_1-score.

We choose XGBoost for further optimization since it achieved both the highest ROC AUC score and the highest F_1-score. It also has a relatively high recall: the model predicts more True Positives (biased words as biased) than False Negatives (biased words as unbiased). The model suffers from predicting many False Positives (unbiased words as biased) but to a smaller extent than other models with higher recall (Logistic regression, QDA, NB, SVM).

XGBoost is "a scalable end-to-end tree boosting system" [90]. The algorithm is based on gradient boosting—an ensemble method that adds predictors sequentially to an ensemble; each new one is fit to the residual errors made by the previous one [168]. Thus, the final model—a combination of many weak learners—is a strong learner. In addition to the fact that XGBoost already achieved the best results on our data set, it provides several advantages: it accounts for sparsity caused by one-hot encoding [90], allows for fine parameter tuning using a computationally efficient algorithm [57], and allows to estimate feature importance since we do not have reliable prior information about the importance [55].

Table 5.5 Performance of algorithms for bias word detection

Model	ROC AUC (sd)	F_1 (sd)	P (sd)	R (sd)
Logistic regression	.82 (.03)	.38 (.05)	.26 (.05)	.67 (.06)
LDA	.82 (.04)	.41 (.04)	.50 (.08)	.35 (.06)
QDA	.76 (.03)	.19 (.00)	.10 (.00)	**.99 (.02)**
NB	.82 (.03)	.35 (.04)	.23 (.03)	.74 (.05)
KNN	.70 (.03)	.21 (.04)	.45 (.09)	.14 (.03)
DT	.62 (.03)	.31 (.04)	.30 (.05)	.33 (.05)
RF	**.84 (.03)**	.26 (.04)	**.71 (.12)**	.16 (.04)
SVM (linear kernel)	.83 (.02)	.38 (.04)	.26 (.04)	.70 (.06)
SVM (rbf kernel)	.78 (.02)	.35 (.04)	.39 (.06)	.31 (.05)
XGBoost	**.84 (.03)**	**.42 (.04)**	.32 (.04)	.64 (.07)
MLP	.63 (.03)	.34 (.06)	.35 (.07)	.33 (.06)

We fine-tune five hyper-parameters that help to control overfitting.[10]

For the fine-tuned model, we quantitatively evaluate the performance and feature importance. Table 5.6 shows that fine-tuning yields an insignificant performance improvement of $F_1 = 1$p.p. We find that the model suffers from underfitting since performance is also low on training ($F_1 = 0.51$) and validation sets ($F_1 = 0.50$). Comparing XGBoost performance to the defined baselines, we see that XGBoost significantly outperforms the random baseline (B1) but fails to significantly outperform the naive usage of the negative sentiment lexicon (B2). However, when analyzing results in a confusion matrix, we see that using just the negative dictionary, in fact, predicts 53% of biased words incorrectly as non-biased words, whereas XGBoost predicts only 23% incorrectly. High F_1-score and ROC AUC of baseline B2 is mostly due to the low number of False Positives, but it essentially equals simply predicting all words as non-biased.

Table 5.6 Excerpt of models and their performance

Model	ROC AUC	F_1	P	R
Baselines				
B1: random	.50	.17	.10	.52
B2: negative	.69	.40	.35	.47
B3: neg. & pos.	.68	.32	.22	.57
B4: bias lexicon	.56	.20	**.62**	.12
XGBoost				
All features	**.79**	**.43**	.29	**.77**
Importance ≥ 10	.77	.41	.28	.74
Importance ≥ 400	.69	.40	.36	.47
All but TF-IDF	.77	.42	.29	.75
All but enrichment	.75	.41	.29	.67
All but linguistic	.74	.35	.23	.75
All but LIWC2015	.76	.40	.28	.72
All but bias lexicon	.77	.41	.28	.75
All but context	.78	**.43**	.30	.75

---

[10] We find the following values to be optimal. max-depth = 6, min-child-weight = 18, subsample = 1, colsample-bytree = 1, and eta = .2. Other hyper-parameters are set to the default values. The maximum number of boosting rounds is set to 999, and early stopping is applied if the F_1-score for the validation set does not increase within ten rounds. The model is weighting the imbalanced classes. The evaluation metric is the F_1-score averaged on five-fold cross-validation.

5.2 Experiments

Since we do not have prior information on which features are the most contributing to media bias detection, we first trained the classifier on all the available features. When analyzing feature importance, we find that the most important features are the occurrence of a word in a negative lexicon (gain = 1195) and being a proper noun (gain = 470). The bias lexicon that we created semi-automatically is among the top 10 important features (gain = 106). Among linguistic features proposed by Recasens et al. [341] as indicators of bias, only sentiment lexica, subjectivity lexica, and assertive verbs are among the top 30 most important features. While report verbs and hedges still have minor importance, factive and implicative verbs have zero importance.

We train several models feeding them with features that have different importance. Excluding features with low feature importance does not improve the performance (Table 5.6). Besides, we test how the model performs when different feature groups are not included. Thus, we train a model with all features except one particular feature or group of features. We notice that the performance drops significantly only when linguistic features are not used, most likely because of the negative sentiment lexicon's high importance.

Lastly, we qualitatively investigate automatically detected bias candidates. Examples of correctly classified biased words (TPs) include mostly emotional words that can be considered biased even without context. Words that can be described as causing negative emotions occur more often than those causing positive emotions. 12.5% of TPs correctly indicate less obvious bias, which is most likely generally rare. The following examples illustrate (1) obvious negative bias, (2) obvious positive bias, and (3) slightly more subtle bias among correctly classified words.

1. Large majorities of both parties seem to like the Green New Deal, despite efforts by Fox News to paint it as **disastrous**.[11]
2. Right-wing media sprung into action to try to discredit her, of course, by implying that a woman who graduated summa cum laude with an economics degree is a bimbo and with Twitchy using a screenshot to make the usually **genial** Ocasio-Cortez somehow look like a ballbuster.[12]
3. As leading 2020 Dems advocate spending **big** on the Green New Deal, it turns out most Americans are worried about other issues.[13]

---

[11] https://www.alternet.org/2019/04/just-a-cover-for-sexism-and-white-nationalism-paul-krugman-explains-why-the-rights-attacks-on-new-democratic-lawmakers-are-bogus/, accessed on 2020-10-31.
[12] https://www.alternet.org/2019/01/alexandria-ocaio-cortez-is-absolutely-right-there-shouldnt-be-any-billionaires/, accessed on 2020-10-31.
[13] https://fxn.ws/370GuwZ, accessed on 2020-10-31.

Examples of biased words incorrectly classified as non-biased (FNs) include words that are (1) parts of phrases, (2) ambivalent as to whether they are biased, (3) not generally biased but only in a particular context, (4) mistakes in the annotation, and random misclassifications:

1. By threatening the kids and their families with deportation, the administration's U.S. Citizenship and Immigration Services was effectively delivering <u>death sentences</u>.[14]
2. When the Muslim ban was first enacted, it **triggered** chaos at airports and prompted widespread protest and legal challenges, and it continues to impose devastating costs on families and people who wish to come to the U.S.[15]
3. The **specter** of "abortion regret" has been used by lawmakers and judges alike to impose or uphold rules making it harder for people to get abortions.[16]
4. Gun enthusiasts cannot admit that they like firearms because they fear black **people**.[17]

Examples of non-biased words misclassified by the model as biased (FPs) include words that (1) are ambivalent as to whether they are biased, (2) describe negative or contentious issues, (3) are due to erroneous annotation, and (4) random misclassifications:

1. Justice Sonia Sotomayor, in her dissent, **accused** the majority of weaponizing the First Amendment—an unconscionable position for a person tasked with "faithfully and impartially" discharging the duty to protect the inherent rights of all Americans.[18]

---

[14] https://www.msnbc.com/rachel-maddow-show/trump-admin-backs-plan-deport-critically-ill-children-msna1280326, accessed on 2020-10-31.

[15] https://www.alternet.org/2020/02/conservative-magazine-denounces-trumps-cruel-expansion-of-his-muslim-ban/, accessed on 2020-10-31.

[16] https://www.alternet.org/2020/01/debunking-the-abortion-regret-narrative-data-shows-women-99-percent-of-women-feel-relief-over-their-decision/, accessed on 2020-10-31.

[17] https://www.alternet.org/2019/07/how-far-will-republicans-go-to-destroy-democracy/#.XSY6699P5zg.twitter, accessed on 2020-10-31.

[18] https://thefederalist.com/2018/06/27/was-gorsuch-worth-a-trump-presidency-its-starting-to-look-that-way/, accessed on 2020-10-31.

2. He also denounced the policy of Chancellor Angela Merkel and the attitude of the German media, which "are constantly pushing" for Europe to welcome more and more **migrants**, in opposition to the will of the Hungarian people.[19]
3. Michelle Williams won a Golden Globe for her role in "Fosse/Verdon" on Sunday night, but perhaps her **biggest** moment came during her acceptance speech when she defended abortion rights and encouraged women to vote "in your own self-interest."[20]
4. The case was sent back to lower **courts** to determine whether the gun owners may seek damages or press claims that the amended law still infringes their rights.[21]

5.3 Conclusion

Our semi-automatically created bias lexicon is indeed able to find emotional words and words that convey a strong opinion. However, we conclude that while capturing emotional and negative opinionated words, the lexicon is unlikely to be exhaustive. So far, the approach lacks an additional method on how to expand the lexicon without adding non-biased words.

Overall, our prototypical system achieves an F_1-score of 0.43, precision of 0.29, recall of 0.77, and ROC AUC of 0.79. MBIC was the largest and most transparent in the area at that point in time, and our classifier is the first built on these data, making a direct comparison to other methods unfeasible. On their respective data sets, researchers who detected media bias on the word level achieved an F1-score of 0.26 [139] and 0.31 [11]; researchers, who detected framing on the word level, achieved an F1-score of 0.45–0.46 [55, 181].

We present the most comprehensive collection of features for classification to date, extending the work of Recasens et al. [341] and Hube & Fetahu [200]. Especially Boosters were not used in previous research, but are among the most important features. We will continue our detailed analysis of feature importance for the overall task with our larger crowdsourced data set and the expert data. We will also improve

---

[19] https://www.breitbart.com/politics/2019/01/10/hungarys-orban-says-he-must-fight-french-president-macron-on-immigration/?utm_source=feedburner&utm_medium=feed&utm_campaign=Feed%3A+breitbart+%28Breitbart+News%29, accessed on 2020-10-31.

[20] https://www.nbcnews.com/news/us-news/michelle-williams-champions-woman-s-right-choose-globes-acceptance-speech-n1110986?cid=public-rss_20200106, accessed on 2020-10-31.

[21] https://www.reuters.com/article/us-usa-court-guns/u-s-supreme-court-sidesteps-major-gun-rights-ruling-but-more-cases-loom-idUSKCN22920S, accessed on 2020-10-31.

the quality of our features. For example, for implicative verbs, Pavlick and Callison-Burch [317] introduced a method to automatically predict the implicativeness of a verb based on the known constraints on the tense of implicative verbs. We could also expand our sentiment and subjectivity lexicons by using WordNet, a de facto lexico-semantic network [142, 287], or SentiWordNet 3.0, a lexical resource that assigns sentiment scores to each synset of WordNet [40].

While recognizing around 77% of biased words correctly, our approach misclassifies around 20% of non-biased words. Due to the classes' imbalance, 20% of the misclassified majority class significantly decreases overall performance. Especially words that are biased only in a particular context are rarely classified correctly, highlighting how media bias is usually very subtle and context-dependent. However, so far, we only accounted for context by using one collective feature for the window of four words surrounding the word.

Overall, we believe the feature-based approach is especially valuable because of its explanatory character, relating bias to specific features, which is impossible with automated feature extraction. It is also not as dependent on the amount of data as a neural network. However, the pure performance even of such an optimized feature-based system as presented above would likely not yield similar results as a deep learning approach. To evaluate in detail what the difference between the two approaches is, the following chapter will introduce neural classifiers to detect media bias automatically built within the dissertation. The code and current system at https://github.com/Media-Bias-Group/Automated-Identification-of-Bias-Inducing-Words-in-News-Articles.

Open Access This chapter is licensed under the terms of the Creative Commons Attribution 4.0 International License (http://creativecommons.org/licenses/by/4.0/), which permits use, sharing, adaptation, distribution and reproduction in any medium or format, as long as you give appropriate credit to the original author(s) and the source, provide a link to the Creative Commons license and indicate if changes were made.

The images or other third party material in this chapter are included in the chapter's Creative Commons license, unless indicated otherwise in a credit line to the material. If material is not included in the chapter's Creative Commons license and your intended use is not permitted by statutory regulation or exceeds the permitted use, you will need to obtain permission directly from the copyright holder.

Neural Media Bias Detection 6

> *Life is made of small moments like this*
>
> Above / & Beyond—*ABGT 350*

We already introduced existing methodologies to automatically detect media bias in Chap. 2. We also saw one major example of a traditional feature-based classification system in the previous Chap. 5. Now, we dive more into neural classification within the domain, particularly the major approaches developed during this dissertation. To shape a common ground and reintroduce the area, we will briefly summarize what deep learning means: Deep learning is a subfield of machine learning inspired by the brain's structure and function, specifically the neural networks that make up the brain. These neural networks comprise layers of interconnected nodes, or "neurons," that process and transmit information. The depth of a neural network refers to the number of layers, and deep learning models typically have many layers, hence the name "deep learning" [368].

Deep learning models can learn and represent very complex and abstract concepts and have been incredibly successful in a wide range of applications, including image and speech recognition or natural language processing. One of the key reasons deep learning models are so effective is that they are able to automatically learn useful representations of the input data, rather than requiring the input data to be hand-engineered, as performed even by us in Chap. 5. This is achieved through the use of multiple layers in the neural network, where each layer learns to extract a different level of abstraction from the input data [368].

Supplementary Information The online version contains supplementary material available at https://doi.org/10.1007/978-3-658-47798-1_6.

Additionally, deep learning models can learn from very large amounts of data, which is crucial in many applications, such as image and speech recognition, where large labeled datasets are readily available. Another important factor is the use of GPUs to train deep learning models, which allows for significant speedup in training time. This speedup makes it feasible to train models with many layers, which would otherwise be too computationally expensive to train [368]. Overall, deep learning's ability to learn useful representations of data, the ability to learn from large amounts of data, and the use of GPUs all contribute to its effectiveness in a wide range of applications. In the electronic supplementary material, Appendix **A**, we will dive more into the history of deep learning. In the following, we introduce the experiments performed to build our own media bias detection models.

6.1 Neural Classification With Distant Supervision

Research Objective
Implement an automated media bias classification system based on deep learning.

Our first experiment bases upon the BABE dataset introduced in Chap. 4. We train and present a neural BERT-based classifier that outperforms existing approaches such as the one we presented in Chap. 5 Spinde et al. [22]. Even though, as shown in Chap. 2 neural network architectures have been applied to the media bias domain [92, 201], their data sets created using crowdsourcing do not exhibit similar quality to BABE. Therefore, conducting an experiment with a neural setup together with our new dataset seemed promising. We include five state of the art neural models in our comparison of models and extend two of them in a distant supervision approach [115, 385]. Leveraging large amounts of distantly labeled data, we formulate a pre-training task helping the model to learn bias-specific embeddings by considering bias information when optimizing its loss function. For the classification presented in this paper, we focus on sentence level bias detection[1]. We publish all our code and resources for the model on https://github.com/Media-Bias-Analysis-Group/Neural-Media-Bias-Detection-Using-Distant-Supervision-With-BABE.

---

[1] During our work at [22], we believed the usage of words would be more suitable since words can be more easily aggregated to sentences. However, we found that too much context gets lost by looking at only words, which is also the consensus in existing work [18].

6.1.1 Methodology

We propose the use of neural classifiers with automated feature learning capabilities to solve the given media bias classification task. A distant supervision framework, similar to Tang et al. [385], allows us to pre-train the feature extraction algorithms leading to improved language representations, thus, including information about a sample's bias. As obtaining large amounts of pre-training labeled data using humans is prohibitively expensive, we resort to noisy yet abundantly available labels that provide supervisory signals.

Learning Task Given a corpus X and a randomly sampled sequence of tokens $x_i \in X$ with $i \in \{1, ..., N\}$, the learning task consists of assigning the correct label y_i to x_i where $y_i \in \{0, 1\}$ represents the *neutral* and *biased* classes, respectively. The supervised task can be optimized by minimizing the binary cross-entropy loss.

Learning task

$$\mathcal{L} := -\frac{1}{N} \sum_{i=1}^{N} \sum_{k=\{0,1\}} f_k(x_i) \cdot log(\hat{f}_k(x_i)). \tag{6.1}$$

where $f_k(\cdot)$ is a binary indicator triggering 0 in the case of neutral labels and 1 in the case of a biased sequence. $\hat{f}_k(\cdot)$ is a scalar representing the language model score for the given sequence.

Neural Models We fit $\hat{f}_k(\cdot)$ using a range of state-of-the-art language models. Central to the architectural design of these models is Vaswani et al. [390]'s encoder stack of the Transformer relying solely on the attention mechanism. Specifically, we use the BERT model [116] and its variants DistilBERT [360] and RoBERTa [265] that learned bidirectional language representations from the unlabeled text. DistilBERT is a compressed model of the original BERT, and RoBERTa uses a slightly different loss function with more training data than its predecessor. We also evaluate models built on the transformer architecture but differ in the training objective. While DistilBERT and RoBERTa use masked language modeling as a pre-training task, ELECTRA [97] uses a discriminative approach to learn language representations. We also include XLNet [416] in our comparison as an example of an autoregressive model. We systematically evaluate the models' performance on the media bias sentence classification task. We also investigate the impact of an additional pre-training task introduced in the next section on the BERT and RoBERTa models' classification capabilities.

Distant Supervision Fine-tuning general language models on the target task has proven beneficial for many tasks in NLP [196]. The language model pre-training followed by fine-tuning allows models to incorporate the idiosyncrasies of the target corpus. For text classification, the authors of ULMFiT [196] demonstrated the superiority of task-specific word embeddings. Before fine-tuning, we introduce an additional pre-training task to improve feature learning capabilities considering media bias content. The typical unsupervised setting used in the general pre-training stage does not include information on language bias in the learning of the embedded space. To remedy this, we incorporate bias information directly in the loss function (equation 6.1) via distant supervision. In this approach, distant or *weak* labels are predicted from noisy sources, alleviating the need for data labeled by humans. Results by Severyn and Moschitti [369] and Deriu et al. [115] demonstrated that pre-training on larger distant datasets followed by fine-tuning on supervised data yields improved performance for sentiment classification.

A pre-training corpus is compiled consisting of news headlines of outlets with and without a partisan leaning to learn bias-specific word embeddings. The data source, namely, the news outlets, are leveraged to provide distant supervision to our system. As a result, the large amounts of data necessary to learn continuous word representations are gathered by mechanical means alleviating the burden of collecting expensive annotations. The assumption is that the distribution of biased words is denser in some news sources than in others. Text sampled from news outlets with a partisan leaning according to the Media Bias Chart[2] is treated as biased. Text sampled from news organizations with high journalistic standards is treated as neutral. Thus, the mapping of bias and neutral labels to sequences is automatized. The data collection resembles the collection of the ground-truth data performed in BABE (see Chap. 4). The defined keywords reflect contentious issues of the US society, as we assume slanted reporting to be more likely among those topics than in the case of less controversial topics. The obtained corpus consisting of 83,143 neutral news headlines and 45,605 biased instances allows for encoding a sequence's

---

[2] The already mentioned https://www.allsides.com/media-bias/media-bias-chart, accessed on 2021-04-13.

6.1 Neural Classification With Distant Supervision

bias information in the embedded space. The news headlines corpus serves to learn more effective language representations, it is not suitable for evaluation purposes due to its noisy nature. We ensure that no overlap exists between the distant corpus and BABE to guarantee model to guarantee model integrity with respect to training and testing.

6.1.2 Experiments

Training Protocol. We implement the neural models with HuggingFace's Transformer API [410]. The model components are instantiated with their pre-trained parameters. Parameters of the classification components are uniformly instantiated and learned. First, we fine-tune and evaluate neural models on BABE. Second, we identify the best performing model of the first run and include the distant supervision pre-training task.

Implementation. The hyperparameters remain unchanged for pre-training on the distant corpus and fine-tuning on BABE. Sentences are batched together with 64 sentences per mini-batch because estimating gradients in an online learning situation resulted in less stable estimates. To optimize $\mathcal{L}$, we use the Adam optimization with a learning rate of 5^{-5} [224]. Training on the distantly labeled corpus is performed for one epoch. While training on BABE, convergence can be observed after three to four epochs. A monitoring system is in place that stops training after two epochs without improvement of the loss and restores the parameters of the best epoch. All computations were performed on a single Tesla T4 GPU. All in all, pre-training and training of all models is executed in 5 hours.

Baseline. To assess the benefit of modern language models for the domain of media bias, we compare their performance to a traditional feature-based model (Baseline). We use the work by Spinde et al. [22] as our baseline method, as it offers the most complete set of features for the media bias domain. The authors use syntactic and lexical features related to bias words such as dictionaries of opinion words [198], hedges [204] and assertive and factive verbs [194]. Spinde et al. [22]'s classifier serves as a baseline to evaluate our approach. As feature-based models operate on the word level, we provide comparability by implementing the classification rule that the presence of a predicted biased word leads to the overall sentence being labeled as biased. In contrast, if the baseline model does not label words as biased in a given sequence, the sequence will be classified as neutral.

Evaluation Metric. Given the relatively small size of 3,700 sequences in BABE, we report performance metrics averaged on a 5 fold cross-validation procedure to stabilize the results. Because the class distribution in SG1 is slightly unbalanced, we use stratified cross-validation to preserve this imbalance in each fold. Following the standard in the literature, we report a weighted average of F_1-scores.

6.1.3 Results

Table 6.1 summarizes our performance results. Our baseline using engineered features exhibits low scores of 0.511 and 0.569 for SG1 and SG2, respectively.[3] BERT improves over the baseline by a large margin of 0.251 points on SG1 and 0.220 points on SG2. DistilBERT exhibits a lower performance for both corpora, whereas RoBERTa is the strongest representative of BERT-based models. Both models based on a different training approach than BERT, namely ELECTRA and XLNet, do not match the performance of BERT and its optimized variants. These results reaffirm established findings of the attention mechanism's advantage over traditional models [188] and indicate the benefits of large pre-trained models' for media bias detection.

Table 6.1 Stratified 5-fold cross-validation results

Model	Macro F_1	
	SG1	SG2
Baseline	0.511 (0.008)	0.569 (0.008)
BERT	0.762 (0.019)	0.789 (0.011)
DistilBERT	0.758 (0.029)	0.777 (0.009)
RoBERTa	0.775 (0.023)	0.799 (0.011)
ELECTRA	0.742 (0.020)	0.760 (0.013)
XLNet	0.760 (0.042)	0.797 (0.015)
BERT + distant	0.778 (0.017)	**0.804** (0.014)
RoBERTa + distant	**0.798** (0.022)	0.799 (0.017)

Standard errors across folds in parentheses. The first model block shows the best results of feature-based models. The second block of models consists of BERT and optimize variants. The models in the third block use new architectural or training approaches. The fourth block refers to models having learned bias-specific embeddings from the distantly supervised corpora.
The best results are printed in **bold**.

---

[3] In this Section, we show three decimal places to account for detailed model differences.

Models trained and evaluated on SG2 generally perform better due to the larger corpus size. The increase is around 0.02 points in the macro F_1-score for all models except RoBERTa + distant, where the improvement is insignificant. Overall, we believe this indicates that extending the dataset in the future will be valuable.

The results of the fourth block of Table 6.1 show that the distant supervision pre-training task leads to an improvement over BERT and RoBERTa. Our best-performing model, BERT + distant on SG2, achieves a macro F_1-score of 0.804, improving over the BERT model by 0.02 points. Media bias can be better captured when word embedding algorithms are pre-trained on the news headlines corpus with distant supervision based on varying news outlets. With the added data, information on a sequence's bias is incorporated into the loss function, which is not the case in general purpose language models.

Our results show how traditional machine learning models, although more interpretable [22], are outperformed by recurrence and attention-based models. This highlights a trade-off between performance and explainability. Traditional models offer better interpretability (by clearly showing which feature has which impact on the result), making it easier to understand and explain the decisions made by the model. On the other hand, recurrence and attention-based models, despite being less interpretable, provide superior performance. The neural models achieve higher accuracy and better capture the nuances of media bias, but their decision-making process is less transparent.

This was our first experiment based on the BABE dataset, which provided multiple takeaways and ideas for implementing more experiments introducing deep learning into the media bias domain. Specifically, we considered stronger domain-adaptive pretraining and multi-task learning, which appeared to be promising approaches for leveraging cross-domain knowledge in a field where datasets (especially high-quality ones) are sparsely available. We implemented both of these approaches after our initial experiment, and we will provide an overview of them in the following two sections.

6.2 Domain-Adaptive Pre-Training

Research Objective
Implement an automated media bias classification system that extends our previous models capabilities by taking domain-specific knowledge into account stronger.

We have seen in Chap. 2 and in Chap. 4 how studies focusing on the automated detection of media bias either rely on noisy and marginally bias-related training data [18]. Even more, they do not always fully exploit highly bias-related data by incorporating only sub-samples of bias corpora into pre-training [17].

In this section[4] we propose an effective domain-adaptive pre-training approach that relies on a highly relevant bias-related encyclopedia data set. Similar approaches have been shown to yield substantial performance boosts for similar tasks within the news, biomedical, and scientific domains [56, 177, 183, 243, 379, 396]. To the best of our knowledge, domain-adaptive pre-training had not yet been explored in the media bias domain before. Like before, we based our experiments on the BABE dataset.

Primarily, we assess the effects of domain-adaptive pre-training on the media bias detection performance of several large-scale language models. Therefore, we leverage transformer-based models with an understanding of biased language. We perform an intermediate pre-training procedure with *BERT* [116], *RoBERTa* [265], *BART* [251], and *T5* [335] on the *Wiki Neutrality Corpus* (WNC) [333], which contains 180k sentence pairs from *Wikipedia* labeled as biased/neutral [333] and fine-tune the architecture on the state-of-the art media bias data set *BABE* [18]. We publish our domain-adapted models, i.e. *DA-RoBERTa* (DA = domain-adaptive), *DA-BERT*, *DA-BART*, and *DA-T5*, as well as training data and all material on https://github.com/Media-Bias-Group/A-Domain-adaptive-Pre-training-Approach-for-Language-BiasDetection-in-News. DA-RoBERTa achieves a new state-of-the-art performance on BABE (F1 = 0.814), while DA-BERT, DA-BART, and DA-T5 also outperform the baselines and distantly supervised models from prior work [18].

6.2.1 Related Work

In **Sect.** 6.1 we show how we pre-train transformer-based models such as BERT [116], RoBERTa [265], and DistilBERT [360] using Distant Supervision Learning on news headlines from articles with different political leanings and fine-tune it on BABE [18]. In another project of us[5], we train DistilBERT [360] on combinations of bias-related datasets using a Multi-task Learning (MTL) [89, 413] approach [17].

---

[4] Which shows our paper [6]

[5] This project and the domain-adaptive project were closely connected. Due to [17] being the basis for experiments following afterwards in this chapter, I decided to present the domain-adaptive approach first. However, some results of [17], which are described in Sect. 6.3, were already available at the time this paper was written.

6.2 Domain-Adaptive Pre-Training

As we will show in **Sect.** 6.3, our MTL model is outperformed by a baseline model (F1 = 0.782) trained on the WNC dataset. We [17] suggest that improvements can be attributed to the WNC dataset being strongly bias-related, hence equipping the model with bias-specific knowledge. To account for this domain knowledge, in this experiment, we use a similar learning task as in **Sect.** 6.1 [18] and exploit the WNC's bias-relatedness by extending the pre-training of several transformer models on the whole WNC instead of its subset.

6.2.2 Domain-Adaptive Pre-Training Approaches

Our training setup can be considered a form of domain-adaptive pre-training [56, 183, 243] in which a language model is equipped with domain-specific knowledge. Several studies experiment with domain-adaptive learning approaches in different domains (e.g., BioBERT [243], SciBERT [56]), but none of them deals with media bias detection [56, 177, 183, 243, 379].

Sun et al. [379] explore different techniques for domain-adaptive pre-training of BERT for text classification tasks such as sentiment classification, question classification, and topic classification. BERT is additionally pre-trained on data from various domains leading to performance boosts on many tasks if the training data are related to the target task's domain. After training BERT on several sentiment classification datasets, Sun et al. [379] reduced the error rate on the Yelp sentiment data set to 1.87% (compared to 2.28% from BERT baseline initialized with *bert-base-uncased* weights). The results from Sun et al. [379] are supported by Gururangan et al. [177] investigating domain-adaptive pre-training of RoBERTa in four different target domains (i.e., biomedical, computer science publications, news, and reviews) and eight subsequent classification tasks. When pre-training RoBERTa on large amounts of news text, the model's F1-score on a hyperpartisan classification dataset [220] improves from F1 = 0.886 (*roberta-base* weights) to F1 = 0.882. Training the model on a domain outside the domain of interest (*irrelevant domain-adaptive pre-training*) drastically decreases performance to F1 = 0.764.

Our domain-adaptive pre-training approach is performed on the WNC corpus and based on implementations from Sun et al. [379] and Gururangan et al. [177]. Due to drastic performance increases through irrelevant domain-adaptive pre-training in previous research [177], we do not implement respective experiments. We detail our proposed training process in **Sect.** 6.2.3. Since most existing approaches focus on sentence-level bias detection, we follow the standard practice and develop a sentence-level classification model. Compared to cutting-edge but convoluted studies in media bias detection [16, 18], we perform a more focused and direct training setup on a large amount of highly bias-related data and expect substantial performance improvements.

6.2.3 Methodology

We use neural-based language models, pre-train them on the bias domain (WNC), and perform evaluations on the media bias classification task using BABE as Fig. 6.1 shows.

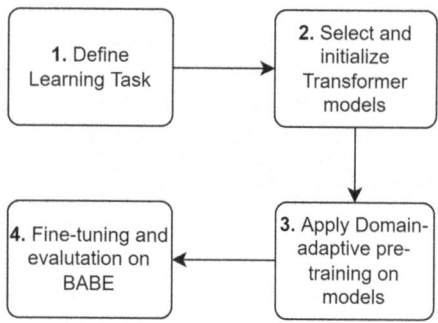

Fig. 6.1 Pipeline for building bias lexicon semi-automatically

We expect that domain-adaptive pre-training improves word representations by adapting them to the data distributions of biased and non-biased news content. Based on BABE, we first define a learning task that is later optimized. Then, we select suitable transformer models and initialize them with pre-trained weights. We adapt the models to the media bias domain by training them on the WNC. Finally, all models are fine-tuned and evaluated on BABE. We will show and detail the individual steps below.

Learning task. The language models are optimized via intermediate training. We have a corpus X containing sentences $x_i \in X$ with $i = 1, ..., N$ and binary bias labels (*Biased* vs. *Non-biased*) encoded as 1 and 0, respectively. The task is to assign the correct label $y_i \in \{0, 1\}$ to x_i. The training objective is to minimize a binary cross-entropy loss.

6.2 Domain-Adaptive Pre-Training

Learning task

$$\mathcal{L} := -\frac{1}{N} \sum_{i=1}^{N} \sum_{k=\{0,1\}} f_k(x_i) \cdot log(\hat{f}_k(x_i)). \qquad (6.2)$$

where $f_k(x_i)$ refers to the true binary label and $\hat{f}_k(x_i)$ indicates the model's predicted score for a sentence.

Transformer-based models. We choose BERT and RoBERTa for our domain-adaptive pre-training as they represent the best-performing models in Spinde et al. [18]. Doing so, we also achieve maximum comparability to previous state-of-the-art bias classifiers. Additionally, we incorporate BART and T5, since encoder-decoder architectures have demonstrated a clear improvement in comparison to BERT in several NLP tasks (e.g., GLUE [399]). We choose the corresponding models to investigate how the combination of autoencoder and autoregressive components (BART), and advanced MTL architectures (T5) perform on our media bias detection task. BERT learns bidirectional word representations on unlabeled text optimizing an unsupervised learning task based on masked language modeling and next sentence prediction (NSP). In contrast to BERT, RoBERTa drops the NSP task and differs slightly in terms of pre-training data. BART uses text manipulations by noising and learns representations by reconstructing the original text sequence. T5 uses an MTL architecture pre-trained on various supervised and unsupervised tasks by converting all training objectives into text-to-text tasks.

Domain-adaptive pre-training. Adapting a pre-trained language model to a specific domain becomes essential when the target domain differs strongly from the pre-training ground truth [56, 183, 243]. Due to tendentious and dubious vocabulary in slanted news, media bias is different from most of the domains BERT-like models are pre-trained on. For example, BERT is trained on English Wikipedia and the BooksCorpus [426] while RoBERTa additionally incorporates commonsense reasoning data, news data, and web text data. To the best of our knowledge, a specific BERT-like model trained on biased language in news does not exist to date. BERT models pre-trained on fake news [66] and political orientation classification [176] do exist. However, the concepts of fake news and political orientation differ substantially from the media bias domain.

Our domain-adaptive pre-training uses the WNC to optimize our learning task (as defined above). The 180k sentence pairs contained in the corpus are manually selected from Wikipedia articles as going against the platform's *Neutral Point of View* (NPOV) standard[6]. The pairs contain an original biased sentence and its manually derived neutral counterpart. Bias forms included in the corpus refer to *epistemological bias*, *framing bias*, and *demographic bias*. Recasens, Danescu-Niculescu-Mizil, and Jurafsky [341] define framing bias as choosing subjective words to embed a particular point of view in the text whereas epistemological bias is described as a modification of a statement's plausibility. Pryzant et al. [333] introduce demographic bias as text containing predispositions towards a certain gender, race, or other demographic category. For a detailed description on sentence selection criteria and the revision process, see Pryzant et al. [333].

Our approach is inspired by Sun et al. [379] and Gururangan et al. [177], which conclude domain-adaptive pre-training is most efficient once pre-training data for the domain adaption is related to the target domain and task. Since WNC (pre-training) and BABE (fine-tuning) have similar bias forms, and are both composed of manually labeled sentences (biased and non-biased), we expect the proposed pre-training task to improve our fine-tuning results.

6.2.4 Experiments

Pre-training. We initialize RoBERTa, BERT, BART, and T5 with pre-trained weights provided by the HuggingFace API[7], and stack a dropout layer (Dropout = 0.2) and randomly initialized linear transformation layer (768,2) on top of the model. All models are used in their base form.

For the domain-adaptive pre-training, sentences are batched together with 32 sentences per batch. For model optimization, we use the AdamW optimizer[8] with a learning rate of $1e^{-5}$, and model performance is evaluated on binary cross-entropy loss. Model convergence can be observed after one epoch and a runtime of ≈ 5 hours on a Tesla P100-PCIE GPU with 16GB RAM.

Fine-tuning. We fine-tune and evaluate the model on BABE Spinde et al. [18] with a batch size = 32. We again use the AdamW optimizer (learning rate = $1e^{-5}$), and model convergence based on cross-entropy loss can be observed after 3–4 epochs.

---

[6] https://en.wikipedia.org/wiki/Wikipedia:Neutral_point_of_view
[7] https://huggingface.co/
[8] https://huggingface.co/docs/transformers/main_classes/optimizer_schedules

6.2 Domain-Adaptive Pre-Training

Due to the small data size of 3700 sentences, we report the model's F1 score in the binary bias labeling task averaged by 5-fold cross-validation. Fine-tuning is performed on a Tesla K80 GPU (12GB RAM) in $\approx$ 15 minutes.

Baseline. For every domain-adaptive language model, we compare its sentence classification performance on BABE to the same architecture merely fine-tuned on BABE (without domain-adaptive pre-training as an intermediate training step). Thereby, we can assess the effect of our training approach. Since Spinde et al. [18] achieve state-of-the-art results on BABE with Distant Supervision Learning [18], we additionally compare our F1 scores to their scores achieved by training BERT and RoBERTa on news headlines distantly labeled as biased and non-biased. We provide statistical significance tests for our domain-adapted models vs. fine-tuned-only models.

Test for Statistical Significance. In their review of existing NLP studies, Dror et al. [122] report that most approaches lack statistical tests inspecting the significance of experimental results. The authors recommend various parametric and non-parametric tests to compare performances of Machine Learning models. For our approach, we select the *McNemars test* which is a non-parametric test to compare the performance of two algorithms on a target task. Since we do not have information on the distribution of our target metric (F1 score), a non-parametric approach is a suitable option to test for significance. The test is based on a $2x2$ contingency table showing the models' predictions on n instances of a target tasks' test set. Under the null hypothesis H_0, the test assumes that both algorithms output the correct/incorrect label for the same proportion of instances from the test set. Accordingly, the alternative hypothesis H_1 states that both algorithms differ significantly in terms of their agreement on items from the test set. The test statistic follows a χ^2 distribution and is suitable for NLP tasks such as binary text classification [117, 122]. For a more detailed introduction to statistical significance tests for NLP use cases, see Dror et al. [122].

Table 6.2 shows the F1 scores (averaged over 5-fold CV split) of our transformer-based experiments on the binary sentence classification task. All domain-adapted models (third block) outperform the baseline models (first block) and the distantly supervised models (middle block) trained by us previously [18].

The best-performing model that achieves a new state-of-the-art on BABE is DA-RoBERTa (F1 = 0.814), which surpasses the baselines and its Distant Supervision variant by 1.5 %. DA-BERT, DA-BART, and DA-T5 achieve a lower F1-score of 0.809, 0.809, and 0.798, yet outperform BERT, BART, and T5 by 2%, 0.8%, and 1.2%, respectively. However, DA-BERT increases sentence classification performance by only 0.5% compared to BERT trained via Distant Supervision [18]. To the best of our knowledge, a distantly supervised variant for BART and T5 is not available.

Table 6.3 shows results of the McNemar statistical significance tests comparing our domain-adapted models with respective baselines. On a significance level of $\alpha = 0.05$, we can observe significant F1-score improvements for BERT vs. its domain-adapted variant ($\chi^2 = 5.65, p = 0.031$) as well as for RoBERTa vs. DA-RoBERTa ($\chi^2 = 3.844, p = 0.049$) and T5 vs. DA-T5 ($\chi^2 = 4.86, p = 0.027$). Adapting BART to the bias domain seems not to significantly improve the sentence classification performance ($\chi^2 = 3.629, p = 0.057$).

We show that all domain-adapted models outperform their baselines and distantly supervised models published previously by us [18]. Our results can be considered a contribution towards a sufficiently accurate bias detection tool. However, some significance tests comparing the performance of domain-adapted models vs. distantly supervised models are missing due to limited resources.

While working on the methodology described above, and searching for useable datasets, we saw the need for systems detecting various sub-forms of bias (Like ones described in Chap. 2 accurately. We believed that MTL approaches trained

Table 6.2 Stratified 5-fold cross-validation results

Model	Macro F_1 (error)
BERT	0.789 (0.011)
RoBERTa	0.799 (0.011)
BART	0.801 (0.009)
T5	0.786 (0.008)
BERT-distant [18]	0.801 (0.014)
RoBERTa-distant [18]	0.799 (0.017)
DA-BERT	0.809 (0.010)
DA-RoBERTa	**0.814** (0.004)
DA-BART	0.809 (0.009)
DA-T5	0.798 (0.009)

Note: Standard errors across folds in parentheses.
The first block shows results of baseline approaches without intermediate pre-training. The second block shows results from [18] based on Distant Supervision Learning (BART and T5 are not incorporated in our previous study). Results from our domain-adaptive approach are shown in the third block.
The best result is printed in **bold**.

on different bias categories might be a a promising direction for future models. Within such model architectures, we would also be able to verify how even more robust and general NLP models benefit from intermediate pre-training. In particular, we got inspired by state-of-the art NLP models such as the recently published *ExT5* [37], incorporating extensive MTL on 107 tasks from different domains, and further exploiting domain-adaptive learning effects. We integrated our inspiration in two MTL approaches, the second one of them being the most sophisticated freely available media bias classifier to date. However, to build the model, a preliminary experiment was needed first. We describe it in the following.

6.3 Multi Task Learning

Research Objective
Evaluate the performance of Multi Task Learning in the media bias domain.

As mentioned above, another one of our models incorporates MTL [353], which allows for increasing performance by sharing model representations between related tasks [203, 264, 379]. The use of cross-domain data sets in our model is particularly relevant for the media bias domain as multiple sources can provide a more robust model. MTL approaches have shown to be helpful when high-quality data sets in the domain are scarce, but text corpora covering general related concepts are available [203, 264, 379, 380, 399]. For example, [203] report that MTL applied on BERT yields an accuracy increase of 1.03% compared to the baseline BERT in a subjectivity detection task. MTL might be a suitable training paradigm for media

Table 6.3 Results of the McNemar test for statistical significance between baseline

Models	McNemar test statistic	
	χ^2	p
BERT vs. DA-BERT	5.65	0.031*
RoBERTa vs. DA-RoBERTa	3.84	0.049*
BART vs. DA-BART	3.63	0.057
T5 vs. DA-T5	4.86	0.027*

Note: $*p < .05$

bias identification systems since sufficiently sized bias corpora with qualitative hand-crafted annotations do not exist. Therefore, we propose the first neural MTL media bias classifier composed of inter-domain and cross-domain data sets. To the best of our knowledge, the MTL paradigm has not been explored in existing work on media bias. Our research question is therefore to assess whether MTL can improve models to classify media bias automatically. We exploit MTL in the media bias context by computing multiple models based on different combinations of auxiliary training data sets. All our models, data, and code are publicly available on https://bit.ly/3cmiQgB. As mentioned, this experiment gave us grounds to build another experiment on top, which we describe in the subsequent **Sect.** 6.3.1.

6.3.1 Methodology

We explore how fine-tuning a language model via MTL can improve the performance in detecting media bias on the sentence level. Computational costs are an important consideration for us since we train multiple large-scale MTL models. For this reason, we employ a distilled modification of BERT [116], called DistilBERT [360], which achieves a 40% reduction in size while simultaneously accelerating the training process by 60% and retaining 97% of language understanding capabilities on NLP benchmark tasks [399]. DistilBERT represents an appropriate architecture, keeping resource consumption and performance balanced. The incorporation of larger models trained via MTL is left to future research.

Our MTL technique is based on *hard parameter sharing* in which all hidden model layers are shared between auxiliary training tasks [353]. Task-specific layers are added on top of the last hidden state, accounting for the label structure of auxiliary data sets. The MTL paradigm we propose is architecture-independent and can be adjusted to future NLP architectures.

For our training procedure, we distinguish between models trained on in-domain and cross-domain data sets. For in-domain data sets, the creation process included concepts related to media bias, such as subjectivity [310]. Conversely, cross-domain data sets include data points that are not directly annotated for or related to media bias, but are retrieved from tasks that bear some connection to it. The auxiliary data sets we use comprise a diverse set of NLP tasks requiring two different losses for the learning process—the Cross-Entropy (CE) loss [112] and the Mean Squared Error (MSE) loss [282]. The origin and number of the data used for the training of our models, as well as their respective original tasks and used loss functions, are shown in Table 6.4. We use in-domain (ID) and cross-domain (CD) data sets used in other MTL studies within the language processing domain [203, 264, 379].

6.3 Multi Task Learning

Table 6.4 Auxiliary data sets incorporated in the MTL models (n = number of instances)

Data set	Domain	n	Task	Loss	Description
Reddit data set (Reddit) [202]	ID	6861	Single Sentence Regression	MSE	Reddit comments labeled on a continuous scale ranging from 0 (supportive) to 1 (discriminatory)
Subjectivity data set (Subj) [310]	ID	10000	Single Sentence Classification	CE	Movie reviews labeled as *objective* or *opinionated*
IMDb [268]	ID	50000	Single Sentence Classification	CE	Movie reviews containing positive and negative sentiment labels
Wikipedia data set (Wiki)[1] [333]	ID	180000	Single Sentence Classification	CE	Neutral and biased sentence pairs from articles going against Wikipedia's NPOV rule
Semantic Textual Similarity Benchmark (STS-B) data set [85]	CD	10943	Pairwise Sentence Similarity	MSE	Multilingual and cross-lingual sentence pairs labeled in terms of similarity
Stanford Natural Language Inference (SNLI) corpus[1] [73]	CD	570000	Pairwise Sentence Classification	CE	Sentence pairs labeled for linguistic relations within the labels *entailment*, *neutral*, or *contradiction*

[1] We only use 50000 text instances from these corpora in our MTL approach to keep the size of training sets balanced.

Figure 6.2 outlines our in-domain MTL model consisting of DistilBERT's encoder, whose parameters are shared across tasks, and the added task-specific layers[9]. The represented model is based on the maximum number of possible data sets within the approach. In our experiments on MTL, we try various combinations, including at least three in-domain and five cross-domain data sets, respectively.

---

[9] The cross-domain model is published at https://bit.ly/3cmiQgB.

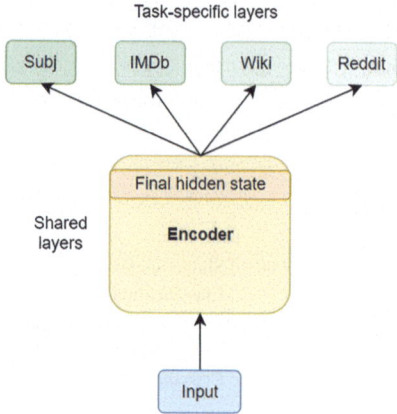

Fig. 6.2 Outline of in-domain MTL model consisting of a shared encoder block and task-specific layers. (*Note*: We implement multiple MTL models based on different combinations of the presented data sets)

For preprocessing and MTL training, we took the same approach as [264]. Initially, pre-trained parameters are loaded from *huggingface*[10]. We split up data for a fixed-size subset of tasks into batches, and batches are merged and shuffled to guarantee the model does not train on too many subsequent batches of a single task. The preprocessing step is repeated every epoch. Batches are then passed on by the data loader one by one to the model, which outputs task-specific predictions and the respective loss. Finally, the loss is backpropagated, and parameters are updated.

6.3.2 Experiments

To investigate the benefit of MTL to identify media bias on a fine-grained linguistic level, we train ten models using MTL, which we compare to five baseline models. As a consequence of a lack of robust guidelines for selection criteria for auxiliary corpora, we choose a variety of auxiliary tasks to fine-tune the DistilBERT model via MTL that have previously been used successfully in MTL studies [203, 264, 379]. Each of our MTL models is trained using a different combination of a sample of six popular data sets, where IMDb [268], Subj [310], Wiki [333], and Reddit

---

[10] https://huggingface.co/transformers/model_doc/distilbert.html

6.3 Multi Task Learning

[202] are considered in-domain data sets, and STS-B [85], and SNLI [73] comprise examples of cross-domain data sets[11].

The in-domain models are based on bias-related data sets[12]. Combining the in-domain corpora yields five different models (Table 6.5, M1–M5): four use triple combinations, and one model relies on all in-domain data sets. The cross-domain models extend the pool of experiments by adding the STS-B and SNLI data sets to each of the five in-domain models (Table 6.5, M6–M10). The approaches are oriented on the MTL fine-tuning approaches applied in [379]. In their experiments based on BERT, the authors apply MTL on domain-related and domain-unrelated data yielding a performance boost for sentiment classification.

All experiments are performed on a *Google Colab NVIDIA Tesla K80*[13]. We choose the *AdamW optimizer* [224] and a batch size of 32. All downstream task layers are based on a hidden state dimensionality of 768. All performance metrics are calculated based on 5-fold cross-validation [77]. Thus, we divide the final bias data set containing 1700 instances into five different train and tests[14]. The models are then iteratively trained on all five training sets and evaluated on the respective held-out test set. Finally, the performance metrics on the test sets are averaged, yielding the cross-validated model performance. Each respective model is trained over four epochs with an early stopping criterion based on validation CE loss. In many cases, the model stops learning after two epochs. The MTL fine-tuning is based on a learning rate of $5 \cdot 10^{-5}$.

As far as we know, there are no related works applying MTL in the media bias domain. Therefore, we compare the performances of our MTL approaches to a set of baseline models (Table 6.5; B1–B5). We report the performance scores achieved from pre-trained DistilBERT provided by *huggingface* (B1). Furthermore, we train four DistilBERT models on each of the in-domain data sets (B2–B5). Thus, we can observe whether the assumed performance boost of our MTL models results from MTL rather than domain-relatedness of the training data.

We expect that fine-tuning via MTL leads to an improvement of DistilBERT's bias identification power. Mainly, we want to analyze whether the MTL technique yields a substantial performance boost compared to simple Transfer Learning (TL) approaches training the model on only a single data set. Therefore, we run several experiments.

---

[11] A detailed description of the data sets is published at the repository mentioned before.
[12] IMDb, Subj, Wiki, Reddit
[13] https://colab.research.google.com/notebooks/intro.ipynb
[14] We use a subset of BABE to evaluate the MTL models.

6.3.3 Results and Discussion

We show the performance indicators of our model on our expert-labeled media bias data set in Table 6.5, according to F_1, precision, recall, and loss. Since the highest macro F_1 score does not necessarily match with the lowest loss, we elaborate on the results from the perspective of both metrics.

Among all MTL-trained models the highest F_1 score is achieved from the in-domain M4 model with 0.776. The best cross-domain model regarding macro F_1 is reached by M8 with 0.771. Compared to DistilBERT, M4 achieves a 3% increase in macro F_1, while B5 achieves the highest macro F_1 for TL-based models at 0.782, which is not surpassed by any MTL approach. Although all MTL models outperform DistilBERT, the highest macro F_1 score of all MTL models is 0.6% lower than that of B5. Overall, MTL improves the B1 baseline macro F_1 score in a range from 0.3% (M9) to 3% (M4). When considering the models from a loss-based perspective, the performance ranks change slightly: M4 remains as the best in-domain MTL model, but M7 (the second to last in terms of macro F_1 performance) reaches the lowest loss within the cross-domain approaches. Compared to DistilBERT, M4 shows a decrease in loss of 4.9%. B5 prevails as the best TL model with a CE loss of 0.466. In contrast to the macro F_1-based perspective, however, M4 achieves the lowest overall loss, outperforming B5 by 0.2%.

In general, our MTL approaches surpass the baseline methods. However, the best overall model based on macro F_1 was a TL model trained on a data set containing revised Wikipedia excerpts (B5), which is the model we, as described, base our experiment from **Sect.** 6.2 on. Based on CE loss, only one MTL model slightly outperform this TL model. Thus, at this point, we cannot state whether Transformer-Based MTL improves media bias detection on the sentence level. Since the results here are not convincing, and the MTL models can not outperform a single task model, we assume that our selection of auxiliary data sets might not have been sufficiently comprehensive. Even more, in our MTL approaches so far, updating DistilBERT's parameters only required the computation and back-propagation of binary CE loss and MSE loss. [353] argues that well-performing MTL approaches must be trained on NLP tasks, including multiple loss functions.

After seeing these results, we decided to follow up on the experiment. It seemed promising to use cross-domain data in the domain since related datasets are so scarce. However, the performance seemed to be insufficient in our small early-stage experiment. We came across the work by Aribandi et al. [37], who built a model of 107 tasks, evaluated them in detail, and decided to continue working on MTL in the media bias domain. Our next approach is more detailed than the early-stage experiment and returns sophisticated results. However, for the publication, I was not

6.3 Multi Task Learning

Table 6.5 Results for all baseline models, i.e., the *huggingface* model or models obtained by TL, as well as the models trained using MTL considering only in-domain data sets or also incorporating cross-domain data. For each metric we have denoted the best performance in bold

	Model	Data sets						macro F_1	micro F_1	binary F_1	Precision	Recall	CE Loss
		Subj	IMDb	Reddit	Wiki	STS	SNLI						
TL	B1			*huggingface* DistilBERT				0.746	0.750	0.711	**0.805**	0.640	0.513
	B2	✓						0.744	0.744	0.730	0.744	0.716	0.545
	B3		✓					0.761	0.762	0.746	0.770	0.725	0.491
	B4			✓				0.743	0.746	0.709	0.790	0.646	0.497
	B5				✓			**0.782**	**0.782**	**0.7695**	0.785	0.754	0.466
ID MTL	M1	✓	✓					0.768	0.768	0.753	0.778	0.731	0.482
	M2	✓	✓					0.760	0.760	0.746	0.766	0.729	0.495
	M3	✓		✓				0.773	0.774	0.762	0.777	0.755	0.482
	M4	✓	✓	✓	✓			0.776	0.777	0.759	0.794	0.727	**0.464**
	M5	✓		✓	✓			0.772	0.771	0.757	0.778	0.737	0.473
CD MTL	M6	✓	✓	✓	✓	✓		0.766	0.766	0.758	0.756	0.763	0.492
	M7	✓	✓	✓	✓	✓	✓	0.765	0.765	0.751	0.770	0.735	0.474
	M8	✓		✓	✓	✓	✓	0.771	0.771	0.762	0.765	0.761	0.491
	M9		✓	✓	✓	✓	✓	0.749	0.750	0.759	0.714	**0.812**	0.499
	M10	✓	✓	✓	✓	✓	✓	0.769	0.770	0.751	0.789	0.720	0.480

the main author. I proposed, developed, supervised, and wrote the paper together with the other authors, but since a larger collaboration was performed (and another author took the major workload), the paper is only mentioned here, and not extensively detailed. In this second study investigating MTL in the media bias domain, we introduce the model MAGPIE as an advanced approach to detect media bias through MTL, significantly enhancing performance across various bias detection tasks [5]. We first build the Large Bias Mixture (LBM) framework, consisting of 59 diverse bias-related tasks, which is central to MAGPIE's methodology. LBM facilitates the comprehensive training of a new MTL model, which employs a RoBERTa-based encoder. The results demonstrate a significant improvement, particularly a 3.3% increase in the F1-score on the BABE dataset. MAGPIE's performance is notably superior in 5 out of 8 tasks within the MBIB benchmark (see below), underscoring the effectiveness of multi-task learning in improving both the accuracy and efficiency of media bias detection systems. The approach contrasts with traditional single-task models by reducing the need for extensive finetuning (Using a RoBERTa encoder, MAGPIE needs just 15% of finetuning steps compared to single-task approaches), thereby setting a new benchmark in the field of neural media bias classification and highlighting the potential of combining large-scale pre-training with multi-task learning strategies. For more detail, here, we refer to the paper.

Open Access This chapter is licensed under the terms of the Creative Commons Attribution 4.0 International License (http://creativecommons.org/licenses/by/4.0/), which permits use, sharing, adaptation, distribution and reproduction in any medium or format, as long as you give appropriate credit to the original author(s) and the source, provide a link to the Creative Commons license and indicate if changes were made.

The images or other third party material in this chapter are included in the chapter's Creative Commons license, unless indicated otherwise in a credit line to the material. If material is not included in the chapter's Creative Commons license and your intended use is not permitted by statutory regulation or exceeds the permitted use, you will need to obtain permission directly from the copyright holder.

Visualization and Perception of Media Bias 7

Life is made of small moments like this

Above & Beyond—*ABGT 350*

As we discuss throughout the thesis, media bias plays a significant role in shaping individual and collective perceptions of news, which can have profound implications on how people form opinions and make decisions based on the information they consume. In order to address the potential negative consequences of media bias, it is crucial to explore effective communication strategies that can counteract its effects. However, existing research on the theoretical foundations of bias messages and visualizations is limited, with neither visualization theory nor bias theory providing comprehensive insights into effective approaches for addressing this issue within their respective domains.

In the following chapter, we delve into the theoretical background that serves as the foundation for our investigation into effective communication and visualization techniques for addressing media bias. Beginning in **Sect. 7.1**, we provide a thorough review of the existing literature on visualization and bias theories. This review lays the groundwork for our empirical studies presented in **Sect. 7.2** and **Sect. 7.3**, where we report on the first set of experiments designed to test how to effectively communicate and visualize media bias to various audiences.

In a third study, we seek to understand whether there is a direct relationship between the degree of bias present in news articles and the perception of such articles

---

Supplementary Information The online version contains supplementary material available at https://doi.org/10.1007/978-3-658-47798-1_7.

on social media platforms, specifically Twitter. We present the methodology, results, and implications of our investigation in **Sect.** 7.4.

Our long-term objective is to combine the automated detection of media bias with automated visualization techniques in order to develop a comprehensive system that facilitates media bias-aware news consumption, promotes news literacy, and encourages critical reading habits among consumers. By integrating these components, we aim to empower individuals to make more informed decisions, engage in constructive discourse, and navigate the complex media landscape with a heightened awareness of the potential influence of bias on their perceptions. While we presented early stage results, we see that much future is required for a such a system to be successfully implemented. We address this again in **Sect.** 8.1.

7.1 Theoretical Background

In Chap. 2, we summarize how exposure to biased information can lead to negative societal outcomes, including group polarization, intolerance of dissent, and political segregation [377]. It can also affect collective decision-making [8]. The implications of selective exposure theory intensify the severity of biased news coverage: Researchers observed long ago that people prefer to consume information that fits their worldview and avoid information that challenges these beliefs [239]. By selecting only confirmatory information, one's own opinion is reaffirmed, and there is no need to re-evaluate existing stances [217]. In this way, the unpleasant feeling of cognitive dissonance is avoided [144]. Isolation in one's own filter bubble or echo chamber confirms internal biases and might lead to a general decrease in the diversity of news consumption [377]. This decrease is further exacerbated by recent technological developments like personalized overview features of, e.g., news aggregators [10]. How partisans select and perceive political news is thus an important question in political communication research [41]. Therefore, in the studies within this chapter, we try to test ways to increase the awareness of media bias (which might mitigate its negative impact) and the partisan evaluation of the media through transparent bias communication.

To create media bias awareness, revealing the existence and nature of media can be an essential route to attain media bias awareness and promote informed and reflective news consumption [10]. For instance, visualizations may generally help to raise media bias awareness and lead to a more balanced news intake by warning people of potential biases [98], highlighting individual instances of bias [10], or facilitating the comparison of contents [296]. Although knowledge of how to communicate media bias effectively is crucial, visualizations and enhanced perception of media bias have only played a minor role in existing research, and several approaches have not yet been investigated. Therefore, we test how effectively different strategies promote media bias awareness and thereby may also help understand common barriers to informed media consumption.

Although knowledge of how to communicate instances of media bias effectively is crucial, visualizations and enhanced perception of media bias have only played a minor role in existing research, and several approaches have not yet been investigated. The literature describes ways to present news, e.g., news aggregators [316], but currently lacks measuring effectiveness and efficiency of how to visualize and communicate single instances of media bias to enable news consumers to become aware of bias and aid them in understanding its effects on their perception of news topics. User studies like the one by Park et al. [315, 316] confirm that bias-aware visualizations in general help users to become aware of bias, compared to baseline visualizations that were bias-agnostic. An et al. [32] gave a prototypical visualization of media bias on Twitter. While they showed how their model could help people receive balanced news information, they also deemphasized "the potential benefit of such political diversity because not everyone prefers to receive diverse political opinions" [32]. A user study on NewsCube 2, a crowdsourcing system for framing in the news, showed that exposing opposing viewpoints on one topic can lead "readers to read more articles covering different aspects" [316] and help them to develop more balanced views.

7.2 Survey A: Visualization Comparison

Research Objective
Testing visual aids for media bias communication on text level (highlights of bas instances with explanation) and overview level (articles from different political perspectives)

In this study, as in our second study (**Sect.** 7.3), we test the effectiveness of communicating bias-related news characteristics using different visualization types and components. Our experiments include tests on an overview level, e.g., showing multiple news topics, related articles, and an aggregated measure of slanted language, as well as on an article level, e.g., showing a selected article's text and in-text bias instances. After an extensive literature review on user-related variables that may affect users' perceptions of bias, such as their political background, we devise and test a questionnaire for assessing the perception of bias and four visualizations: two control group visualizations (bias agnostic) as well as two treatment visualizations (bias aware). We mainly report three contributions:

C1 Analysis of the influence of participant-related factors on understanding biased coverage.
C2 Analysis of the efficacy of mitigating echo chamber effects by presenting users with different perspectives on the same topic.
C3 Comparison of the efficacy of bias agnostic and bias aware visualization types as to enabling news consumers to understand the presence and degree of biased coverage.

7.2.1 Study Setup

Our study employs a conjoint analysis [179] to test how visualizations can improve users' understanding or awareness of media bias in news articles. In our design, we show a fully randomized selection of visualization variants to each participant and then ask a series of questions regarding the perception of bias in the articles viewed. We base our selection of variables for this prototypical study, as shown in Table 7.1.

Table 7.1 Participant-related variables presumed to influence bias perception

Variable	Category	Source
Gender, age, education, religion, residence	Demogr.	[135]
Political orientation, esp. party affiliation	Pol. bg.	[165]
Opinion on pre-selected, political topics	Pol. bg.	[242]
Engaging in political discussions	Pol. bg.	[135]
Belief in hostile media	Pol. bg.	[135]

First, participants answer questions on their background, based on the variables which we show in Table 7.1. Second, we randomly assign respondents (1) to an order of three pre-selected topics (to mitigate any influence of the order in which topics are viewed [181]), (2) to seeing the overview visualization or not (to measure contribution C2), and (3) to one of the four article visualizations (to measure C3). The design of the overview follows allsides.com, per topic showing three articles that are representative of three political categories, as depicted in Fig. 7.1.

7.2 Survey A: Visualization Comparison

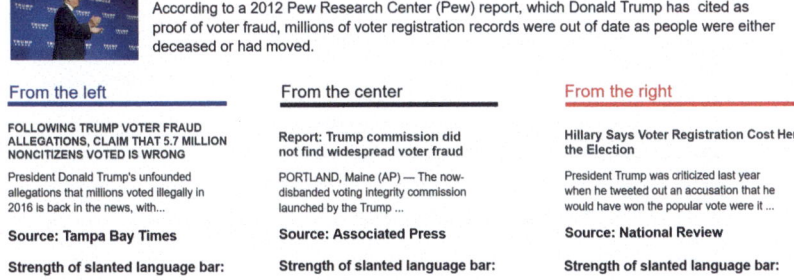

Fig. 7.1 Excerpt from the news overview page

For each of our study participant groups, we show the texts of three articles and visualize the articles differently: (1) plain, i.e., as it would be shown in a news aggregator or on a news website, or (2) with visually highlighted phrases that represent the facts most important to an article's event. The treatment groups see the text enhanced with either (3) visually highlighted framing effects, or (4) visually highlighted annotations of biased or unbalanced language (Fig. 7.2. In variant 4, we also show reasons why the text is biased. Variant 4 aims to represent instances of bias found using the currently most effective form of bias analysis, i.e., we conduct an inductive content analysis with 6 coders. Variant 3 aims to represent what the state-of-the-art in automated bias identification is able to detect [181], e.g., target-dependent sentiment classification, a basic yet effective way to catch the effects of biased coverage.

We gather the annotations used within the visualizations for each of the articles by a brief questionnaire, where three students per article and type of annotation, i.e., framing (3) and biased language (4), mark text phrases based on their judgment. Another three students check their results manually, before we integrate all results into one common set of annotations for each article, by discarding annotations that are not found by at least two of the three students in both groups. To facilitate the appearance of bias, we select a publicly controversial and politically polarizing topic (immigrant voter Fraud Allegations and immigration restrictions) as well as one topic related to the fake university in Farmington.

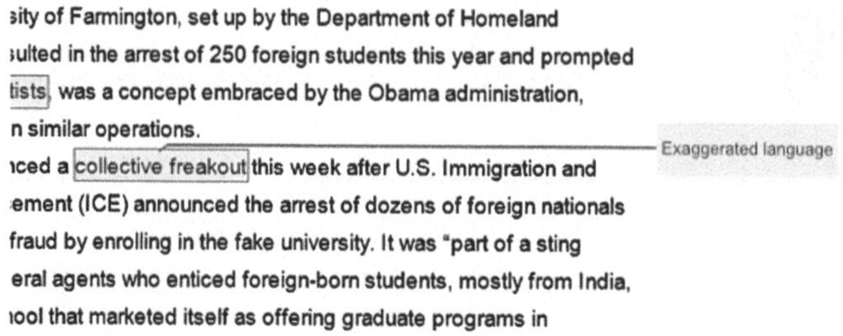

> sity of Farmington, set up by the Department of Homeland
> sulted in the arrest of 250 foreign students this year and prompted
> tists, was a concept embraced by the Obama administration,
> n similar operations.
> iced a collective freakout this week after U.S. Immigration and ⸺ Exaggerated language
> ement (ICE) announced the arrest of dozens of foreign nationals
> fraud by enrolling in the fake university. It was "part of a sting
> eral agents who enticed foreign-born students, mostly from India,
> iool that marketed itself as offering graduate programs in

Fig. 7.2 Excerpt from one article with visually highlighted annotations of biased language

After reading the article, we ask participants three questions to measure if and how strongly they became aware of the presence or absence of bias within the article. Two of these are control questions, e.g., about the article's content, to verify that they had read the article. For example, for the immigration topic, we ask: "How many illegal immigrants are believed to might have voted, according to the article?" To further understand whether participants rather agree or disagree with the opinion voiced in the article, we ask how much participants agree with a polarizing statement from the current article and how much they believe that the public agrees with that statement. For example, for the first article, we ask how much the participant agrees with the statement: "Trump has made repeated claims about massive voter fraud and election rigging." Most importantly, we ask (3) how the participants estimate the degree of the bias of the article's author, how politically extreme they perceive the news article, and how impartial and one-sided they think it was in dealing with the actual issue. The questions are indirectly asking for bias perception, as we assume a strong emotional and personal effect when asking for bias directly. In all groups the type of visualization and order of articles were randomized.

7.2.2 Results

Participants in the study are US Turkers on Amazon Mechanical Turk (MTurk). To reduce the number of low-quality answers, we accept only Turkers with MTurk's Masters qualification [267]. In total, 123 workers complete the study. Afterward, we perform a manual quality analysis and discard the low-quality results from one Turker.

7.2 Survey A: Visualization Comparison

We find that for all of our variables (C1), random effects show high variation between the three articles. While our set of experimental variables does not lead to significant differences in means, a multilevel model shows that perceived journalist bias is directly and significantly related to the perceived political extremeness and impartiality of the article. The model can also be inspected online (see **Sect. 7.2.3**). We do not find any influence of the time at which participants see an article on bias perception, e.g., as the first or last one of the three we show them.

Exposure to divergent perspectives in the overview visualization, e.g., article excerpts representing the political spectrum of the same topic, does not significantly alter the awareness of media bias in the articles viewed afterward (C2). While this is, on one hand, unintuitive (people will become aware of other perspectives), on the other hand, it aligns with findings by An et al. [32], i.e., readers are resistant to views different from their own. Forcing users to view different perspectives may increase hesitance even further. We believe that future research should focus on raising interest in users to view opposing perspectives (see **Sect. 7.2.3**).

The results show no strong effects of becoming aware of the bias of the treatment groups compared to the control group (C3), which is partially in line with prior work on echo chambers (see also C2) and that news readers tend to prefer reading articles matching their views [32]. However, we notice some effects of different visualizations. For example, Fig. 7.3 shows that the hand-annotated bias visualization (first column), which reveals biased vs. neutral language, most effectively communicates bias instances to users. Based on a significance level of 10%, our multilevel model from C1 confirms this. The framing visualization (second) yields slight improvements and the important-fact visualization (third) yields no improvements compared to the control group. Lastly, we find that readers can determine if and how much an article is biased, e.g., impartial or politically extreme since different users usually agree regarding their rating on the same article. Fig. 7.3 also shows strong differences between the articles shown in the study, e.g., article A1 (red) is deemed more biased as to multiple variables, such as political extremeness and journalist's unfairness, than A2 (green).

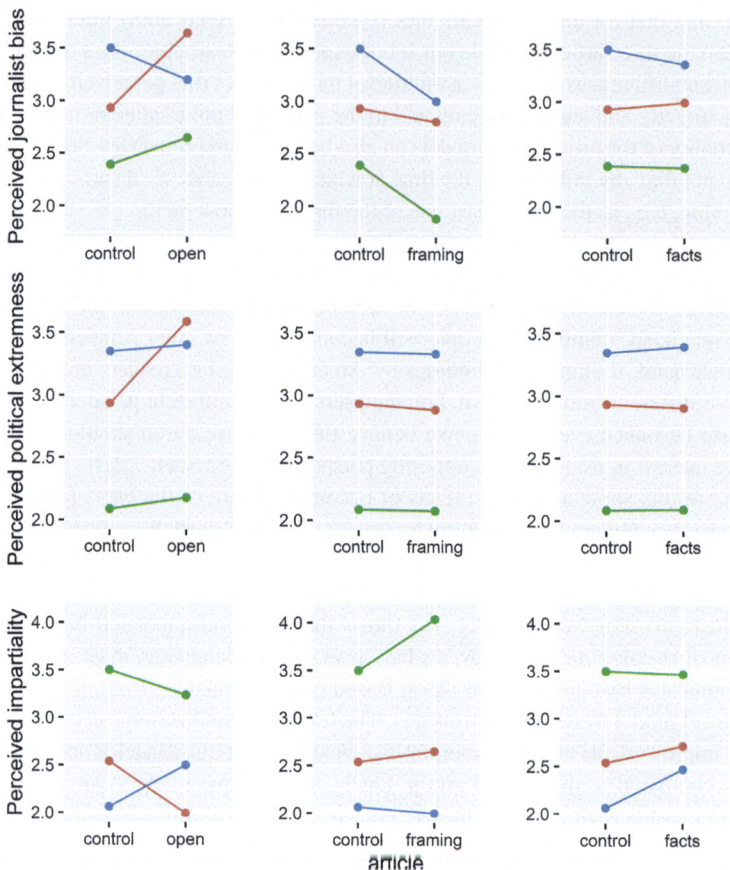

Fig. 7.3 Perceived level of political extremeness, fair perspective, and impartiality (each in one row) on a scale from 1 (least) to 5 (most), comparing the visualizations with the control group (columns). Red: C1, Green: C2, Blue: C3

7.2.3 Conclusion

We present the results of a user study on the effectiveness of communicating slanted bias coverage and, more specifically, individual instances of media bias in news articles to news consumers using different visualizations[1]. Specifically, we investigate

---

[1] We publish the survey materials, including questionnaires, articles, visualizations, data, and results freely at: https://zenodo.org/record/3627995#.Xi3uOyNCeUk.

three parts that may influence the perception of slanted coverage: readers' background (contribution C1), viewing a bias-aware news overview (C2), and different visualizations for reading an article (C3). While on the one hand, the study finds no statistically significant factors influencing bias perception in users, on the other hand, we find several indicative factors that gave ground to our follow-up study, **Sect. 7.3**.

For C1, we find that random effects show strong variation dependent on the article. Perceived political extremeness, journalist bias, and impartiality were closely and significantly related. We confirmed readers' aversion against other views [32] by our overview test (C2). We plan to investigate alternatives to forcing users to view different perspectives, e.g., indicating different word choices of one fact within an article. We will also investigate whether there exist differences in bias perception when forcedly seeing a specific article after an overview page or when there exists a free article choice, which could be a major difference to the news aggregator by Park et al. [315]. We find that participants become aware of bias when presented with bias-aware visualizations (C3): visualizing annotations stemming from a manual content analysis are most, followed by highlighting targets as to their sentiment.

7.3 Survey B: Automated Classification Assessment

Research Objective
Testing the effectiveness of a forewarning message, text annotations, and a political classification on facilitating bias awareness

In our second study on visual indicators of media bias, we test how effectively different strategies promote media bias awareness and thereby may also help understand common barriers to informed media consumption. As before, we test three ways to increase the awareness of media bias which might mitigate its negative impact and the partisan evaluation of the media through transparent bias communication. Their effectiveness to raise awareness is tested in an online experiment. We select three major methods in related work [10, 98] to analyze how they facilitate the detection of media bias in one combined study. The visual and textual aids come in the form of (a) a forewarning message, (b) text annotations we tested in preliminary work (see **Sect.** 7.2), and (c) political classifiers. In the online study, we randomized 985 participants to receive a biased liberal or conservative news article in any combination of the three aids. Meanwhile, their subjective perception of media bias in this article, attitude change, and political ideology was assessed. Both the forewarning message and the annotations increased media bias awareness, whereas the political classification showed no effect. Incongruence between an article's political position and individual political orientation also increased media bias awareness. Visual aids did not mitigate this effect. Likewise, attitudes remained unaltered.

Forewarning Message According to socio-psychological inoculation theory [279], it is possible to pre-emptively confer psychological resistance against persuasion attempts by exposing people to a message of warning character. It is similar to the process of immunizing against a virus by administering a weakened dose of the virus: A so-called inoculation message is expected to protect people from a persuasive attack by exposing them to weakened forms of the persuasion attempt. Due to the perceived threat of the forewarning inoculation message, people tend to strengthen their own position and are thus more resistant to influences of imminent persuasion attacks [327]. Therefore, one strategy to help people detect bias is to prepare them ahead of media consumption for the occurrence of media bias, thereby "forewarning" them against biased language influences. Such warnings have been widely established in persuasion and shown to be effective in different applied contexts [48]. Furthermore, such warnings also seem to help not only to protect attitudes against influences but also to determine the quality of a piece of information [69, 129, 259] and communicate the information accordingly [323]. For biased language, this may work specifically by focusing the reader's attention on a universal motive to evaluate the accuracy of information while relying on the individual's capacity to detect the bias when encountered [69, 323].

Annotations Other than informing people in advance about bias occurrence, a further approach is to inform them during reading, thereby increasing their awareness of biased language and providing direct help to detect it in an article. Recently, there has been a lot of research on media bias from information science, but it is mainly concerned with its identification and detection [10, 20, 92, 201]. However, whereas some research concerning the effects of visualizations of media bias in news articles to detect bias are promising (here: flagging fake news as debunked [75], others did not find such effects, potentially also due to the technical issues in accurately annotating single articles [10]. Still, they offer a good prospect to enable higher media bias awareness and more balanced news consumption. We show our annotation visualization in Fig. 7.4.

7.3 Survey B: Automated Classification Assessment

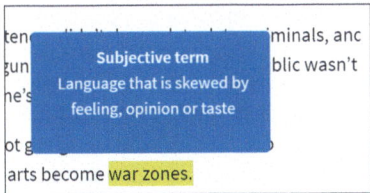

Fig. 7.4 Example of the bias annotation "subjective term". Boxed annotation appeared by moving the cursor/finger over the highlighted text section

Political Classification Another attempt to raise media bias awareness is a political classification of biased material after readers have dealt with it. An et al. [32] proposed an ideological left-right map where media sources are politically classified. The authors suggest that showing a source's political leaning helps readers question their attitudes and even promotes browsing for news articles with multiple viewpoints. Likewise, several other studies indicate that feedback on the political orientation of an article or a source may lead to more media bias awareness and a more balanced news consumption [10]. Additionally, exposing users to multiple diverse viewpoints on controversial topics encourages the development of more balanced viewpoints [316]. A study by Munson and colleagues (2013) further suggests that a feedback element indicating whether the user's browsing history consists of biased news consumption modestly leads to more balanced news consumption. Based on these findings, we will test whether the sole representation of a source's leaning helps raise bias awareness among users on the condition that the article is classified as politically skewed. We show our political classification bar in Fig. 7.5.

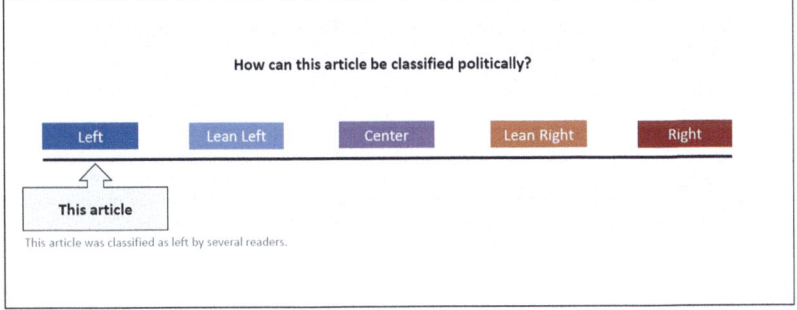

Fig. 7.5 Example of an article classification as being politically left-oriented

Partisan Media Bias Awareness Individuals perceive biased content that corresponds to their opinion as less biased [141] and biased content that contradicts their viewpoints as more biased [394] (see Chap. 2). This partisan effect suggests that incongruence between the reader's position and the news article's position may increase media bias perception of the article, whereas congruence may decrease it. Thus, partisan media consumers may engage in motivated reasoning to overcome cognitive dissonance experienced when encountering media bias in any news article generally in line with their viewpoints (e.g. [212]). Exposure to messages inconsistent with one's beliefs could create cognitive dissonance, which a person generally tries to avoid to reduce negative emotions [144]. Raising media bias awareness could increase experienced cognitive dissonance and thereby lead to even more partisan ratings of bias. Further, content is considered appropriate in media coverage dependent on one's political identity [171]. Other researchers focus on the inattention to the quality of news and the motive to only support truthful news [324]. Both approaches lead us to expect opposite results for the partisanship of the media bias ratings with increased media bias awareness as created by our proposed visualizations: Partisanship of ratings should decrease rather than increase as people are reminded of more general norms and accuracy motives [69].

Study Aims and Hypotheses This project aims to contribute to a deeper understanding of effective media bias communication. To this end, we create a set of bias visualizations revealing bias in different ways and test their effectiveness to raise awareness in an online experiment. Following the respective literature elaborated above for each technique, we would expect enhanced media bias awareness by all visualizations:

Hypothesis H1
a A forewarning message prior to news articles increases media bias awareness in presented articles.
b Annotations in news articles increase media bias awareness in presented articles.
c A political classification of news articles increases media bias awareness in presented articles.

7.3 Survey B: Automated Classification Assessment

Another goal of this study is to understand better the reader's political orientation in media bias awareness. In line with the findings of partisan media bias perception [389], we adopt the following hypothesis:

Hypothesis H2
Presented material will be rated less biased if consistent with individual political orientation.

Furthermore, we assume, following the attentional and normative explanation of partisanship in ratings rather than cognitive dissonance theory, the following effect:

Hypothesis H3
Bias visualizations will mitigate the effects of partisan bias ratings.

7.3.1 Study Setup

A total of 1002 participants from the US were recruited online via Prolific in August 2020. A final sample of N = 985 was included in the analysis (51% female; age: M = 32.67; SD = 11.95). The excluded participants did not fully complete the study or indicated that their data might not be trusted in a seriousness check. The target sample size was determined using power analysis, so that small effects (f = 0.10) could be found with a power of .80 (Faul et al., 2007). The online study was scheduled to last approximately 10 minutes, for which the participants received £1.10 as payment.

The experiment was conducted online in Qualtrics (https://www.qualtrics.com). It operated with fully informed consent, adheres to the Declaration of Helsinki, and was conducted in compliance with relevant laws and institutional guidelines, including the ones of the University of Konstanz ethics board. All participants confirmed their consent in written form and were informed in detail about the study, the aim, data processing, anonymization, and other background information.

After collecting informed consent and demographic information, we conducted an initial attitude assessment which asked for their general perception of the presented topic on three dimensions and personal relevance. Next, participants read one randomly selected biased news article (either liberal or conservative), randomly supplemented by any combination of the visual aids (forewarning message, annotations, political classification). Thus, the study had a 2x2x2 forewarning message (yes/no) x annotations (yes/no) x political map (yes/no) between design. The article also varied between participants in both article positions (liberal/conservative) and article topics (gun law/abortion) to determine the results' partialness and generalizability. Finally, attitudes towards the topic were reassessed, followed by a seriousness check.

7.3.1.1 Visual Aids

Forewarning Message. The forewarning message consisted of a short warning and was displayed directly before the news article. It reads: "Beware of biased news coverage. Read consciously. Don't be fooled. The term 'media bias' refers to, in part, non-neutral tonality and word choice in the news. Media Bias can consciously and unconsciously result in a narrow and one-sided point of view. How a topic or issue is covered in the news can decisively impact public debates and affect our collective decision making." Besides, an example of one-sided language was shown, and readers were encouraged to consume news consciously.

Annotations. Annotations were directly integrated into the news texts. Biased words or sentences were highlighted [23], and by hovering over the marked sections, a short explanation of the respective type of bias appeared (Fig. 7.4). For example, if moving the cursor over a very one-sided term, the following annotation would be displayed: "Subjective term: Language that is skewed by feeling, opinion or taste." Annotations were based on the ratings of six members of our research group, where phrases had to be nominated by at least three raters[2].

Political Classification. A political classification in the form of a spectrum from left to right indicated the source's political ideology (Fig. 7.5). It was displayed

---

[2] The final annotations can be found in the supplementary preregistration repository accompanying this article at https://osf.io/e95dh/?view_only=d2fb5dc2d64741e393b30b9ee6cc7dc1. We followed the guidelines applied in existing research to teach annotators about bias and reach higher-quality annotations [18]. In future work, we will further increase the number of raters, as we address in the discussion.

7.3 Survey B: Automated Classification Assessment

immediately after the presented article and based on the rating of the webpage AllSides.

7.3.1.2 Selected Articles

We used four biased news articles that varied in topic and political position. Each participant was assigned to one article. The two topics covered were gun law and the debate on abortion, with either a liberal or conservative article position. Topics were selected because we considered them controversial issues in the United States that most people are presumably familiar with. To ensure that articles were biased, they were taken from sources deemed extreme according to the AllSides classification. Conservative texts were taken from Breitbart.com; liberal articles were from Huffpost.com and Washingtonpost.com. We also conducted a manipulation check to determine whether participants perceived political article positions in line with our assumptions: Just after reading the article, participants were asked to classify its political stance on a visual analogue scale (-5 = very liberal to 5 = very conservative). To ensure comparability, articles were shortened to approximately the same length, and respective sources were not indicated. All article texts used are listed together with their annotations in the supplementary preregistration repository accompa.

7.3.1.3 Measures

Media Bias Awareness. Five semantic differentials assessed media bias awareness on fairness, partialness, acceptableness, trustworthiness, and persuasiveness [161, 355] on visual analogue scales ("I think the presented news article was..."). Media bias awareness was established by averaging the five items and recoded to range from -5 = low bias awareness to 5 = high bias awareness ($\alpha = .88$).

Political Orientation. The variable political orientation was measured on a visual analogue scale ranging from -5 = very conservative to 5 = very liberal), introduced with the question "Do you consider yourself to be liberal, conservative, or somewhere in between?" adopted by Spinde and colleagues [10, 15]. Likewise, we assessed the perceived stance of the read article on the same scale introduced with the question "I think the presented news article was...".

Attitudes Towards Article Topic. Attitudes were assessed before and after the article presentation by a three-item semantic differential scale (wrong-right, unacceptable-acceptable, bad-good) evaluating the two topics ("Generally, laws restricting abortion/ the use of guns are..."; α = .99). The three items were averaged per topic to yield a score from (-5 = very conservative attitude to 5 = very liberal attitude). Besides, we assessed topic involvement by one item before the article presentation ("To me personally, laws restricting the use of guns/ abortions are...irrelevant-relevant") on a scale from -5 to 5.

Statistical Analysis. To test the effects of the visual aids on media bias perception, we used ANOVAs with effect-coded factors in a forewarning message (yes/no) x annotations (yes/no) x political map (yes/no) x2 article position (liberal/conservative) x2 article topic (gun law/abortion) between design. For analyses testing political ideology effects, this was generalized to a GLM with standardized political orientation as an additional interacting variable followed by a simple effects analysis. The same model was applied to the second attitude rating, with the first attitude rating and topic involvement as covariates for attitude change.

7.3.2 Results

7.3.2.1 Manipulation Check and Other Effects on Perceived Political Stance of the Article

Overall, the positions of the political articles were perceived as designed (article position: $F(1,953) = 528.67, p < .001, \eta_p^2 = .357$): Articles assigned a liberal position were perceived as more liberal (M = 1.60, SD = 2.70), whereas conservative articles were rated more conservative (M = -1.98, SD = 2.26). This difference between the conservative and the liberal article was more pronounced, when a forewarning message ($F(1,953) = 7.33, p = .007, \eta_p^2 = .008$), annotations ($F(1,953) = 3.96, p = .047, \eta_p^2 = .004$), or the political classifications were present ($F(1,953) = 9.12, p = .003, \eta_p^2 = .009$; see Fig. 7.6). The combination of forewarning and classification further increased the difference ($F(1,953) = 5.28, p = .022, \eta_p^2 = .006$).

7.3 Survey B: Automated Classification Assessment

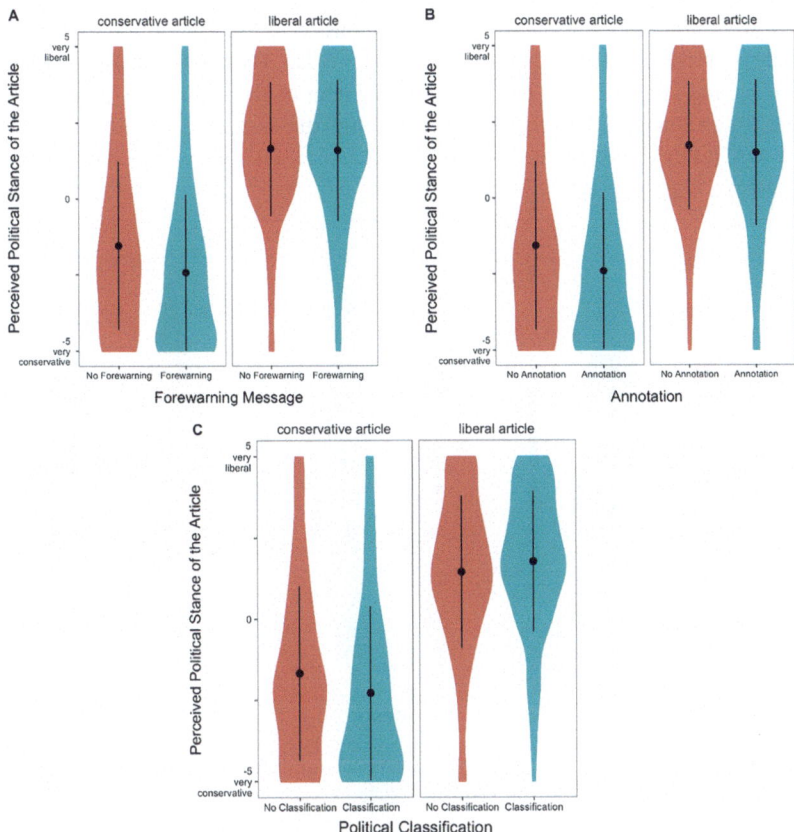

Fig. 7.6 Across all conditions, liberal articles were perceived to be more liberal and conservative articles more conservative. The interventions increased the differences between the two ratings. Dots represent means, and lines are standard deviations

7.3.2.2 Effects of Visual Aids on Media Bias Perceptions

Testing the effects of the visual aids on media bias perceptions in general, we found that both the forewarning message ($F(1,953) = 8.29$, $p = .004$, $\eta_p^2 = .009$) and the annotations ($F(1,953) = 24.00$, $p < .001$, $\eta_p^2 = .025$) increased perceived bias, which we show in Fig. 7.7. However, we found no effect of the political classification ($F(1,953) = 2.56$, $p = .110$, $\eta_p^2 = .003$) and no systematic higher-order interaction involving any of the manipulations ($p \geq .085$, $\eta_p^2 \leq .003$). Moreover, there were differences in media bias perceptions of the specific articles (topic x article position: $F(1,953) = 24.44, p < .001, \eta_p^2 = .025$). The two found main effects were by and large robust when testing it per item of the media bias perception scale (forewarning had no significant effect on partialness and persuasiveness) or in a MANOVA (forewarning: $F(5,949) = 5.22, p < .001, \eta_p^2 = .027$; annotation: $F(5,949) = 6.25, p < .001, \eta_p^2 = .032$).

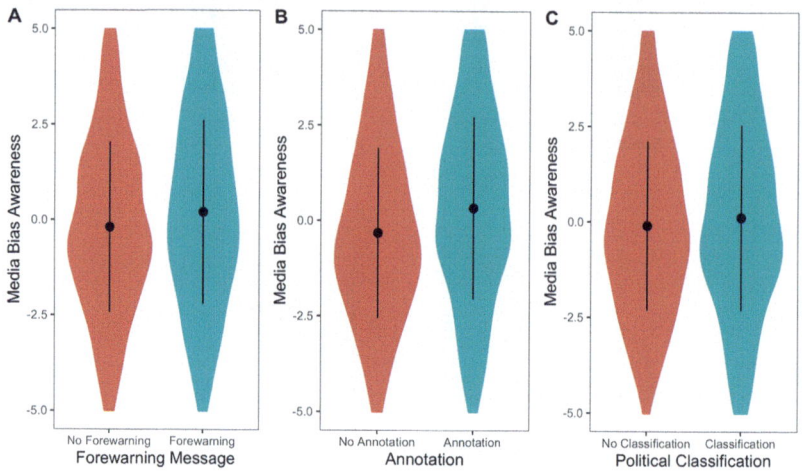

Fig. 7.7 The forewarning message, as well as annotations, increased media bias awareness. Dots represent means, and lines are standard deviations

7.3.2.3 Partisan Media Bias Ratings

When considering self-indicated political orientation and its fit to the article position, we found that media bias was perceived less for articles consistent with the reader's political orientation ($F(1,921) = 113.37, p < .001, \eta_p^2 = .110$): For conservative articles, liberal readers rated conservative articles more biased than conservative readers ($\beta = 0.32; p < .001; 95\%CI[0.25; 0.38]$). Conversely, liberal articles were rated less biased by liberals ($\beta = -0.20; p < .001; 95\%CI[-0.27; -0.13]$), indicating a partisan bias rating for both political isles, which we show in Fig. 7.8.

7.3 Survey B: Automated Classification Assessment

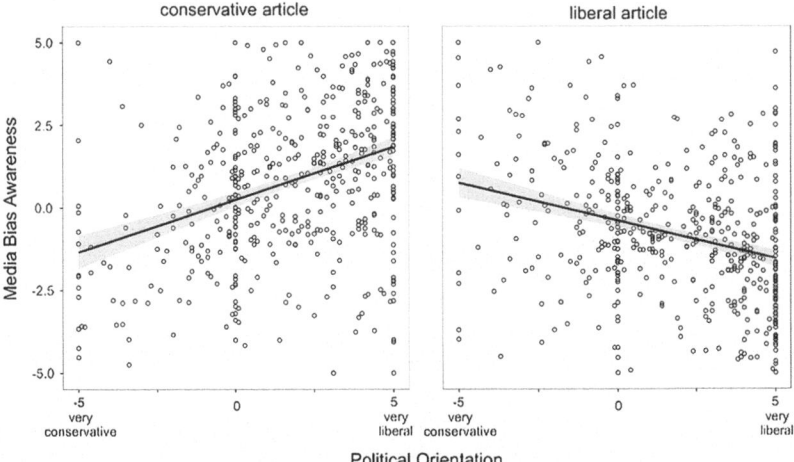

Fig. 7.8 Bias awareness increases when the article is not aligned with the persons' political position. Shades show 95% confidence intervals of the regression estimation

This partisan rating of articles was unaffected by forewarning ($F(1,921) = 1.52$, $p = .218$, $\eta_p^2 = .002$), annotations ($F(1,921) = 0.26$, $p = .612$, $\eta_p^2 < .001$), and political classification ($F(1,921) = 2.72$, $p = .010$, $\eta_p^2 = .003$). Yet, with the increasing liberalness of the reader, the combination of forewarning and annotation was slightly less effective in the detection of bias ($F(1,921) = 4.19$, $p = .041$, $\eta_p^2 = .005$). Furthermore, there were some topic-related differences irrelevant to the current hypotheses (higher bias was perceived for the gun laws articles (topic: $F(1,921) = 11.32, p < .001, \eta_p^2 = .012$) and specifically so for the liberal one (topic x article position: $F(1,921) = 23.86, p < .001, \eta_p^2 = .025$) with some uninterpretable minor higher-order interaction (forewarning x annotation x classification x political orientation x topic: $F(1,921) = 4.10, p = .043, \eta_p^2 = .004$)).

7.3.2.4 Effects on Attitudes

By and large, attitudes on the topics were not affected by the experiment: While attitudes after reading the article were in line with prior attitudes ($F(1,919) = 2415.42$, $p < .001, \eta_p^2 = .724$) and individual political orientation ($F(1,919) = 34.54, p < .001$, $\eta_p^2 = .036$), neither article position ($F(1,919) = 2.63$, $p = .105$, $\eta_p^2 = .003$) nor any of the visual aids had any general impact ($p \geq .084$, $\eta_p^2 \leq .003$). Likewise, neither of the aids interacted with the factor article position ($p \geq .298$, $\eta_p^2 \leq .001$). Solely, there were some additional minor topic-specific significant effects of the annotation combined with the forewarning ($F(1,919) = 4.77$, $p = .0292$, $\eta_p^2 = .005$) and an increased liberalness of attitude with higher topic involvement ($F(1,919) = 4.31$, $p = .038$, $\eta_p^2 = .005$), that we want to disclose, but deem irrelevant to our hypotheses and research questions.

7.3.3 Discussion

In this study, we tested different techniques to communicate media bias. Our experiment revealed that presenting a forewarning message and text annotations enhanced awareness of biased reporting, while a political classification did not. All three methods (forewarning, annotation, political classification) impacted the political ideology rating of the presented article. Furthermore, we found evidence for partisan bias ratings: Participants rated articles that agreed with their general orientation to be less biased than articles from the other side of the political spectrum. The positive effect of the forewarning message on media bias ratings, albeit small, is in line with a few other findings of successful appeals to and reminders of accuracy motives [323]. In addition, it accords with the notion that reflecting on media bias involves some efforts [233, 324], so motivating people to engage in this process can help detect bias. Regarding the effects of in-text annotations, our finding differs from a previous study of a similar design [10], which did not identify the effect due to a lack of power and less optimal annotations. While news consumers may generally identify outright false or fake [322] news, detecting subtle biases can profit from such aids. This indicates that bias detection is far from ideal, particularly in more ambiguous cases. As in-text annotation and forewarning message effects were independent of each other, participants seemingly do not profit from the combination of aids. On the other hand, the political classification could solely improve the detection of the political alignment of the text (which was also achieved by both other methods) but not help detect biased language. Subsequently, the detection of biased language and media bias itself does not appear to be directly related to an article's political affiliation. Our study also replicates findings that the detection of media bias and fake news is affected by individual convictions [389]: We found that participants could detect media bias more readily if there was an incongruence between the participant's and the article's political ideology. Such a connection may be particularly true for detecting more subtle media biases and holding an article in high regard compared to successfully identifying outright fake news, for which a reversed effect could be found in some instances [324]. In addition, interventions were ineffective to lower such partisan effects. Similarly, attitudes remained relatively stable and were

7.3 Survey B: Automated Classification Assessment

not affected by any of the visual aids. Making biased language more visible and reminding people of potential biases could apparently not help them overcome their ideology in rating the acceptance of an article when there is no clear indication that the information presented in the article is fake but solely biased. Likewise, the forewarning message successfully altered the motivation to look for biased language, but did not decrease the effects of political identity on the rating: While being able to detect the political affiliation of an article, it seems that participants were not capable of separating the stance of the article from its biased use of language, even when prompted to do so. In the same vein, effects were not more pronounced when the political classification was further visualized, potentially pointing to the notion that the stance is also detected without help (after all, while the manipulations increased the distinction between liberal and conservative articles, the article's position was reliably identified even without any supporting material) and that partisan ratings are not a deliberate derogatory act. Furthermore, the problem of partisan bias ratings also did not increase with increased media bias awareness via the manipulations, as could have been expected by cognitive dissonance theory. For future work, we will improve the representativeness of the surveyed sample, which limits far-reaching generalizations at this point. Additionally, we will increase the generalizability by employing articles that are politically neutral or exhibit comparatively low bias. Both forewarning and annotations may have increased ratings in this study, but it is unclear whether they also aid in identifying low-bias articles and leading to lower ratings, respectively. Improving the quality of our annotations by including more annotators is an additional step towards exhausting potential findings. We will also investigate how combinations of the visualizations and strategies work together and conduct expert interviews to determine which applications would be of interest in an applied scenario. Still, the current study shows that two of our interventions raised attention to biased language in media, giving a first insight into the yet sparsely tested field of presenting media bias to news consumers. Furthermore, there is a great challenge in translating these experimental interventions to applications used by news consumers in the field. While forewarning messages could be implemented quite simply in the context of other media, for instance, as a disclaimer (see [323]), we hope that automated classifiers on the sentence level will prove to be an effective tool to create instant annotating aids for example as browser add-ons. Even though recent studies show promising accuracy improvements for such classifiers [92, 201], we still want to note that much research needs to be devoted to finding stable and reliable markers of biased language. Future work also has great potential to consider these strategies as teaching tools to train users in identifying bias without visual aids. This could offer a framework for a large-scale study in which additional variables measuring previous news consumption habits could be employed.

7.3.4 Conclusion

In the context of our digitalized world, where news and information of differing quality are available everywhere, our results provide important insights for media bias research. In the present study, we were able to show that forewarning messages and annotations increased media bias awareness among readers in selected news articles. Also, we could replicate the well-known hostile media bias that consists of people being more aware of bias in articles from the opposing side of the political spectrum. However, our experiment revealed that the visualizations could not reduce this effect, but partisan ratings rather seemed unaffected. In sum, digital tools uncovering and visualizing media bias may help mitigate the negative effects of media bias in the future.

7.4 Twitter Comments and News Article Bias

> **Research Objective**
> Analysis of the relation between news article bias and users' reactions to these articles on Twitter.

The dissemination of news does not occur in isolation, but rather the interaction of readers with (biased) news is closely linked to how other users react to a given article. And while past research has recognized the close link between media bias and two key concepts related to news dissemination online—hate speech and sentiment (or valence)—there is, to the best of our knowledge, no prior work that has considered all three concepts simultaneously.

In this study, we address this research gap by examining the characteristics of user reactions (or comments) to news articles via Twitter in terms of sentiment and hate (henceforth called comment characteristics) and putting these in relation to the bias of the respective article. The overall question driving our research is whether there are significant differences between the comment characteristics of articles

7.4 Twitter Comments and News Article Bias

that are more biased compared to those of less biased articles. That is, we examine whether reactions to an article indicate its level of bias.

In addressing our research question, we make three distinct contributions:

- The construction of a first-of-its-kind dataset for the combined study of media bias, sentiment of user reactions, and hate speech.
- Detecting characteristics of reactions to news articles by building two text classifiers, one for hate speech detection and one for sentiment analysis.
- Conducting a multi-level regression analysis of comment characteristics that sheds light on indicators of the articles' biases.

Our work bases on a literature review upon media bias and hate speech, for which we refer to Chap. 2. In subsection 7.4.3, we discuss the methodological approach used, and we present the results of our analysis in subsection 7.4.4. The section concludes by discussing the limitations of this work, and we provide an outlook for future research in this area within subsection 7.4.5. We publish all of our models and code at https://github.com/Media-Bias-Group/TwitterBiasAnalysis, to enhance the transparency and reproducibility of our work.[3]

7.4.1 Research Gap

The majority of the literature on media bias we reviewed focuses on explaining (A) why bias occurs in the news, (B) how to detect bias in a statement, an article, or on reporting level, and (C) why news consumers perceive news as biased at all.

At the same time, prior research has recognized that hate speech and sentiment analysis are two concepts of high informational value for media bias research [25]. To the best of our knowledge, and despite all three concepts being closely connected, there is no study to date that conducts a combined study of all three. In this paper, we aim to address this research gap. Osmundsen et al. [308] show that biased news on Twitter is explicitly shared for partisan polarization. If successful, such polarization should be mirrored in how individuals react to or comment on an article online. Our study's main objective is to examine users' social media comments about articles (henceforth called comment characteristics) regarding their sentiment and level of hate. We aim to put these comment characteristics in relation to the articles' bias.

---

[3] Due to the licensing of Twitter, not all data can be shared. Please contact us for any questions in this regard.

The goal is to establish whether reactions to a news article posted on social media can indicate its bias.

No large-scale standard data for analyzing the impact of media bias, hate speech, or sentiment in news articles on their social media perception currently exists [15]. Our literature review did not yield any results connecting news article bias to news perception on a large scale. We argue that, by now, methods are sufficiently advanced to execute studies analyzing the impact of news article bias on social media reactions. To facilitate this kind of analysis and address our research questions, we provide the first large-scale dataset connecting news article bias and their comments on Twitter, called BAT – **B**ias **A**nd **T**witter.

7.4.2 Research Question and Hypotheses

In addressing our first research question *whether user comments on a news article are an indicator of the article's bias* (RQ1), we start from the premise that: 1) hateful language might be an indicator of bias, and 2) a statement's polarity (positive or negative) might be an indicator for bias. Assuming these assumptions hold true, user comments that contain hate or strong sentiment can be considered biased. To derive our hypotheses, we mainly focus on the two papers mentioned above: [421] observed that new articles with certain linguistic characters attract more hateful comments than those without these characteristics. Similarly, the research of [308] suggests that the level of polarization of a news article should be mirrored in comments to the article. Both papers suggest that article characteristics are a crucial factor and that these characteristics and the comments and article receives online are highly connected. Specifically, more biased coverage in a given article corresponds to more extreme reactions to that article. Building upon these findings, we derive the following hypotheses.

Hypotheses

a The more hateful the comments on an article, the more biased this article is.

b The stronger the comments' polarity for a given article, the more biased this article is.

7.4.3 Methodology

7.4.3.1 Research Design

The first set of data we collected are news articles and article-related data, including information on the bias of an article. We accessed these data from Ad Fontes media,[4] a corporation that rates news articles with respect to their reliability and their political bias. Ad Fontes media's website provides a list of English-speaking articles from various U.S.-based and international outlets that have been manually labeled according to their level of political bias and reliability. The rated articles cover various topics, for example, COVID-19, politics, or lifestyle topics. The political bias score defines how politically influenced an article is, ranging from −42 (most extreme left) to +42 (most extreme right). The reliability score indicates how much truthfulness the article contains. Here, the values range from 0 (least reliable, contains inaccurate/fabricated info) to 64 (most reliable, original fact reporting). The existing literature suggests that labels provided by Ad Fontes media are suitable for media bias-related tasks and are of high quality [92]. However, especially since it relies on manual labels, the Ad Fontes article set does not cover the full range of political and non-political, recent and less recent, or controversial and non-controversial topics. The article selection by Ad Fontes media thus likely introduces bias into the dataset. Ideally, media bias datasets are based on a balanced and comprehensive article selection [6, 18]; we address this point again in subsubsection 7.4.5.3.

The second data source we rely on is user-generated content collected from Twitter. Its up-to-date content covers a large variety of topics [285]. It is therefore considered a valuable data source for all kinds of text processing tasks like sentiment analysis [126, 427] and hate speech detection [373]. Lastly, Twitter is one of the most popular micro-blogging sites [126] with roughly 436 million active users.[5] In a survey of the Reuters Institute, 25% of all Twitter users worldwide stated that they use Twitter to get the latest news [299]. Although 25% might not seem much, compared with other popular Social Media platforms, Twitter is the most popular for news consumption [299]. Following this reasoning, for the purposes of this study Twitter is considered a suitable data source to track reactions to news articles.

After data collection, tweets commenting on a specific article must be processed to ascertain their characteristics. However, media bias is a multifaceted concept comprised of various subtasks, which complicates its direct transferability to social media comments, especially given their brevity. Therefore, we examine comments in terms of two proxy features. First, a transfer learning method is applied to detect

---

[4] https://adfontesmedia.com
[5] https://www.statista.com/statistics/272014/global-social-networks-ranked-by-number-of-users/

the sentiment polarity of the tweets. Transfer learning is particularly useful when handling limited data [17]. The same approach is subsequently used to ascertain whether the comments contain hateful language.

Our motivation for analyzing sentiment and hatefulness specifically is twofold:

1. Both categories are major types of bias, pervasive in social media analyses [293, 346].
2. Both have demonstrated high classification accuracy, especially in the context of social media data [125, 293].

The first point suggests that they provide substantial informational value for detecting media bias. The second point acknowledges that other media bias categories, such as linguistic bias or text-level context bias, present more significant challenges for automatic detection [25]. This is primarily due to the subtle nature of these bias indicators and the necessity for more contextual information.

Regarding both article-level media bias and comment-level hate speech and polarity, appropriate and delineated data are available, making these categories a suitable starting point for investigating a potential link. However, we will revisit and discuss these choices and their implications in the subsection 7.4.5. As using deep neural network models for text classification has become increasingly popular, we propose fine-tuning XLNet, "a generalized autoregressive pretraining method that enables learning bidirectional contexts" [416, p. 1]. XLNet outperforms other established methods, like BERT, in various tasks, including sentiment analysis [416].

After examining the comments with regard to their characteristics, we apply a multi-level statistical model to estimate the relationship between different article features and their outreach and impact on Twitter. The data we collected contains information on the article-level and on the outlet-level, i.e., it has a hierarchical structure with articles nested within news outlets. In such cases, multi-level models are recommended, as they allow examining the influence of individual and cluster-level covariates [131].

The general workflow of this study is presented in Fig. 7.9. First, we start by collecting the required data (1), relying on the two data sources introduced above: Ad Fontes Media (1a) and Twitter (1b). In the second step, we propose two XLNet-based text classifiers to identify the comment characteristics of the article comments (2). Precisely, we fine-tune XLNet for sentiment analysis (2a) and hate speech detection (2b). Lastly, the data is analyzed by applying a multi-level regression model (3). We measure both the effects of the predictors (3a) and the interaction effects (3b).

7.4 Twitter Comments and News Article Bias

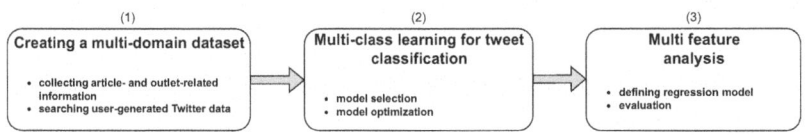

Fig. 7.9 Analysis pipeline used in the study

7.4.3.2 Data Collection

For this study, data on statement-level (i.e., user-comments on articles) and data on article-level (i.e., the bias of the articles) is required. We scrape articles from Ad Fontes Media's website to collect their respective political bias and reliability scores.[6] To obtain the scores for the articles, each article was rated by a group of three Ad Fontes media analysts, randomly drawn from their pool of over 40 analysts. Each group consists of analysts that identify across the political spectrum, i.e., left, center, and right. The analysts rate the articles using defined metrics and multiple sub-factors. The three scores are then averaged, producing the overall article scores.

The selected articles are exclusively in English, and the sources are primarily U.S.-based news agencies. They are selected based on how prominently they are featured on the news outlet's website. Usually, at least 15 articles are rated per outlet. However, for more prominent outlets, there can be more. The list is periodically updated by adding new articles.

We manually exclude those outlets that only received an overall ranking but of which no article has been rated. Given the remaining outlets (henceforth called relevant outlets), the following article-related metrics are scraped: article headline, article URL, political bias score of the article, and reliability score of the article. Some of the articles' headlines had to be manually corrected, as the information embedded on Ad Fontes Media's website is incorrect. In addition, for each outlet, the following outlet-related metrics are scraped: overall bias score, overall reliability score, bias class, reliability class, and the outlet's name.

Once we have collected all data on the article level, the challenging part is identifying user reactions or comments related to the articles in our sample. To access the user comments, we use the Twitter API,[7] but manual preparation is required before the search process can be automated. This includes creating a period for each outlet that defines its outlet-specific publication period. This outlet-specific publication period makes the Twitter scraping process more efficient by setting an

---

[6] https://AdFontesmedia.com/rankings-by-individual-news-source/; accessed on 2021-10-26.

[7] https://developer.twitter.com/en/products/twitter-api

individual start and end date for each outlet, such that only tweets that fall into that period are scraped. The start date is the earliest date an outlet published an article in our sample minus three days. The end date is the latest date an outlet published an article plus seven days.

The user comments are then collected gradually. First, the outlets' tweets referencing one of the rated articles (henceforth called original tweets) are searched and in a second step the comments to these tweets are collected as well as the quoted retweets. Together these constitute our final dataset, which we refer to as BAT—Bias And Twitter. BAT covers 2,800 (bias-rated) news articles from 255 different English-speaking (mainly U.S.) news outlets and 175,807 comments and retweets referring to these articles.

7.4.3.3 Examining Comment Characteristics

To examine the collected tweets with respect to their level of hate and sentiment polarity, we propose a fine-tuned XLNet approach. We access the pre-trained model via the Hugging Face library[8] and work with the base-cased version due to limited computational resources.

For the sentiment training data, we use Sentiment140,[9] the Stanford Twitter Sentiment dataset [163] containing roughly 1.6 million tweets labeled for sentiment polarity (positive, neutral, negative). We consider this dataset a good choice due to its size and the number of researchers who used Sentiment140 for sentiment analysis [51, 163, 427]. The training set of the Sentiment140 accessed via the Hugging Face library contains encoded labels for positive and negative sentiment. To keep the time requirements of the fine-tuning procedure of the XLNet within limits, a smaller subset is created by random sampling 24,000 of the 1.6 million tweets. The class distribution is roughly equal, with 12,017 tweets labeled as negative and 11,983 as positive.

For the hate speech training data, we use the HatebaseTwitter dataset [110], a collection of tweets labeled as hate speech, offensive language, or neither. For the purposes of this study, we do not distinguish between hateful and offensive language. Given the definition of hate speech, the existence of both hateful and offensive language is considered biased. The HatebaseTwitter dataset [110] available via the Hugging Face library,[10] is highly imbalanced, with 19,190 tweets labeled as offensive, 1,430 tweets labeled as hateful, and only 4,163 tweets labeled as non-hate. For this reason, we add another dataset, also available via the Hugging

---

[8] https://huggingface.co/transformers/v2.0.0/pretrained_models.html
[9] http://help.sentiment140.com/for-students
[10] https://huggingface.co/datasets/hate_speech_offensive

7.4 Twitter Comments and News Article Bias

Face library,[11] which contains additional 31,962 tweets, of which 29,720 tweets are labeled as neutral, and 2,242 tweets are labeled as hateful. To create the dataset used for fine-tuning, both hate datasets are combined, and then 24,000 tweets are randomly sampled, of which 9,721 are labeled as hate and 14,279 labeled as non-hate.

Before proceeding, the tweets in both training datasets are preprocessed. This includes removing text passages that contain no cues regarding a statement's sentiment or hatefulness. Once the preparation is completed, the pre-trained base-cased XLNet is fine-tuned once for sentiment analysis using the sentiment training data, and once for hate speech detection using the hate speech training data. For both approaches, the input data is split into three parts: a training set (50%), a test set (25%), and a validation set (25%). The models' hyperparameters defined for each fine-tuning are displayed in Table 7.2.

Table 7.2 Hyperparameters defined for the fine-tuning procedures for both sentiment and hate classification

Parameter	XLNet_Sentiment	XLNet_Hate
batch size	8	8
max length	400	512
optimization function	AdamW	AdamW
learning rate	$3e^{-5}$	$3e^{-5}$
dropout rate	10%	10%
nr. of epochs	2	2

Table 7.3 and Table 7.4 show the classification results for the two models. To better understand the classification results of XLNet_Sentiment, 90% confidence intervals were calculated by repeating the training and evaluation ten times, making use of the high amounts of unused available training data from the Sentiment140 dataset (the confidence intervals can be found in Table 7.3 and the average classification results in the paper's Zenodo repository[12]). Since only little unused data

---

[11] https://huggingface.co/datasets/tweets_hate_speech_detection
[12] https://zenodo.org/record/7141335

for the XLNet_Hate fine-tuning is available 5-fold cross-validation was used to assess the classification results. The 5-fold cross-validation was repeated ten times with randomly re-sampled bins for each iteration resulting in 50 model training and evaluation steps. The classification results were then used to also calculate 90% confidence intervals (the confidence intervals can be found in Table 7.4 and the average classification results in the paper's Zenodo repository). The classification results for the XLNet_Sentiment suggest that the fine-tuned `xlnet-base-cased` provides good performance with an F1-Score of 0.82%. The classification report shows that the model performs slightly better at detecting negative sentiment than positive sentiment. Observing the learning curves for the XLNet_Sentiment shows evidence for model overfitting, hence the respective performance.

In contrast, the overall F1-score of the XLNet_Hate model is 95.5%, which is a surprisingly high performance for hate speech detection. The classifier's unusually high performance on the test dataset can be explained by the particularities of this specific task, i.e., a comparably open definition of what constitutes hate speech and a low threshold of when something was classified as hate speech. To check how well XLNet_Hate generalizes, we tested it on the HateXplain benchmark dataset by [274]. On HateXplain, the classifier performs much less well with an F1-score of 63.8%.

Table 7.3 Results from the classification report obtained by fine-tuning XLNet for sentiment analysis (90% confidence intervals in brackets)

	Precision	Recall	F1-Score	Support
Negative	0.820 (0.807, 0.822)	0.815 (0.824, 0.842)	0.818 (0.818, 0.829)	3023
Positive	0.814 (0.820, 0.835)	0.818 (0.800, 0.817)	0.816 (0.814, 0.822)	2977
Accuracy			0.818 (0.816, 0.825)	6000
Macro Average	0.817 (0.816, 0.825)	0.817 (0.816, 0.825)	0.817 (0.816, 0.825)	6000
Weighted Average	0.817 (0.817, 0.825)	0.817 (0.816, 0.825)	0.817 (0.816, 0.825)	6000

7.4 Twitter Comments and News Article Bias

Table 7.4 Results from the classification report obtained by fine-tuning XLNet for hate speech detection (90% confidence intervals in brackets)

	Precision	Recall	F1-Score	Support
No Hate	0.962 (0.938, 0.961)	0.963 (0.961, 0.964)	0.962 (0.948, 0.962)	3569
Hate	0.946 (0.893, 0.954)	0.944 (0.885, 0.947)	0.945 (0.889, 0.950)	2431
Accuracy			0.955 (0.932, 0.955)	6000
Macro Average	0.954 (0.915, 0.958)	0.953 (0.925, 0.954)	0.953 (0.918, 0.956)	6000
Weighted Average	0.955 (0.920, 0.958)	0.955 (0.932, 0.955)	0.955 (0.924, 0.957)	6000

7.4.3.4 Multi-Level Modeling

Multi-level models are statistical models that enable the examination of hierarchical data structures, to analyze the influence of individual (i.e., Level 1) and cluster-level (i.e., Level 2) covariates [131, 197]. Based on the structure of the data we collected, we deal with two levels where the comment characteristics are level-1 predictors and the outlets' overall scores are level-2 predictors.[13] Level-1 predictors usually have variance on both levels [131, 197], and level-2 predictors typically have only variance on the upper-level [131, 197]. Multi-level models offer the possibility to investigate interaction effects, i.e., the moderating effect of the level-2 predictor on the relationship between level-1 predictors and Y. The basic model set up for such a scenario is as follows:

$$\begin{aligned} Y_{ij} = & \gamma_{00} + \gamma_{01} Z_{1j} + \gamma_{02} Z_{2j} \\ & + \gamma_{10} X_{1ij} + \gamma_{11} Z_{1j} X_{1ij} + \gamma_{12} Z_{2j} X_{1ij} \\ & + \gamma_{20} X_{2ij} + \gamma_{21} Z_{1j} Z_{2ij} + \gamma_{22} Z_{2j} X_{2ij} \\ & + u_{0j} + u_{1j} X_{1ij} + u_{2j} X_{2ij} + e_{ij} \end{aligned} \quad (7.1)$$

The two terms $\gamma_{01} Z_{1j}$ and $\gamma_{02} Z_{2j}$ in the first line describe the effects of the level-2 predictors Z_{1j} and Z_{2j} respectively on the outcome Y. The second and third lines of the Equation represent the effects of the level-1 predictors X_{1ij} and X_{2ij} on the

---

[13] The variance on level 1 is referred to as within-group variance, the variance on level 2 as between-group variance respectively [131].

outcome Y. Note, that these effects are potentially moderated by the level-2 predictors. This means, the regression coefficients γ_{11}, γ_{12}, γ_{21}, and γ_{22} express the interaction effects. Lastly, the fourth line of the Equation combines all residual errors at the class level.

We want to obtain "pure" effects of our level-1 and level-2 predictors on Y, without the effects of the level-1 predictors being influenced by the level-2 predictors. Centering of our parameters achieves this and provides better interpretability of the coefficients ([131]). We applied both main centering mechanisms typically used, grand mean centering and grouped mean centering (see subsubsection 7.4.4.3). When centering around the grand mean (henceforth denoted by the subscript CGM), the overall mean gets subtracted from each value of the variable [131]. In contrast, when centering around the group mean (henceforth denoted by the subscript CWC), for each value of the variable its respective group mean is subtracted [131].

Keeping in mind the two research questions stated in subsection 7.4.1 and subsection 7.4.2, we focus on two effects of interest: 1) the effect of comment characteristics on the article's bias, and 2) the influence of the outlet's characteristics on the article's bias. We observe the effects of level-1 variables (i.e., hatefulness and sentiment polarity of the comments) on Y as well as the effects of level-2 variables (i.e., the outlet's overall bias and overall reliability) on Y. We can ideally estimate the effects of both the level-1 and level-2 predictors to provide meaningful interpretations. Specifically, we center our level-1 and level-2 predictors as follows: 1) We group mean center the two level-1 predictors hate score and sentiment polarity; 2) We grand mean center the two level-2 predictors overall bias and overall reliability; and 3) We additionally grand mean center the two level-1 group means for hate score and sentiment polarity.

Hence, the final multi-level regression model reads as follows. For simplicity reasons, interaction effects are not included here, as these are only relevant in case a significant relationship between level-1 predictors and Y can be observed[14] [131]:

$$Y_{ij} = \gamma_{00} + \gamma_{01}Z_{1jCGM} + \gamma_{02}Z_{2jCGM} + \gamma_{03}Z_{3jCGM} + \gamma_{04}Z_{4jCGM}$$
$$+ \gamma_{10}X_{1ijCWC} + \gamma_{20}X_{2ijCWC} \qquad (7.2)$$
$$+ u_{0j} + u_{1j}X_{1ij} + u_{2j}X_{2ij} + e_{ij}$$

---

[14] See subsection 7.4.4.

7.4 Twitter Comments and News Article Bias

The regression coefficients of Equation 7.2 can be interpreted as follows:

- γ_{00}: The mean intercept.
- γ_{01} & γ_{02}: Predict the effects of the level-2 predictors Z_1 (γ_{01}) and Z_2 (γ_{02}) on the outcome variable. For example, if γ_{01} is positive, the outcome variable is higher when the value for Z_1 is higher.
- γ_{10} & γ_{20}: Predict the effects of the level-1 predictors X_1 (γ_{10}) and X_2 (γ_{20}) on the outcome variable. For example, if γ_{10} is positive, the outcome variable is higher when the value for X_1 is larger. Hence, these two regression coefficients indicate the within-group variance.
- γ_{03} & γ_{04}: Predict the variance of the two level-1 predictors hate score and sentiment polarity on level-2. Hence, these two regression coefficients indicate the between-group variance.

7.4.4 Results

7.4.4.1 The BAT Dataset

Ad Fontes media in total provides outlet-related information about 321 news outlets. As the focus lies on the article-related metrics in the first place, only those outlets have been considered where at least one article has been rated. Hence, the data collection process as described in subsubsection 7.4.3.2 results in the BAT dataset containing a total of 2,800 rated news articles from 255 different news outlets.

The majority of articles have low bias scores, with most articles being centered around a political bias score of 0 (i.e., not politically biased). However, there are slightly more left-skewed articles than right-skewed articles (see Fig. 7.10a. Overall, the articles are predominantly rated as reliable, with only a few articles having low-reliability scores (see Fig. 7.10b). A similar pattern is observed for the political bias and reliability scores of the outlets (see Fig. 7.11a and Fig. 7.11b). The majority of rated outlets are left-biased with fewer right-skewed outlets. Overall, the outlets are mostly considered to be reliable.

Figure 7.12a indicates a relationship between the level of bias of an article and its level of reliability. From the plot, it appears that more biased articles are also less reliable. Figure 7.12b shows the same relationship on the outlet-level. Both plots highlight a similar pattern, which shows that the outlet's level of bias increases its articles' bias.

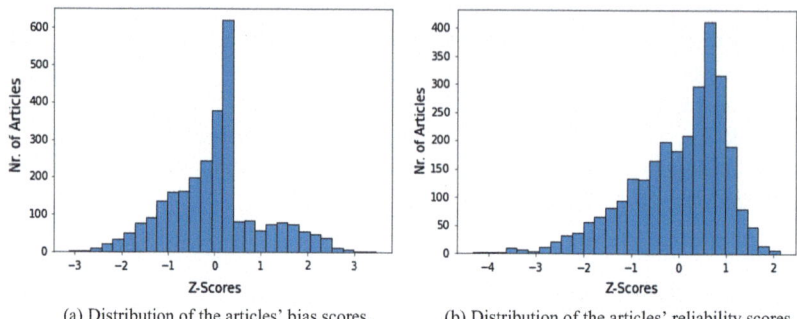

(a) Distribution of the articles' bias scores.   (b) Distribution of the articles' reliability scores.

Fig. 7.10 The distribution of the articles' political bias scores (Fig. 7.10a) and reliability scores (Fig. 7.10b). The data was z-normalized, and the optimal number of bins (here: 28) was estimated by Rice's Rule

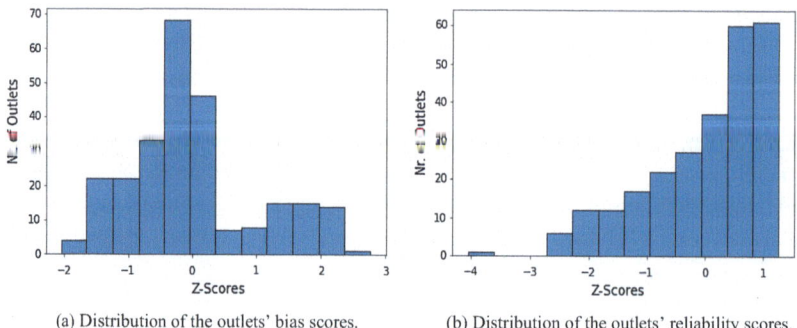

(a) Distribution of the outlets' bias scores.   (b) Distribution of the outlets' reliability scores.

Fig. 7.11 The distribution of the articles' political bias scores (Fig. 7.11a) and reliability scores (Fig. 7.11b). The data was z-normalized, and the optimal number of bins (here: 28) was estimated by Rice's Rule

7.4 Twitter Comments and News Article Bias

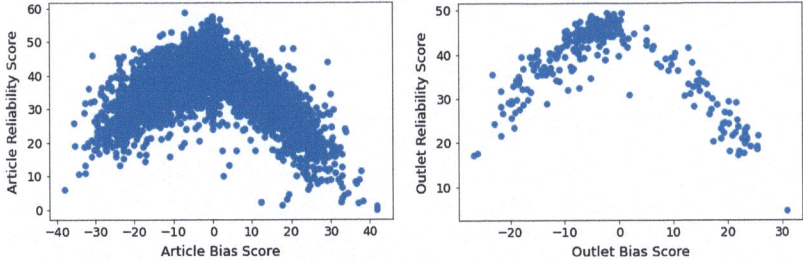

(a) Pattern between the political bias of the articles and their reliability. It is observable that more biased articles tend to have lower reliability scores.

(b) Pattern between the political bias of outlets and their reliability. It is observable, that more biased outlets tend to have lower reliability scores.

Fig. 7.12 Political bias vs. reliability for (a) articles and (b) outlets

Based on the articles collected from Ad Fontes media, we found a total of 7,059 original tweets. However, some of these tweets link to the same article. This is the case, for example, when the outlet posts a tweet referencing a news story multiple times. In total, from the 6,345 articles collected from Ad Fontes media, only 3,473 articles from 268 outlets remain; for 15 outlets, no original tweets have been found, or no tweets have been posted at all. The reasons for that are either that no tweets have been posted within the dedicated time period, no tweets referencing the respective articles have been posted, or the matching process was unsuccessful. A detailed overview of included and excluded outlets is provided in the paper's Zenodo repository.[15]

In the next step, we collected all comments and quoted retweets on these 7,059 original tweets. As explained in subsection 7.4.3.2, we considered comments that are directly posted below the original tweet, as well as the quoted retweets. Our final dataset contains a total number of 175,807 comments and quoted retweets. Henceforth, all direct comments and quoted retweets are referred to as comments, as the distinction between direct comments and quoted retweets is no longer necessary. These 175,807 collected comments refer to 2,800 articles from 255 news outlets. We excluded an additional 13 outlets since no comments on the original tweets were posted.

After matching with Twitter comments, we overall had to exclude roughly two-thirds of the data accessible on the Ad Fontes media website. The reasons for that are that either no original tweets have been found or the original tweet has not been

---

[15] https://zenodo.org/record/7141335

commented on. The plots below show the distribution of bias and reliability scores for all articles and outlets included in the final dataset. Overall, the amount of left- and right-biased articles, shown in Fig. 7.13a, in the final dataset is roughly similar compared to the full Ad Fontes media data. The same applies to the reliability levels of the articles, shown in Fig. 7.13b, although some of the articles with medium to high reliability have been removed. In contrast, the distribution plot for the bias scores among all outlets, displayed in Fig. 7.14a, as well as the plot for the distribution of reliability scores, shown in Fig. 7.14b, have not changed significantly. Hence, we can conclude that removing the respective articles and outlets after matching them with Twitter comments did not change the underlying structure of BAT.

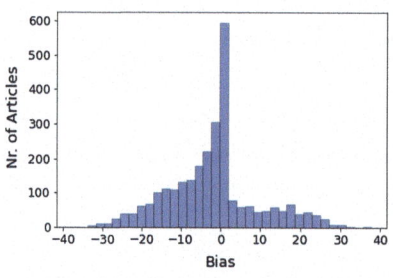

(a) Distribution of the articles' bias scores over the dataset, where the bias ranges from -42 (hyperpartisan left) to +42 (hyperpartisan right).

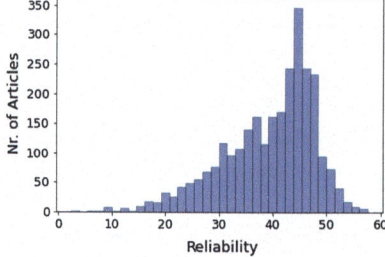

(b) Distribution of the articles' reliability scores over the dataset, where the score ranges from 0 (most unreliable) to +64 (most reliable).

Fig. 7.13 The distribution of the articles' (a) political bias scores and (b) reliability scores

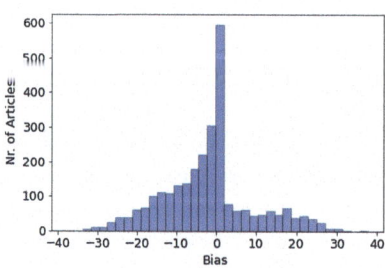

(a) Distribution of the outlets' bias scores over the dataset, where the bias ranges from -42 (hyperpartisan left) to +42 (hyperpartisan right).

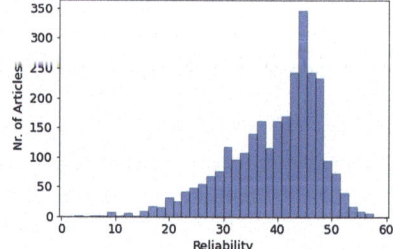

(b) Distribution of the outlets' reliability scores over the dataset, where the score ranges from 0 (most unreliable) to +64 (most reliable).

Fig. 7.14 The distribution of the outlets' (a) political bias scores and (b) reliability scores

7.4.4.2 Examining Comment Characteristics: Classification Results

XLNet for Sentiment Analysis Using the fine-tuned XLNet_Sentiment for text classification, we classify tweets according to their sentiment polarity. The classifier returns two scores, one for positive sentiment and one for negative sentiment. Both scores range between 0 and 1, where the positive sentiment score indicates the likelihood of the tweet being positive, and the negative sentiment score indicates the likelihood of the tweet being negative. An example is provided in Table C.7 (Table 7.5).

Table 7.5 Examples of how the fine-tuned XLNet_Sentiment classifies text into positive or negative sentiment. As described in subsubsection 7.4.3.3, the tweet text has been cleaned for a better text understanding

Tweet Text	Positive Score	Negative Score	Label
Cool Never going back to work masked forever	0.163	0.837	negative
Excellent choice as is I feel so lucky as a Californian to have such amazing representation	0.994	0.006	positive

Of all 175,807 tweets in the dataset, 59.53% have been classified to have overall negative sentiment and 40.47% of the tweets as positive. The distribution of the sentiment scores is quite distinct with sentiment values being either close to 0 or close to 1. Given the sentiment scores, we added a third sentiment-related attribute to BAT, which captures the strength of the polarity independent of its direction. Since the sentiment scores lie between 0 and 1, with both ends of the range indicating negative and positive sentiment, respectively, the actual polarity strength is not adequately captured by those scores. For example, considering a negative sentiment score of 0.95 simultaneously means that the positive sentiment score is 0.05. Hence, the statement is classified as negative because the negative sentiment score exceeds the positive score. However, that score does not indicate how strong the sentiment is, i.e., how much it deviates from a neutral value. The value for neutral sentiment is 0.5, as it is the exact middle value between the two extremes. Therefore, to obtain the polarity strength, we consider the absolute differences for each sentiment score to 0.5. Because of the scores' mutuality, it does not make a difference which scores we use for this calculation, the absolute distances to 0.5 are the same for both positive and negative scores. Lastly, to keep this attribute on a comparable scale with the other comment characteristics, the polarity strengths are transformed onto a scale ranging from 0 to 1, using min-max normalization. **XLNet for Hate Speech Detection** The XLNet_Hate classifies tweets as either hateful or not. Similar to the sentiment classifier, this classifier also returns two scores, one indicating the likelihood that the text is hateful and the other that it is not. Again, both scores range between 0 (non-hate) and 1 (hate) and add up to 1. Examples of the hate speech classification results are provided in Table C.8 (Table 7.6).

Table 7.6 Examples of how the fine-tuned XLNet_Hate classifies text into hate or non-hate. As described in subsubsection 7.4.3.3, the tweet text has been cleaned for a better text understanding

Tweet Text	Positive Score	Negative Score	Label
Because she is a better person than I am	0.016	0.984	non-hate
let's see if he listens or does the same pigheaded shit he did with USDA	0.985	0.015	hate

Of all 175,807 tweets in BAT, only 15.7% have been classified as hate, whereas the vast majority of 84.3% tweets have been classified as non-hate.

To summarize, BAT consists of a total number of 175,807 tweets reacting (or commenting) on 2,800 articles. Overall, 255 news outlets have been included in the dataset. In total, BAT contains 21 attributes that can be divided into three types: 1) comment characteristics, 2) article-related metrics, and 3) outlet-related metrics. The comment characteristics refer to all the attributes that determine the tweets' characteristics: the positive and negative hate scores (*pos_score_hate*, *neg_score_hate*), the hate value (*hate_value*), the positive and negative sentiment scores (*pos_score_sentiment*, *neg_score_sentiment*), the sentiment value (*sentiment*), and the polarity strength (*polarity_strength*). Second, article-related metrics refer to all information on article-level that have been collected from Ad Fontes media. Those attributes are the political bias score (*bias_score*) and the reliability score (*reliability_score*). Lastly, outlet-related metrics have also been collected from Ad Fontes media. They are the outlet's overall political bias score (*overall_bias*) and respective political bias class (*bias_class*), and the outlet's overall reliability score (*overall_reliability*) and its reliability class (*reliability_class*). We provide a detailed description of all attributes of the dataset in the paper's Zenodo repository.[16]

---

[16] https://zenodo.org/record/7141335

7.4 Twitter Comments and News Article Bias

Human Assessment of BAT Since the article- and outlet-related metrics are based on human annotations, the confidence in labels is high. However, especially with hate speech where classifications can be ambiguous, the automatically generated labels require a certain degree of human control. To verify the classifications of XLNet_Hate, 100 tweets were therefore randomly sampled and manually annotated. The manual annotations were then compared to XLNet_Hate's predictions. Excluding a small fraction of tweets that could not be labeled because they did not contain any text, the agreement rate lies at 78%. A confusion matrix showing the annotation differences can be found in Table 7.7. This overall increases our confidence in the comment characteristics.

Table 7.7 Confusion Matrix showing the differences between manually annotated and XLNet_Hate's labels

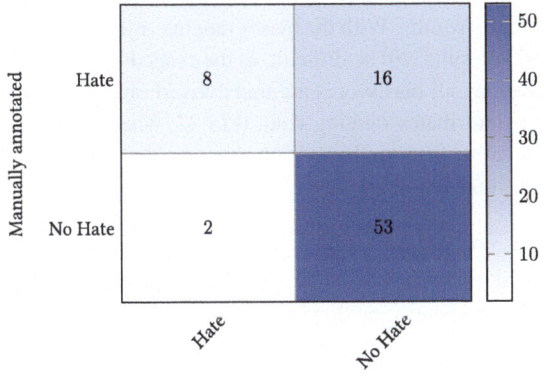

Annotated by XLNet_Hate

7.4.4.3 Multi-level Regression Analysis

The following multi-level regression is conducted only with a subset of the available attributes, which are considered to be most meaningful. Specifically, we exclude several attributes that do not add explanatory value. Recall that both classifiers each returned two scores, a positive and negative sentiment score and a positive and negative hate score respectively. As described in subsection 7.4.4.2, we used the two sentiment scores to construct a third sentiment attribute ("polarity_strength"). Consequently, the two sentiment scores are excluded from the set of attributes as they would not add any additional explanatory value to the multi-level-regression.

For the hate scores, we decided to include only the positive hate score, following the same reasoning as for the sentiment scores.

This results in an attribute set consisting of two level-1 predictors, two level-2 predictors, and two outcome variables. The predictors on level 1 are hate score and polarity strength. The positive hate score is interpreted such that the higher the score, the more hateful the comment. For polarity strength a higher score indicates greater comment polarity. Note that whether polarity is positive or negative, is not captured by this score as we are only concerned with how extreme a comment is. The predictors on level 2 are the outlet's overall political bias and overall reliability. The two outcome variables are also on level 1 and refer to the article's bias score and the article's reliability score. As both outcome variables are of interest, the regression analysis is conducted once for bias score as the dependent variable and once for the reliability score as the dependent variable.

Before we execute the multi-level regression model, the two bias scores need to be prepared to obtain meaningful results. With the biases ranging from -42 to $+42$, the interpretation of regression results will be difficult, as the exact direction cannot be uniquely identified. Therefore, all bias scores are transformed onto the positive scale, which leads to the two attributes ranging from 0 to 42, where 0 indicates no bias and 42 indicates the most extreme bias. With this operationalization, the direction of the effects can be unambiguously interpreted.

Effects of Level-1 and Level-2 Predictors We specified the multi-level regression used to estimate the effects of the predictors in Equation 7.2. The model consists of two level-1 predictors and two level-2 predictors. To obtain meaningful results with interpretable regression coefficients, the predictors are centered accordingly. Table 7.8 provides an overview of the model parameters, the regression coefficients, the corresponding predictors of the model, and which centering method has been applied.

Table 7.8 Description of the parameters in Equation 7.2

Parameter	Regression Coefficient	Variable	Centering Method
$X_{1_{CWC}}$	γ_{10}	hate_cwc	CWC
$X_{2_{CWC}}$	γ_{20}	polarity_cwc	CWC
$Z_{1_{CGM}}$	γ_{01}	overall_bias_cgm	CGM
$Z_{2_{CGM}}$	γ_{02}	overall_reliability_cgm	CGM
$Z_{3_{CGM}}$	γ_{03}	gmean_hate_cgm	CGM
$Z_{4_{CGM}}$	γ_{04}	gmean_polarity_cgm	CGM

7.4 Twitter Comments and News Article Bias

As stated above, the multi-level regression is conducted once for the articles' bias scores as the outcome variable and once for the article's reliability score, respectively. Table 7.9 shows the parameter estimates for the two models, where (1) refers to the model setup with the bias score as the dependent variable, and (2) refers to the model setup with the reliability score as the dependent variable.

Table 7.9 Results for Level-1 and Level-2 Effects

	Dependent variable:	
	bias_score_abs	reliability_score
	(1)	(2)
hate_cwc	4.065***(0.792)	−2.099***(0.702)
polarity_cwc	0.756(1.009)	−1.528(1.036)
overall_bias_cgm	0.793***(0.046)	−0.099**(0.050)
overall_reliability_cgm	−0.057(0.039)	0.638***(0.043)
gmean_hate_cgm	0.977(2.182)	−2.953(2.400)
gmean_polarity_cgm	−0.711(2.694)	2.087(3.036)
Constant	8.469***(0.136)	39.252***(0.144)
Observations	2,800	2,800
Log Likelihood	−8,602.005	−9,014.642
Akaike Inf. Crit.	17,232.010	18,047.280
Bayesian Inf. Crit.	17,315.130	18,100.720

Note: $^*p < 0.1$; $^{**}p < 0.05$; $^{***}p < 0.01$

Comment Characteristics and Article Bias

The parameter estimates of the first model provide valuable insights into the relationship between comment characteristics and article bias. Starting with the level-1 predictors, the only significant relationship is the one between the level of hate in the comments and the article bias. However, this effect refers to the within-group variance. Hence, it can be interpreted as the relationship between the comments' hatefulness and the article's bias. The relationship is positive, and the regression coefficient is 4.065, which means that if the comments' hatefulness increases by 1 score point, the bias of the article increases by 4.065 score points. The association between comments' polarity strength and bias of the article is 0.756. However, the estimate is not significant. In contrast, the between-group variance predicts how a group's average value affects the average outcome value. These effects are estimated by including the two grand mean-centered group means of hate score and polarity strength. The regression coefficients estimating the between-group variance are not significant.

For the level-2 predictors, the relationship between the outlet's overall bias and the outcome is positive and significant, meaning that the bias score of articles is higher when the outlet is generally considered to be more biased. There is no significant relationship between the outlet's overall reliability and the outcome. In addition, it has been assumed that the slopes for the two level-1 predictors vary across outlets. However, only the variance of the hate score is significant. The variance of the polarity strength is not. This means, for polarity strength, the hypothesis that the slope is varying across outlets can be rejected [197]. Hence, we can assume that polarity strength is not varying across outlets.

Comment Characteristics and Article Reliability

The parameter estimates obtained from the second multi-level regression (2) provide similar results as the first regression. As for the level-1 predictors, again, the only significant relationship is observed between the level of hate in the comments and the article's reliability. The value for the regression coefficient is -2.099 and significant at $p < 0.01$, illustrating the relationship between the comments' hate score and the article's reliability on level 1. This is interpreted as increasing of the comments' hate score by 1 score point, decreases the article's reliability by 2.099 score points. Similar to the results described above, there does not appear to be a significant direct relationship between comments' polarity strength and the article's reliability, as well as no significant between-group variances.

For the level-2 predictors, however, both have a significant relationship with the outcome. For the overall bias, the regression coefficient is -0.099 and significant at $p < 0.05$. This result indicates that the article's reliability decreases with an increase in the outlet's overall bias score. For the overall reliability, the regression coefficient is 0.638 and is significant at $p < 0.01$. This is interpreted as an article's reliability score increasing if the outlet's overall reliability score increases. In addition, for this model, the variances of the two level-1 predictors are both not significant, allowing the conclusion that the slopes for hate score and polarity strength do not vary across outlets [197]. This means that both level-1 predictors can be assumed to not vary across outlets.

In sum, these two analyses provide evidence that the hate score of the comments is positively correlated with an article's bias. This is true for both outcomes, article bias, and article reliability. In contrast, no significant relationship can be observed for the polarity strength. Lastly, the results show significant effects of the outlet's overall bias and the outlet's overall reliability on the article's bias. For the regression on the article's bias score, our analysis points to the article's bias score being higher

7.4 Twitter Comments and News Article Bias

for outlets rated as more biased. For the regression on the article's reliability score, the parameter estimates indicate that the article's reliability is less for more biased outlets but higher for more reliable outlets.

Interaction Effects of Level-2 Predictors

We emphasized in subsection 7.4.3.4 that in the case of significant relationships between level-1 predictors and the outcome variable, interaction effects can be interpreted. To get estimates for the interaction effects, only the four regression coefficients γ_{11}, γ_{12}, γ_{21}, and γ_{22} are required, which is why we discarded the grand mean centered group means here.

For all of our regressions, we only observed significant relationships between the hate score and the article's bias and the hate score and the article's reliability. Hence, we define our final interaction model as shown in Equation 7.3. The parameters have the same meaning as stated in Table 7.8.

$$Y_{ij} = \gamma_{00} + \gamma_{01} Z_{1jCGM} + \gamma_{02} Z_{2jCGM}$$
$$+ \gamma_{10} X_{1ijCWC} + \gamma_{11} Z_{1jCGM} X_{1ijCWC} + \gamma_{12} Z_{2jCGM} X_{1ijCWC} \quad (7.3)$$
$$+ u_{0j} + u_{1j} X_{1ij} + u_{2j} X_{2ij} + e_{ij}$$

Table 7.10 presents the parameter estimates for the interaction effects between hate score and overall bias as well as hate score and overall reliability. The analysis was again performed twice: once for the bias score as the dependent variable (3) and once for the reliability score as the dependent variable (4).

The Moderating Effect on Hate-Bias Relationship

The parameter estimates for the first regression (3) suggest that both interaction effects are significant. The first regression coefficient for the interaction effect between overall bias and hate score is 0.703 and significant at $p < 0.01$. This means that the effect of hateful comments on the article's bias is more prominent for more biased outlets.

The regression coefficient for the interaction effect between overall reliability and hate score is 0.435 and is significant at $p < 0.05$. This can be interpreted as the effect of hateful comments on the article's bias being larger for outlets that are considered to be more reliable.

Table 7.10 Results for Interaction Effects

	Dependent variable:	
	bias_score_abs	reliability_score
	(3)	(4)
hate_cwc	3.786***(0.762)	−2.022***(0.709)
polarity_cwc	0.684(1.008)	−1.498(1.037)
overall_bias_cgm	0.775***(0.046)	−0.112**(0.049)
overall_reliability_cgm	−0.070*(0.040)	0.634***(0.042)
hate_cwc:overall_bias_cgm	0.703***(0.252)	−0.296(0.235)
hate_cwc:overall_reliability_cgm	0.435**(0.217)	−0.226(0.202)
Constant	8.461***(0.136)	39.257***(0.145)
Observations	2,800	2,800
Log Likelihood	−8,597.700	−9,014.854
Akaike Inf. Crit.	17,223.400	18,047.710
Bayesian Inf. Crit.	17,306.520	18,101.140

Note: $^*p < 0.1$; $^{**}p < 0.05$; $^{***}p < 0.01$

The Moderating Effect on Hate-Reliability Relationship

The parameter estimates for the second regression (4) provide no evidence for the existence of interaction effects. The two regression coefficients for the interaction effect between overall bias and hate score and overall reliability and hate score are both not significant. **Implications of the Regression Results** In conclusion, the two multi-level regression models (1) and (2) provide support for H1. Both models yield parameter estimates that indicate a significant relationship between the hatefulness of comments and the article's bias. In contrast, no evidence has been found that confirms H2, indicating that the polarity strength does not seem to correlate with an article's bias. Lastly, both regression models (1) and (2) show a positive relationship between the outlet's overall bias and the article's bias.

In addition, model (3) provides evidence for the existence of interaction effects, suggesting that the effect of hateful comments on the article's bias is even worse when the outlet is more biased. These findings underpin the above-described results of the direct effects. Hence, providing additional support for H1 respectively.

With regard to the two expectations formulated in subsection 7.4.2, we can therefore conclude that, first, comment characteristics can indeed be an indicator of an article's bias. However, this has only been observed for the hate score of the comments. The polarity strength seems to have no effect on the article's bias. Second, we find evidence that the outlet's bias also influences how biased the articles are.

7.4 Twitter Comments and News Article Bias

Hence, the outlets' stance is an additional important factor, next to the comment characteristics.

7.4.5 Discussion & Future Work

7.4.5.1 Implications

This study has both theoretical and practical implications. The results of our regression models provide support for the hypothesis that the more hateful the comments or reactions to an article, the more biased this article is (H1). This also means that future research can utilize the hatefulness of comments as a proxy for an article's bias. We do not find support for the hypothesis that the polarity of comments related to great article bias (H2). Even though only one of our two hypotheses is supported, we can still overall conclude that the characteristics of the comments and an article's bias are connected. This is in line with existing research that provides evidence that the article's characteristics and the comments are article receives are highly connected [308, 421]. It is worth emphasizing that this connection is potentially of grave societal concern as it implies that biased articles not only misinform the reader but foster more hateful behavior on the internet. Our study thus not only just offers researchers a tool to measure bias but also points to the importance of striving for stronger media bias awareness. Finally, BAT offers researchers an accessible resource to further empirically investigate the article-comment relationship.

7.4.5.2 Limitations

One of the key limitations of our approach has already been pointed out in subsubsection 7.4.3.3. The learning curves of the fine-tuning of the XLNet for sentiment analysis indicate that the model suffers from overfitting. Our qualitative evaluation[17] confirms that the results are sufficiently precise to permit our analysis, yet the classifier performance should be improved in future work. Several solutions exist for how overfitting can be prevented. The most straightforward solution is to find the appropriate number of training epochs. If the model is trained too long, it remembers the structure of the training data too well and hence results in overfitting [418]. However, here the model suffers from overfitting already after the second epoch. Therefore, a more suitable solution is to increase the quality and the size of the training data, as the model's performance can be significantly affected by the quantity and quality of the training dataset used [418]. Ideally, the model is fine-tuned on large amounts of high-quality training data, potentially even applying

---

[17] Based on a manual re-evaluation of 100 classifications on new and out-of-training sample texts.

regularization techniques like experimenting with the dropout rate [418]. We did not pursue this approach further for this study given limited computational resources, time constraints, and the fact that the performance achieved was already sufficient to answer our research questions.

In general, the classification of Twitter data regarding hate speech and sentiment polarity is difficult. This stems from the nature of Twitter as a microblogging service. In general, tweets are short messages with a maximum of only 280 characters. Therefore, users in English tweets often tend to use abbreviations, smileys, and other Twitter-specific language to express their opinions [427]. In addition, language models generally have difficulties understanding subtle nuances in language, like negations, sarcasm, or slang. In addition, labels of the dataset used for training do not necessarily represent a true gold standard. One problem with manually annotated data is that it is prone to contain racial bias or other kinds of biases introduced by the annotator [361]. When training a classifier with biased data, the algorithm will adopt this bias, and hence, the classifier then also tends to return biased classification results [292].

Therefore, to obtain a high-quality, fine-tuned language model for the respective task, a collection of the most common language models should have been considered. By doing so, a baseline performance could be established against which the performance of other models can then be evaluated, for example, following the approach of Spinde et al. [18]. We also note that in addition to the XLNet, other established language models could have been applied. The current state-of-the-art models for text classification include BERT, RoBERTa, DistilBERT, XLM, or T5 [63]. In addition, different approaches can be tested against each other, for example, pursuing the approach presented by Rodríguez, Argueta, and Chen [345], who applied sentiment and emotion analysis to detect hateful language. Arguably hate speech detection and sentiment analysis are two-class classification problems, but approaches exist where the classification task is considered a multi-class problem. For hate speech detection, some datasets contain three or four labels, specifying the tweets, for example, into hateful language, offensive language, or neither [110, 401, 402]. The same applies to sentiment datasets, where the vast majority of datasets contain at least the three labels positive, negative, and neutral [163, 210].

In general, more Twitter data can be collected by recursively collecting comments and quoted retweets. In this paper, only the comments and quoted retweets on level 1 have been collected. This means only the comments that have been posted directly on the original tweet as well as the quoted retweets of that original tweet. One could, for example, recursively collect all comments to the quoted retweets as well as quoted retweets of those retweets.

7.4.5.3 Future Work

There are, aside from the limitations discussed above, some avenues for future work that go beyond the scope of the current study.

One next logical step could be to include further indicators for an article's bias. Given the hierarchical structure of our data, we could add additional information. For example, a third level can be introduced to the multi-level regression model by conducting topic modeling. The data would then contain articles nested into outlets, which would be nested into topics. One factor contributing to cognitive bias is the level of involvement. For example, [135] state that the more an individual is involved with a topic, the more likely it is that news is perceived as biased. Therefore, one logical assumption is that articles on generally more polarizing topics receive more and more valenced comments. Additionally, future work should consider other comment features besides sentiment analysis and hate speech. Additional features might be able to further increase the media bias prediction results. Potential categories could be linguistic bias or political bias.

In general, considering additional information sources could reveal valuable insights for future studies. For instance, methodologies exist where researchers assess the bias of an article by classifying its headline [336]. This approach could be extended by investigating whether the headline of an article influences the degree of pronounced characteristics in the comments. One potential research direction is to analyze whether sensationalist headlines attract more emotionally charged comments. Moreover, the dataset of articles from Ad Fontes is limited. As discussed in subsection 7.4.3, ideal media bias datasets should consider a comprehensive selection of articles covering various topics with distinct characteristics, such as political relevance, topicality, and controversy [15]. Thus, future work should focus on constructing a larger and more comprehensive dataset of rated articles. Ratings for such articles could be provided by experts or through crowdsourcing to improve scalability [23].

In our work, we concentrate on the relationship between hate speech and polarity in the comments and media bias in the news article. We chose these as easily identifiable concepts with a clear data basis. Further analysis of all concepts (see [25]) would require that all concepts are recognized in the data, which is out of the scope of this work.

Lastly, considering the fact that Twitter is an enormously large database that collects all kinds of user-generated data, conducting a user-group analysis might provide additional valuable insights. Adapting ideas of already existing user group analysis approaches [206, 331], one could investigate demographics of users like the user's age, gender, or political orientation by conducting text-based (i.e., the user's tweet content) or community-based (i.e., the user's followers) analyses. This user-specific information can then be used in different contexts, for example, to investigate within- and between-group dynamics of the comments on articles of different outlets.

7.4.6 Conclusion

In this paper, we focus on analyzing whether users react differently to more biased reporting. Specifically, we examine whether Twitter comments or replies to news articles can serve as indicators for the actual level of bias in a given article. After discussing the theoretical background of media bias, we present BAT (**B**ias **A**nd **T**witter), the first dataset connecting reliable human-made media bias classifications of news articles with the reactions these articles elicited on Twitter. Using BAT, we related comment sentiment and hate to the article bias annotations within a multi-level regression. The results provide interesting insights into the complexity of media bias and show that the comments made about an article are indeed an indicator of its bias, and vice-versa. We present evidence that biased articles have significantly higher amounts of hatefulness within their Twitter reactions. Our analysis also shows that the news outlet's individual stance reinforces the hate-bias relationship. In future work, we will extend the dataset and analysis, including with additional concepts related to media bias.

Open Access This chapter is licensed under the terms of the Creative Commons Attribution 4.0 International License (http://creativecommons.org/licenses/by/4.0/), which permits use, sharing, adaptation, distribution and reproduction in any medium or format, as long as you give appropriate credit to the original author(s) and the source, provide a link to the Creative Commons license and indicate if changes were made.

The images or other third party material in this chapter are included in the chapter's Creative Commons license, unless indicated otherwise in a credit line to the material. If material is not included in the chapter's Creative Commons license and your intended use is not permitted by statutory regulation or exceeds the permitted use, you will need to obtain permission directly from the copyright holder.

Conclusion and Future Work 8

> *There is a way out of every box, a solution to every puzzle;*
> *it's just a matter of finding it.*
>
> Captain Jean-Luc Picard—*Star Trek*

This chapter summarizes and concludes the contribution of this thesis in **Sect.** 8.1 and **Sect.** 8.2, respectively. **Sect.** 8.3 provides an overview of future work projects and the ethical implications of working on media bias.

8.1 Summary

This dissertation puts forth a promising, cross-disciplinary solution to a critical and ongoing issue in computer science, computational linguistics, and related fields: identifying linguistic biases in news articles (and even other texts). Many people consider such articles a reliable source of information about current events, even though it is also broadly believed and academically confirmed that news outlets are biased [411]. Given the trust readers put into news articles and the significant influence of media outlets on society and public opinion, media bias may potentially lead to readers adopting biased views [10]. The news, therefore, play an essential part in forming public opinion on political and other current issues [248]. Simultaneously, unrestricted access to unbiased information about any topic is crucial to develop a balanced viewpoint on different events [22]. The severity of biased news coverage is amplified further by the fact that regular news consumers are typically not fully aware of its degree and scope [10]. A first important step to increase awareness of media bias is developing methods to detect it automatically since the sheer volume of digital information available nowadays is not manually manageable. Additionally, it is crucial to comprehend how all discoveries in this research field can be utilized to enhance media literacy and address bias from a non-expert perspective. By developing a system that not only highlights bias but also sensitizes readers to the topic, we can effectively confront this issue.

Our review of prior work in this field showed that existing automated methods for detecting media bias often produce only superficial or ambiguous results, despite having good technical performance. The biases they uncover are often technically significant but not socially relevant, and fail to effectively reveal the slants present in news coverage. The primary cause of these mixed outcomes is that previous methods have regarded bias as an ambiguously defined concept, failing to encapsulate diverse perspectives effectively. Even more, already in 2018, Hamborg, Donnay, and Gipp [181] concluded that the interdisciplinarity of media bias research should be improved in the future, and (C) that approaches in computer science did not account for bias having many different forms and usually only focus on very narrow bias definitions. To address this shortcoming, we structured and reviewed the concept of media bias to support a more common understanding of bias across research domains. We introduced the media bias framework, the first coherent overview of the current state of research on media bias from different perspectives. We connected the various existing concepts so that other projects, including the classification approaches mentioned in this thesis, can a) be more easily categorized into the problem they tackle precisely and b) have an easier review to find concepts within the media bias domain that can be valuable additions to other experiments. The media bias framework we presented in this dissertation is the first step in establishing a common ground for more clearly defined media bias research. As shown in Chap. 2, we split media bias into five major bias categories: linguistic, cognitive, text-level context, reporting level, as well as related concepts. We also introduce subgroups for all of these concepts. Throughout the process of writing this dissertation, our framework's definitions and structure underwent numerous discussions and revisions, illustrating a vast array of possibilities for defining media bias.

Not only did Hamborg, Donnay, and Gipp [181] highlight in 2018 the need for a clearer overview of concepts, but they also emphasized how advanced computational methods, such as word embeddings and deep learning, had yet to be fully incorporated into the automated detection of media bias. To evaluate the progression of methodologies within computer science three years later, we provide a comprehensive review of recently published literature on computer science methods and datasets for media bias detection.

In total, we manually reviewed over 1,528 papers related to computer science research on the topic from 2019 to May 2022, following an initial automatic

8.1 Summary

filtering of over 300,000 keyword-related publications. Our review yielded valuable insights into best practices and trends in the field of research. As in many other applications of computer science [258], transformer models have quickly become the most frequently used method for media bias detection or within debiasing pipelines, generally showing more reliable performance [18]. Platforms like Hugging Face[1] facilitate the implementation of the models and their adaption to various tasks [119]. However, the new models have not yet made their way into all subtypes of bias, leaving room for future experiments and adaptions. Also, available media bias classifiers are based mainly on small in-domain datasets. Recent advancements in NLP, especially transformer-based models, show how accurate results can be achieved by unsupervised or supervised training on massive text corpora [37] and by an extensive evaluation of model pre-training using inter and cross-domain datasets [37].

Although much less popular than transformers, graph-based methods show rising applications in media bias detection. However, they are mostly used when analyzing social network content, activities, and structures, and identifying structural political stances within these entities. [170, 378, 425]. Generally, apart from the currently mostly used language models, established methods still find application. Traditional natural language processing approaches, as well as non-transformer-based (deep NN) machine learning models, fulfill invaluable functions. Their simplicity compared to language-model-based approaches makes especially simple traditional machine learning and NLP approaches explainable, which has advantages in many applications where the transparency of classification decisions is key (e.g. [15]). Since they have been applied to media bias identification tasks, these established approaches also serve as a baseline to compare new (transformer-based) approaches. Since they offer higher explainability and have been tested over a comparably much longer time period, we do not expect language models to replace other approaches altogether soon.

In our review, we also showed how the datasets used recently for media bias detection largely ignore the insights obtained in psychological research on the topic. Datasets exhibit low annotator agreement and also neglect annotator background, making their annotations less accurate [18]. The perception of bias often depends on factors other than the content itself, such as the understanding of the related text and the individual background of a reader. Psychological research shows how many individual factors affect the perception of bias, such as topic knowledge, political ideology, or simply age and education. Phenomena like the HMP (Chap. 2) make it hard to objectively determine whether and how an article or clip is biased. Still,

---

[1] https://huggingface.co/

psychological insights on media bias have never been used within research on automated media bias detection methods or media bias datasets on a large scale. So far, no best practice data collection method exists, even though some researchers attempt to create such a framework [18]. For media bias, crowdsourced data often lack annotation quality, while expert annotations are cumbersome and expensive to gather. Even more, we want to highlight that bias will always be a part of datasets created by human annotators [152], and awareness of such bias is not widely distributed among the literature containing datasets.

Beyond the mere conceptualization of the media bias domain and the technical methods employed, we also recognized through our work, particularly in dataset creation, that the perception of media bias had been only marginally studied. Consequently, we chose to develop an initial media bias questionnaire. This instrument incorporates reliable and tested items intended to measure how an individual perceives bias. We conducted a literature search to find 824 relevant questions about text perception in previous research on the topic. In a multi-iterative process, we summarized and condensed these questions semantically to conclude a complete and representative set of possible question types about bias. The final set consisted of 25 questions with varying answering formats, 17 questions using semantic differentials, and six ratings of feelings. We tested each question on 190 articles with 663 participants to identify how well the questions measure an article's perceived bias. Our results show that 21 final items are suitable and reliable for measuring the perception of media bias (Chap. 3).

During our work, we built two major datasets; MBIC and BABE (Chap. 4). MBIC is the first available dataset about media bias reporting detailed information on annotator characteristics and their individual background. It was the first data set we created. Before MBIC, existing data sets did not control for the individual background of annotators, which may affect their assessment and represent critical information for contextualizing their annotations. We, therefore, created a matrix-based methodology to crowdsource such data using a self-developed annotation platform called TASSY [23]. MBIC contains 1,700 statements representing sentence and word level media bias instances, annotated by ten crowdsource annotators per statement. The MBIC dataset attains an inter-annotator agreement of $\alpha = 0.21$. This low agreement level underscores the complexity of the task and aligns with comparable crowdsourcing research in the field [201].

Following our work on MBIC, we concluded that crowdsource workers had difficulties grasping the concept of media bias, even when presented with detailed instructions. This led us to develop the BABE dataset [18]. BABE is a robust and diverse dataset, curated by trained experts for media bias research. We also employed it to explore why expert labeling is crucial within this domain. The data set offers

8.1 Summary

better annotation quality and higher inter-annotator agreement than existing work. It consists of 3,700 sentences balanced among topics and outlets, containing binary (bias or no bias) media bias labels on the word and sentence level. Also, it allowed us to compare expert annotations with the crowdsourced labels provided by [21] to further analyze quality differences between the two groups. Our results show how expert annotators render more qualitative bias labels than crowdsource workers in MBIC. Employing annotators with domain expertise allowed us to achieve an inter-annotator agreement of $\alpha = 0.40$, which is higher than existing data sets [21].

Mainly, we used our datasets (and other datatsets) for five major experiments. First, we built a feature-oriented approach (Chap. 5), which provides strong descriptive and explanatory power compared to deep learning techniques. We identified and engineered various linguistic, lexical, and syntactic features that can potentially be media bias indicators. To the best of our knowledge, our resource collection is the most complete within the media bias research area. We evaluated all of our features in various combinations and retrieved their possible importance both for future research and for the task in general. We also evaluated various possible ML approaches with all of our features. XGBoost, a decision tree implementation, yields the best results. Our approach achieves an F_1-score of 0.43, a precision of 0.29, a recall of 0.77, and a ROC AUC of 0.79, which outperformed current media bias detection methods based on features.

After this experiment, we continued to work on more DL-oriented approaches (Chap. 6). Of these, our first model incorporated distant supervision into automated media bias detection. Within these early-stage experiments, our best-performing BERT-based model was pre-trained on a larger corpus consisting of distant labels. Fine-tuning and evaluating the model on our proposed supervised data set, we achieved a macro F_1-score of 0.804, which, at the time, outperformed existing methods. We saw that using additional labels might be promising, and therefore continued to investigate neural models with greater detail. In particular, this led to our second and third DL experiment. We proposed DA-RoBERTa (achieving a higher F_1-score of 0.814 on the same data as our first experiment). To do so, we equipped several transformer architectures (i.e., BERT, RoBERTa, BART, and T5) with an understanding of biased language, showing that domain-adaptive pre-training significantly improves the classifier's bias detection performance compared to baseline models without intermediate pre-training. We also investigated whether MTL can be a promising direction for media bias research. Since media bias, as shown in Chap. 2, is a multi-task construct, we believed the model specifically accounting for multiple tasks to be a promising research direction. In the inital experiment, we proposed a tbML architecture trained via Multi-Task Learning using six bias-related datasets. Our best-performing implementation achieved a macro F_1 of 0.776, which was a performance boost of 3% compared to our baseline but lower than the performances of the models mentioned before. However, we saw that some individual tasks had a positive impact and decided that, as a final experiment, we should conduct a more large-scale MTL experiment.

In this more large-scale experiment, we introduce the model MAGPIE as an advanced approach to detect media bias through multi-task learning (MTL), significantly enhancing performance across various bias detection tasks [5]. We first build the Large Bias Mixture (LBM) framework, consisting of 59 diverse bias-related tasks, which is central to MAGPIE's methodology. LBM facilitates the comprehensive training of a new MTL model, which employs a RoBERTa-based encoder. The results demonstrate a significant improvement, particularly a 3.3% increase in the F1-score on the BABE dataset. MAGPIE's performance is notably superior in 5 out of 8 tasks within the MBIB benchmark (see below), underscoring the effectiveness of multi-task learning in improving both the accuracy and efficiency of media bias detection systems. The approach contrasts with traditional single-task models by reducing the need for extensive finetuning (Using a RoBERTa encoder, MAGPIE needs just 15% of finetuning steps compared to single-task approaches), thereby setting a new benchmark in the field of neural media bias classification and highlighting the potential of combining large-scale pre-training with multi-task learning strategies.

In light of our classifications, datasets, and literature review, we recognized the need to explore potential applications for the future use of media bias classifications in practical scenarios. Consequently, we delved into the perception of media bias, particularly concerning potential visualizations. Initially, we assembled a manually annotated dataset of highlighted bias in news articles and subsequently tested three visualization strategies to present these annotations to news readers. Although our results did not indicate a substantial impact on the bias awareness of treatment groups compared to the control group, we observed that a visualization of hand-annotated bias communicated instances of bias is more effective than a framing visualization. As the initial experiment did not yield large effects, we decided to refine our visualization techniques further. Building upon our prior experiment, we improved the quality of the visualizations, selected various elements for enhanced highlighting, and significantly increased the size of the study. Unlike our previous findings, both the forewarning message and the annotations significantly heightened media bias awareness, while the political classification had no observable effect. Incongruence between the political stance of an article and an individual's political orientation also amplified media bias awareness. Visual aids did not mitigate this effect.

Finally, we explored the correlation between bias in news articles and its perception on Twitter. Our findings revealed that comments on an article serve as a reliable gauge of its bias and the reverse is also true. Evidence showed that Twitter users' responses to biased articles are overwhelmingly negative and hateful. Furthermore, our analysis demonstrated a reinforcing link between the news outlet's stance and the relationship between hateful comments and bias.

8.2 Contributions of the Thesis

This thesis has made five main contributions:

1. It presented a systematic literature review, concluding in the first media bias framework, connecting concepts and definitions within the research area. Additionally, the review gave an overview of the status of recent computer scientific work on media bias, identifying recent trends.
2. It filtered and evaluated a comprehensive item set suitable for measuring the perception of media bias.
3. It introduced two new datasets (MBIC and BABE), summarizes their creation process and showcases how the datasets deal with existing drawbacks in prior work.
4. It demonstrated the possibilities of feature-based classification approaches in the domain and introduced multiple neural classification approaches. Concluding with a final multi-task experiment, this thesis presents the most versatile and state-of-the-art media bias classifier currently available to the public. This final model is one of the first to approach media bias detection as a multi-task problem, mirroring the inherent multi-task nature of media bias, a feature we believe to be inescapable in this domain.
5. Lastly, the thesis also showed multiple ways to visualize and highlight media bias. It evaluated how bias in news articles can affect their perception.

These contributions resulted in 23 peer-reviewed publications [1–6, 8, 10–19, 21–23, 25, 376]. The publications were cited 383 times[2] overall. In the following, we briefly summarize the contributions of this thesis for each of the five research tasks that were defined in the introduction, **Sect.** 1.3.

---

[2] According to Google Scholar evaluated on 2024-03-11.

> **Research Task I**
> Create a full comprehensive overview of concepts and definitions, as well as computational methods, existing in the domain.
> *Contributing publications:* [8, 13]

To tackle this research task, we summarize the research on computational methods to detect media bias by systematically reviewing 3140 research papers published between 2019 and 2022. To structure our review and support a mutual understanding of bias across research domains, we introduce the Media Bias Taxonomy, which provides a coherent overview of the current state of research on media bias from different perspectives. We show that media bias detection is a highly active research field in which transformer-based classification approaches have led to significant improvements in recent years. These improvements include higher classification accuracy and the ability to detect more fine-granular types of bias. However, we have identified a lack of interdisciplinarity in existing projects and a need for more awareness of the various types of media bias to support methodologically thorough performance evaluations of media bias detection systems. Concluding from our analysis, we see the integration of recent machine learning advancements with reliable and diverse bias assessment strategies from other research areas as the most promising area for future research contributions.

> **Research Task II**
> Develop a scale that can be used as a reliable standard to evaluate the perception of media bias.
> *Contributing publications:* [8, 15]

Our contribution to this research task is the development of a scale that can be used as a reliable standard to evaluate article bias [15]. We conduct a literature search to find 824 relevant questions about text perception in previous research on the topic. In a multi-iterative process, we summarize and condense these questions semantically to conclude a complete and representative set of possible question types about bias. The final set consisted of 25 questions with varying answering formats, 17 questions using semantic differentials, and six ratings of feelings. We

8.2 Contributions of the Thesis

tested each of the questions on 190 articles with overall 663 participants to identify how well the questions measure an article's perceived bias. Our results show that 21 final items are suitable and reliable for measuring the perception of media bias.

> **Research Task III**
> Create media bias datasets that tackle the problems in existing datasets.
> *Contributing publications:* [8, 16, 18, 21, 23, 405]

Within the work on this thesis, we published two major datasets: MBIC [21] and BABE [18]. MBIC (Media Bias Including Characteristics) is a prototypical yet robust and diverse data set for media bias research. It consists of 1,700 statements representing various media bias instances and contains labels for media bias identification on the word and sentence level. The statements are reviewed by ten annotators each and contain labels for media bias identification both on the word and sentence level. In contrast to existing research, our data incorporate background information on the participants' demographics, political ideology, and their opinion about media in general. We gather MBIC using our own survey platform since existing platform systems did not offer sufficient options to collect text annotations [23].

Building upon MBIC, we have developed BABE, a robust and diverse dataset created by trained experts specifically for media bias research. In this process, we analyzed the crucial role that expert labeling plays in this domain. Our dataset provides superior annotation quality and higher inter-annotator agreement compared to existing works. Comprising 3,700 sentences balanced across topics and outlets, it includes media bias labels at both the word and sentence levels. To date, BABE stands as the largest available dataset created by experts for studying media bias by word choice.

> **Research Task IV**
> Implement a reliable automated media bias classification system, making use of technological advancements in terms of language models.
> *Contributing publications:* [5, 6, 8, 17, 18, 22]

Working on research task IV, we develop multiple classification systems. First, we present early-stage and feature-based classifiers based on the German language [11, 12]. Second, we improve the feature-based approaches by systemically identifying and engineering various linguistic, lexical, and syntactic features that can potentially be media bias indicators [22]. To the best of our knowledge, our resource collection is the most complete within the media bias research area. We evaluate all of our features in various combinations and retrieve their possible importance both for future research and for the task in general. We also evaluate various possible Machine Learning approaches with all of our features. XGBoost, a decision tree implementation, yields the best results. Our approach achieves an F_1-score of 0.43, a precision of 0.29, a recall of 0.77, and a ROC AUC of 0.79, which outperforms current media bias detection methods based on features.

Since neural models show promising performances, we also present deep learning approaches to identify media bias automatically. Our initial model is a BERT-based classifier trained on the BABE dataset. Our best-performing model is pre-trained on a larger corpus consisting of distant labels. Fine-tuning and evaluating the model on our proposed supervised data set, we achieve a macro F_1-score of 0.804, outperforming existing methods. We extend the work on such models in our later works [6, 17], where we introduce domain-adaptive learning and multi-task learning into the domain. Our work shows how important multi-task awareness is in the domain and highlights that sufficient performances for real-world applications can already be achieved. Among the benchmark MBIB [25], which we also publish during the thesis, we show that our models outperform existing other non-commercial solutions.

> **Research Task V**
> Study how bias is perceived and how visualizations can improve a reader's bias awareness.
> *Contributing publications:* [3, 4, 8, 10, 14]

First, we create three manually annotated datasets and test varying visualization strategies [10]. The results show no strong effects of becoming aware of the bias of the treatment groups compared to the control group, although a visualization of hand-annotated bias communicated bias instances more effectively than a framing visualization. Showing participants an overview page, which opposes different viewpoints on the same topic, does not influence a respondent's bias perception significantly. Using a multilevel model, we find that perceived journalist bias is significantly related to the perceived political extremeness and impartiality of the article.

Second, we execute another experiment with a similar outline [14]. We analyze how to facilitate the detection of media bias with visual and textual aids in the form of (a) a forewarning message, (b) text annotations, and (c) political classifiers. In an online experiment, we randomize 985 participants to receive a biased liberal or conservative news article in any combination of the three aids. Meanwhile, we assess their subjective perception of media bias in this article, attitude change, and political ideology. The forewarning message and the annotations increased media bias awareness, whereas the political classification showed no effect. Incongruence between an article's political position and individual political orientation also increased media bias awareness. Visual aids did not mitigate this effect. Likewise, attitudes remained unaltered.

Lastly, we partially analyze the general impact news bias can have. We approach the question from a measurement point of view, examining whether Twitter comments on articles can serve as bias indicators, i.e., whether user comments indicate the actual level of bias in a given article. We first give an overview of media bias research, then discuss key concepts related to how individuals engage with online content, focusing on the sentiment (or valance) of comments and outright hate speech. We then present the first dataset connecting expert media bias classifications of news articles with the reactions these articles had upon publication on Twitter. Our results show that the comments made on an article are indeed an indicator for its bias, and vice-versa. With a regression coefficient of 0.703 ($p < 0.01$), we present evidence that Twitter reactions to biased articles are significantly more hateful. Even more, our analysis shows that the news outlet's individual stance reinforces the hate-bias relationship.

In total, we present multiple studies about how bias can be perceived. However, we understand that the area offers a wide variety of potential future projects, and we address this again in **Sect.** 8.3.3.

8.3 Future Work

8.3.1 Future Dataset and Task Developments

The continuous advancement and expansion of datasets concerning media bias and associated concepts, including hate speech, gender bias, racial bias, sentiment analysis, and others, is important for several reasons, which we detail below. In future work that builds upon this thesis, we[3] will strive to establish and expand existing research structures. Our goal is to develop increasingly reliable and diverse datasets on the topic.

1. Fostering fairness and accountability: The development of extensive datasets on media bias and related issues enables researchers and developers to gain a deeper comprehension of how these biases manifest in media content. This knowledge facilitates the creation of algorithms, tools, and policies that promote fairness and hold media organizations accountable for their content.
2. Curbing the proliferation of misinformation and disinformation: Biased media may contribute to the dissemination of inaccurate or deceptive information. The development of comprehensive datasets on media bias can assist in identifying and mitigating such content, thereby reducing the prevalence of misinformation and disinformation in society.
3. Enhancing AI ethics and diminishing AI bias: As artificial intelligence systems become increasingly integrated into daily life, it is imperative to ensure that these systems are unbiased and ethical. Developing datasets on media bias and associated concepts contributes to the training of AI models in recognizing and mitigating such biases, resulting in more responsible AI deployment.
4. Encouraging diverse perspectives: Media bias can result in a dearth of diversity in perspectives, which may further marginalize underrepresented groups. By perpetually developing datasets capturing various aspects of bias, tools can be created to identify and promote content that represents a multitude of viewpoints, fostering a more inclusive media landscape.
5. Empowering media consumers: Making datasets on media bias and related issues publicly available enables consumers to make more informed decisions regarding the media they consume. This facilitates a better understanding of the biases present in the content they consume and encourages critical thinking.
6. Enhancing media literacy: As datasets on media bias evolve, they can contribute to improved media literacy education. By comprehending the diverse types of biases, consumers can develop the necessary skills to navigate the intricate media landscape and make informed decisions regarding the information they consume.
7. Supporting policy development and regulation: Comprehensive datasets on media bias can serve as invaluable resources for policymakers and regulators seeking to address these issues at a societal level. The data can inform policy

---

[3] In the course of this work, we also founded our own research group. For more information, visit https://media-bias-research.org/.

development and regulatory frameworks, ensuring they are based on a robust empirical foundation.
8. Facilitating interdisciplinary research: Extensive datasets on media bias and related concepts can serve as a foundation for interdisciplinary research, allowing scholars from various fields, such as communication, sociology, psychology, and computer science, to collaborate and develop innovative solutions to address these complex issues.
9. Tracking trends and changes over time: By continuously developing and updating datasets on media bias, researchers can monitor trends and changes in the media landscape over time. This can provide valuable insights into the evolution of bias in media and inform strategies to address these issues.
10. Fostering global collaboration: Addressing media bias and related issues necessitates a global effort, and comprehensive datasets can serve as a common ground for collaboration. By developing and sharing datasets, researchers, organizations, and policymakers from around the world can work together to tackle the challenges posed by media bias and promote a more equitable and inclusive media environment.

8.3.2 Future Language Modeling Experiments

In our work, we primarily advanced media bias detection based on traditional machine learning methods and deep learning approaches. We built systems using domain-adaptive learning, multi-task learning, and distant supervision. Overall, we believe that multi-task learning appears to be the most promising avenue for future media bias research, particularly given the complex and multifaceted nature of media bias. Even more, we believe that developing models that can provide explanations for their predictions, such as explainable AI techniques like LIME, SHAP, and attention mechanisms, can increase transparency and trust in the media bias detection process. Such explanations might also help in possible active learning approaches, where classifications and explanations are given to users for feedback, which is then used to continuously improve the predictions in a loop. While this dissertation primarily focuses on text characteristics, it is important to note that multimodal approaches—integrating information from text, images, audio, and video—have the potential to bolster media bias detection capabilities, providing a more comprehensive understanding of media bias. This is true not only for additional media content types but also for content perspective. Understanding what is reported, where it's reported, and what information is omitted is likely just as important in portraying media bias. Lastly, analyzing the temporal patterns in media bias can offer valuable insights into its dynamics, helping to understand trends and devise strategies to counteract potential negative effects of spreading bias or even misinformation. Finally, addressing biases in training data is crucial for building accurate and robust media bias detection models; techniques like data augmentation, re-sampling, and adversarial training can be used to mitigate biases in the training data and improve model performance.

Apart from core media bias, general language modeling trends develop, and naturally also affect future models on media bias detection. For example, one enduring trend in language modeling is the continuous scaling of model size and computational power. Researchers have consistently observed that larger models with more parameters tend to perform better on a wide range of NLP tasks. This has driven the development of increasingly large models, such as GPT-3 and GPT-4. The demand for greater computational resources has also grown, prompting advances in hardware and distributed training techniques that enable the training of these colossal models. Additionally, the integration of multimodal information and context has become an essential aspect of language modeling—this is not only true for the bias expressed by other forms of content or information, such as mentioned above, but also for improving text classification systems. By incorporating various forms of data, such as images, audio, and video, language models can develop a more comprehensive understanding of the world and its linguistic complexities. Such a multimodal approach has also highlighted the importance of context in language understanding, leading to models that can better capture and represent contextual information.

Lastly, as language models have grown in size and capability, so have concerns surrounding their ethical implications. The potential for models to perpetuate and amplify existing biases present in training data has emerged as a significant challenge in the field. Researchers have increasingly focused on developing techniques and methodologies to address these concerns, with a growing emphasis on fairness, accountability, transparency, and explainability. Bias mitigation strategies, such as data augmentation, debiasing techniques, and adversarial training, have become essential components in the development and evaluation of language models. We will detail about considerations in this area in greater detail within **Sect.** 8.3.4.

8.3.3 Future Experiments on Visualization

In this dissertation, we have presented various studies focusing on the visualization of media bias to news consumers. We aim to show how visually rendering biases in various news sources can aid individuals in recognizing and understanding potential

8.3 Future Work

influences on the information they receive. Ideally, such understanding facilitates informed decisions about the reliability and accuracy of news stories, promoting a more responsible approach to news consumption.

Visualizing media bias aids in the development of media literacy. This means that by grasping how media messages are constructed, disseminated, and consumed, news consumers are better equipped to identify biases, assess the credibility of sources, and discern possible motives behind slanted reporting. Ultimately, these processes could enhance critical reading skills.

Moreover, in addition to fostering media literacy and critical thinking, visualizing media bias could help counteract the effects of echo chambers and filter bubbles. By illuminating media bias, individuals may become more aware of their own consumption habits and intentionally seek out contrasting viewpoints, leading to a more balanced understanding of issues.

Illustrating media bias likely plays a crucial role in enriching the news consumption experience, promoting media literacy, and nurturing critical thinking among news consumers. However, the domain of media bias visualization is still nascent, and the precise relationships between reading, understanding, decision-making, and media bias remain areas for further research.

Future work could beneficially focus on a more detailed exploration of strategies to highlight bias, along with additional research on the overall perception of bias. Projects such as the media bias questionnaire [15] can be continuously updated, while the insight from our studies on visualization [10, 14] need to be integrated with real-world application, to test similar strategies more closely to actual news readers and outside of academic studies. We envision the development of more globally focused applications similar to Allsides[4] and Ground News[5], but with more granular visualizations and a stronger emphasis on language independence. Even more, we believe that news platforms can also help develop datasets—a first prototype was developed in close connected to the work within this thesis. It is accessible here: https://newsunfold.fly.dev/. Furthermore, we have already begun developing a media bias game. This interactive approach not only cultivates critical reading skills in a fun and engaging manner but also facilitates the collection of annotations and feedback about media bias. After concluding this thesis, we plan to devote more effort towards the highlight of media bias, given its substantial potential to enhance awareness and foster critical reading and decision-making skills. In an era of extensive AI availability, where content creation and distribution are increasingly simple, we believe such skills to be of essential importance [14].

---

[4] https://www.Allsides.com, accessed on 2023-01-06.
[5] https://ground.news/, accessed on 2023-01-06.

8.3.4 Ethical Implications

Developing datasets, language models, and visualizations related to media bias involves a range of ethical implications that warrant careful consideration throughout the research and development process. An in-depth explanation of these ethical implications is provided below.

When developing datasets about media bias, several ethical considerations are important. First, data representativeness is crucial; datasets must encompass diverse sources to accurately reflect the media landscape and capture various forms of bias, including political, racial, gender, and sensationalism. This requires sampling from a broad range of media outlets, platforms, and formats, as well as considering underrepresented perspectives to avoid skewed representations.

Privacy is another vital ethical concern in dataset development. Researchers must take steps to anonymize personal information to protect the privacy of individuals involved in creating or sharing media content. This can involve removing or obfuscating personally identifiable information (PII), such as names, email addresses, and other identifiers, to minimize potential harm to individuals.

Addressing potential biases in dataset creation is also essential. Researchers should be cautious about inadvertently introducing their own biases during the labeling process. To minimize this risk, objective and transparent labeling methodologies should be employed, such as using multiple annotators with diverse backgrounds and employing clear, well-defined guidelines for labeling.

In the context of developing language models to analyze media bias, ethical concerns revolve around model fairness, transparency, and unintended consequences. Model fairness is about ensuring that the model does not perpetuate existing biases or create new ones. To achieve this, researchers should utilize diverse and balanced training data, employ techniques to mitigate biases in the model, and perform rigorous evaluations to assess potential bias in the model's outputs.

Transparency in the model's decision-making process is vital for users to understand the basis for the model's analysis and to build trust in the technology. This can involve providing clear explanations of the algorithms, data sources, and assumptions underlying the model, as well as offering mechanisms for users to provide feedback on the model's performance.

Developers must also consider potential unintended consequences of language models, such as the misuse of the model to manipulate media content, create "deepfake" news, or discredit legitimate sources. To address these concerns, developers can incorporate safeguards to prevent misuse, collaborate with stakeholders to develop guidelines and policies for responsible use and engage in ongoing monitoring of the technology's impact.

8.3 Future Work

Visualizations for news readers about media bias come with ethical implications, including accuracy, interpretability, and potential misuse. Visualizations should accurately represent the underlying data and analysis, avoiding distortions or misrepresentations that could mislead users. To ensure accuracy, designers should employ best practices in data visualization, such as choosing appropriate chart types, scales, and color schemes, and providing thorough documentation of the data sources and methodologies.

Interpretability is another critical concern in developing visualizations. Visualizations should be designed to be easily interpretable, providing clear and accessible information to users, regardless of their expertise in the subject matter. This can involve using intuitive visual elements, incorporating explanatory text or tooltips, and offering user-friendly navigation and interaction features.

Potential misuse of visualizations is an essential ethical consideration, as they can be employed to promote a particular agenda or discredit specific media sources. To mitigate this risk, visualizations should be accompanied by contextual information and explanations that provide a balanced perspective and empower users to make informed judgments about media content. Additionally, designers should be transparent about any limitations or uncertainties in the data and analysis, helping users to understand the nuances and complexities of the subject matter.

In conclusion, the development of datasets, language models, and visualizations related to media bias presents numerous ethical implications that require thoughtful attention. Ensuring data representativeness, maintaining privacy, and addressing potential biases are key concerns in creating datasets. Model fairness, transparency, and unintended consequences must be considered when developing language models. Accuracy, interpretability, and potential misuse are crucial ethical aspects of visualizations. Addressing these ethical concerns is vital to promote responsible research and development and to foster a fair, transparent, and accountable media landscape. By prioritizing ethical considerations, researchers and developers can contribute to a better understanding of media bias and its implications, ultimately empowering media consumers to make informed decisions and promoting a diverse and inclusive media environment.

Open Access This chapter is licensed under the terms of the Creative Commons Attribution 4.0 International License (http://creativecommons.org/licenses/by/4.0/), which permits use, sharing, adaptation, distribution and reproduction in any medium or format, as long as you give appropriate credit to the original author(s) and the source, provide a link to the Creative Commons license and indicate if changes were made.

The images or other third party material in this chapter are included in the chapter's Creative Commons license, unless indicated otherwise in a credit line to the material. If material is not included in the chapter's Creative Commons license and your intended use is not permitted by statutory regulation or exceeds the permitted use, you will need to obtain permission directly from the copyright holder.

Glossary

ANN: Artificial Neural Network.
AttnBL: Attention-based Bidirectional Long Short-term Memory.
BiRNN: Bidirectional Recurrent Neural Network.
CNN: Convolutional Neural Network.
DL: Deep Learning.
DS: Distant Supervision.
FMP: Friendly Media Phenomenon.
GCN: Graph Convolutional Network.
GRU: Gated Recurrent Unit.
HAN: Hierarchical Attention Network.
HMP: Hostile Media Effect.
HMP: Hostile Media Phenomenon.
KNN: K-Nearest Neighbors.
LDA: Latent Dirichlet Allocation.
LR: Logistic Regression.
LSTM: Long Short-Term Memory.
ML: Machine Learning.
MLP: Multilayer Perceptron.
MTL: Multi-Task Learning.
NB: Naive Bayes.
NLP: Natural Language Processing.
NN: Meural Metwork.
nNN: Non-Neural Networks.
NSP: Next Sentence Prediction.
ntbML: Non-Transformer-Based Machine Learning.
RF: Random Forest.
RNN: Recurrent Neural Network.

SVM: Support Vector Machine.
tbML: transformer-based Machine Learning.
tNLP: traditional Natural Language Processing.
UMAP: Uniform manifold approximation and projection for Dimension Reduction.
VADER: Valence Aware Dictionary for Sentiment Reasoning.
XGBoost: Extreme Gradient Boosting.

Bibliography of Publications, Submissions & Talks

1. J. Ehrhardt, T. Spinde, A. Vardasbi, and F. Hamborg. "Omission of Information: Identifying Political Slant via an Analysis of Co-occurring Entities". In: *Information between Data and Knowledge*. Vol. 74. Schriften zur Informationswissenschaft. Glückstadt: Werner Hülsbusch, 2021, pp. 80–93. URL: https://epub.uniregensburg.de/44939/.
2. F. Hamborg, T. Spinde, K. Heinser, K. Donnay, and B. Gipp. "How to effectively identify and communicate person-targeting media bias in daily news consumption?" In: *Proceedings of the 15th ACM conference on recommender systems, 9th international workshop on news recommendation and analytics (INRA 2021)*. tex.topic: newsanalysis. 2021-09.
3. S. Hinterreiter, T. Spinde, S. Oberdörfer, I. Echizen, and M. E. Latoschik. "News ninja: Gamified annotation of linguistic bias in online news". In: *CHI PLAY '24 [in review]*. Tampere, Finland, 2024.
4. S. Hinterreiter, M. Wessel, F. Schliski, I. Echizen, M. E. Latoschik, and T. Spinde. "NewsUnravel: Creating a news-reading application that indicates linguistic media bias and collects feedback". In: *ICWSM '24 [in review]*. 2024.
5. T. Horych, M. Wessel, J. P. Wahle, T. Ruas, J. Wassmuth, A. Greiner-Petter, A. Aizawa, B. Gipp, and T. Spinde. "MAGPIE: Multi-task analysis of media-bias generalization with pre-trained identification of expressions". In: *"Proceedings of the 2024 Joint International Conference on Computational Linguistics, Language Resources and Evaluation"*. 2024-02-01. URL: https://media-bias-research.org/wpcontent/uploads/2024/03/Horych2024a.pdf (visited on 2024-02-01).
6. D. Krieger, T. Spinde, T. Ruas, J. Kulshrestha, and B. Gipp. "A Domain-adaptive Pretraining Approach for Language Bias Detection in News". In: *2022 ACM/IEEE Joint Conference on Digital Libraries (JCDL)*. Cologne, Germany, 2022. https://doi.org/10.1145/3529372.3530932. URL: https://media-bias-research.org/wpcontent/uploads/2022/06/Krieger2022_mbg.pdf (visited on 2022-06-01)
7. N. Meuschke, A. Jagdale, T. Spinde, J. Mitrović, and B. Gipp. "A Benchmark of PDF Information Extraction Tools Using a Multi-task and Multi-domain Evaluation Framework for Academic Documents". In: *Proceedings of the 18th International Conference (iConference 2023)*. Vol. 13972. LNCS. Cham: Springer Nature Switzerland, 2023, pp. 383–405. ISBN: 978-3-031-28031-3 978-3-031-28032-0.

8. T. Spinde. "An Interdisciplinary Approach for the Automated Detection and Visualization of Media Bias in News Articles". In: *2021 IEEE International Conference on Data Mining Workshops (ICDMW)*. 2021. https://doi.org/10.1109/ICDMW53433.2021.00144. URL: https://media-bias-research.org/wp-content/uploads/2021/09/Spinde2021g.pdf (visited on 2021-09-30).
9. T. Spinde. "CitizenData: Entwicklung einer Open-Source Crowdsourcing-Plattform fur Datenjournalismus". Bachelorthesis. Universität Passau, 2015.
10. T. Spinde, F. Hamborg, K. Donnay, A. Becerra, and B. Gipp. "Enabling News Consumers to View and Understand Biased News Coverage: A Study on the Perception and Visualization of Media Bias". In: *Proceedings of the ACM/IEEE Joint Conference on Digital Libraries in 2020. Virtual Event China: ACM*, 2020, pp. 389–392. https://doi.org/10.1145/3383583.3398619. URL: https://dl.acm.org/doi/10.1145/3383583.3398619 (visited on 2020-09-19).
11. T. Spinde, F. Hamborg, and B. Gipp. "An Integrated Approach to Detect Media Bias in German News Articles". In: *Proceedings of the ACM/IEEE Joint Conference on Digital Libraries in 2020*. Virtual Event China: ACM, 2020, pp. 505–506. https://doi.org/10.1145/3383583.3398585. URL: https://doi.org/10.1145/3383583.3398585 (visited on 2020-09-19).
12. T. Spinde, F. Hamborg, and B. Gipp. "Media Bias in German News Articles: A Combined Approach". *In: ECML PKDD 2020 Workshops*. Cham: Springer International Publishing, 2020, pp. 581–590. https://doi.org/10.1007/978-3-030-65965-3_41. URL: https://media-bias-research.org/wp-content/uploads/2021/01/Media-Bias-in-German-News-Articles-A-Combined-Approach.pdf.
13. T. Spinde, S. Hinterreiter, F. Haak, T. Ruas, H. Giese, N. Meuschke, and B. Gipp. "The media bias taxonomy: A systematic literature review on the forms and automated detection of media bias". In: *ACM computing surveys (CSUR) [in review]* (2024). tex.pubstate: published tex.tppubtype: article. URL: https://mediabias-research.org/wp-content/uploads/2023/12/spinde2023.pdf (visited on 2023-01-01).
14. T. Spinde, C. Jeggle, M. Haupt, W. Gaissmaier, and H. Giese. "How do we raise media bias awareness effectively? Effects of visualizations to communicate bias". In: *PLOS ONE*. Vol. 17. Issue: 4. Public Library of Science, 2022, pp. 1–14. https://doi.org/10.1371/journal.pone.0266204. URL: https://doi.org/10.1371/journal.pone.0266204.
15. T. Spinde, C. Kreuter, W. Gaissmaier, F. Hamborg, B. Gipp, and H. Giese. "Do You Think It's Biased? How To Ask For The Perception Of Media Bias". In: *Proceedings of the ACM/IEEE Joint Conference on Digital Libraries (JCDL)*. 2021, pp. 61–69. https://doi.org/10.1109/JCDL52503.2021.00018. URL: https://mediabias-research.org/wp-content/uploads/2022/01/Spinde2021e.pdf (visited on 2021-09-01).
16. T. Spinde, D. Krieger, M. Plank, and B. Gipp. "Towards A Reliable Ground-Truth For Biased Language Detection". In: *Proceedings of the ACM/IEEE-CS Joint Conference on Digital Libraries (JCDL)*. Virtual Event, 2021. https://doi.org/10.1109/JCDL52503.2021.00053. URL: https://media-bias-research.org/wpcontent/uploads/2022/01/Spinde2021d.pdf (visited on 2021-09-01).
17. T. Spinde, J.-D. Krieger, T. Ruas, J. Mitrović, F. Götz-Hahn, A. Aizawa, and B. Gipp. "Exploiting transformer-based multitask learning for the detection of media bias in news articles". In: *Proceedings of the iConference 2022*. Virtual event, 2022. https://doi.org/10.1007/978-3-030-96957-8_20. URL: https://media-biasresearch.org/wp-content/uploads/2022/03/Spinde2022a_mbg.pdf (visited on 2022-03-04).

18. T. Spinde, M. Plank, J.-D. Krieger, T. Ruas, B. Gipp, and A. Aizawa. "Neural Media Bias Detection Using Distant Supervision With BABE—Bias Annotations By Experts". In: *Proc. Ann. Meeting Association for Computational Linguistics (ACL)*. Punta Cana, Dominican Republic: Association for Computational Linguistics, 2021, pp. 1166–1177. https://doi.org/10.18653/v1/2021.findings-emnlp.101. URL: https://aclanthology.org/2021.findings-emnlp.101.
19. T. Spinde, E. Richter, M. Wessel, J. Kulshrestha, and K. Donnay. "What do Twitter comments tell about news article bias? Assessing the impact of news article bias on its perception on Twitter". In: *Online Social Networks and Media 37–38 (2023)*, p. 100264. ISSN: 2468-6964. https://doi.org/10.1016/j.osnem.2023.100264. URL: https://www.sciencedirect.com/science/article/pii/S246869642300023X.
20. T. Spinde, L. Rudnitckaia, F. Hamborg, and B. Gipp. "Identification of Biased Terms in News Articles by Comparison of Outlet-specific Word Embeddings". In: *Proceedings of the 16th International Conference (iConference 2021)*. Beijing, China (Virtual Event), 2021. https://doi.org/10.1007/978-3-030-71305-8_17. URL: https://media-bias-research.org/wp-content/uploads/2021/01/Identification-of-Biased-Terms-in-News-Articles-by-Comparison-of-Outlet-specific-Word-Embeddings.pdf.
21. T. Spinde, L. Rudnitckaia, S. Kanishka, F. Hamborg, Bela, Gipp, and K. Donnay. "MBIC—a media bias annotation dataset including annotator characteristics". In: *Proceedings of the iConference 2021*. Beijing, China (Virtual Event), 2021. https://doi.org/10.6084/m9.figshare.17192924. URL: https://media-biasresearch.org/wp-content/uploads/2021/01/Spinde2021a.pdf (visited on 2021-03-01).
22. T. Spinde, L. Rudnitckaia, J. Mitrović, F. Hamborg, M. Granitzer, B. Gipp, and K. Donnay. "Automated identification of bias inducing words in news articles using linguistic and context-oriented features". In: *Information Processing & Management* 58.3 (2021), p. 102505. ISSN: 0306-4573. https://doi.org/10.1016/j.ipm.2021.102505. URL: https://www.sciencedirect.com/science/article/pii/S0306457321000157.
23. T. Spinde, K. Sinha, N. Meuschke, and B. Gipp. "TASSY—A Text Annotation Survey System". In: *Proceedings of the ACM/IEEE Joint Conference on Digital Libraries (JCDL)*. author+an={1=highlight}. Champaign, IL, USA, 2021. https://doi.org/10.1109/JCDL52503.2021.00052. URL: https://media-bias-research.org/wpcontent/uploads/2022/01/Spinde2021c.pdf.
24. Timo Spinde. "Automated detection of bias words in german news articles". Master thesis. Universität Konstanz, 2018.
25. M. Wessel, T. Horych, T. Ruas, A. Aizawa, B. Gipp, and T. Spinde. "Introducing MBIB—the first media bias identification benchmark task and dataset collection". In: *Proceedings of the 46th international ACM SIGIR conference on research and development in information retrieval (SIGIR '23)*. New York, NY, USA: ACM, 2023. https://doi.org/10.1145/3539618.3591882. URL: https://media-biasresearch.org/wp-content/uploads/2023/04/Wessel2023Preprint.pdf (visited on 2023-07-01).

Bibliography

26. V. P. Aires, J. Freire, and F. G. Nakamura. "An Information Theory Approach to Detect Media Bias in News Websites". In: *San Diego* (2020), p. 9.
27. M. Z. Ali, Ehsan-Ul-Haq, S. Rauf, K. Javed, and S. Hussain. "Improving Hate Speech Detection of Urdu Tweets Using Sentiment Analysis". In: *IEEE Access* 9 (2021), pp. 84296–84305. https://doi.org/10.1109/ACCESS.2021.3087827.
28. E. Allaway and K. McKeown. *A Unified Feature Representation for Lexical Connotations*. _eprint: 2006.00635. 2021.
29. H. M. Alonso, A. Delamaire, and B. Sagot. "Annotating omission in statement pairs". In: *Proceedings of the 11th Linguistic Annotation Workshop*. Valencia, Spain: Association for Computational Linguistics, 2017-04, pp. 41–45. https://doi.org/10.18653/v1/W17-0805.
30. K. J. Alsem, S. Brakman, L. Hoogduin, and G. Kuper. "The impact of newspapers on consumer confidence: does spin bias exist?" In: *Applied Economics* 40.5 (2008). Number: 5 Publisher: Routledge _eprint: https://doi.org/10.1080/00036840600707100, pp. 531–539. https://doi.org/10.1080/00036840600707100.
31. K. Alzhrani. "Ideology Detection of Personalized Political News Coverage: A New Dataset". In: *Proceedings of the 2020 the 4th International Conference on Compute and Data Analysis*. event-place: Silicon Valley CA USA. ACM, 2020, pp. 10–15. https://doi.org/10.1145/3388142.3388149.
32. J. An, M. Cha, K. Gummadi, J. Crowcroft, and D. Quercia. "Visualizing media bias through twitter". In: *Proceedings of the International AAAI Conference on Web and Social Media* 6.2 (2021-08), pp. 2–5. https://doi.org/10.1609/icwsm.v6i2.14343.
33. Ananya, N. Parthasarthi, and S. Singh. "GenderQuant: Quantifying Mention-Level Genderedness". In: *Proceedings of the 2019 Conference of the North*. event-place: Minneapolis, Minnesota. Association for Computational Linguistics, 2019, pp. 2959–2969. https://doi.org/10.18653/v1/N19-1303.
34. T. Anthonio and L. Kloppenburg. "Team Kermit-the-frog at SemEval-2019 Task 4: Bias Detection Through Sentiment Analysis and Simple Linguistic Features". In: *Proceedings of the 13th International Workshop on Semantic Evaluation*. event-place: Minneapolis, Minnesota, USA. Association for Computational Linguistics, 2019, pp. 1016–1020. https://doi.org/10.18653/v1/S19-2177.
35. J.-Y. Antoine, J. Villaneau, and A. Lefeuvre. "Weighted Krippendorff's alpha is a more reliable metrics for multi-coders ordinal annotations: experimental studies on emotion, opinion and coreference annotation". In: *Proc. Ann. Meeting Association for Computational Linguistics (ACL)*. Gothenburg, Sweden: Association for Computational Linguistics, 2014-04, pp. 550–559. https://doi.org/10.3115/v1/E14-1058.
36. A. Ardèvol-Abreu and H. Gil de Zúñiga. "Effects of Editorial Media Bias Perception and Media Trust on the Use of Traditional, Citizen, and Social Media News". In: *Journalism & Mass Communication Quarterly* 94.3 (2017-09), pp. 703–724. ISSN: 1077-6990. https://doi.org/10.1177/1077699016654684.
37. V. Aribandi, Y. Tay, T. Schuster, et al. "ExT5: Towards Extreme Multi-Task Scaling for Transfer Learning". In: *CoRR* abs/2111.10952 (2021). URL: https://arxiv.org/abs/2111.10952.

38. F. T. Asr, M. Mazraeh, A. Lopes, et al. "The Gender Gap Tracker: Using Natural Language Processing to measure gender bias in media". In: *PloS one* 16.1 (2021-01-29). Number: 1 Publisher: Public Library of Science, e0245533-e0245533. ISSN: 1932-6203. https://doi.org/10.1371/journal.pone.0245533.
39. L. Atkins. Skewed: *A Critical Thinker's Guide to Media Bias*. G—Reference, Information and Interdisciplinary Subjects Series. Prometheus Books, 2016. ISBN: 978-1-63388-165-5. URL: https://books.google.de/books?id=otd5jgEACAAJ.
40. S. Baccianella, A. Esuli, and F. Sebastiani. "SentiWordNet 3.0: An Enhanced Lexical Resource for Sentiment Analysis and Opinion Mining". In: *LREC*. 2010.
41. M. Bachl. "Selective Exposure and Hostile Media Perceptions During Election Campaigns". In: *International Journal of Public Opinion Research* 29.2 (2017-06), pp. 352–362. ISSN: 0954-2892. https://doi.org/10.1093/ijpor/edw014.
42. P. Badjatiya, M. Gupta, and V. Varma. "Stereotypical Bias Removal for Hate Speech Detection Task using Knowledge-based Generalizations". In: *The World Wide Web Conference on—WWW '19*. event-place: San Francisco, CA, USA. ACM Press, 2019, pp. 49–59. https://doi.org/10.1145/3308558.3313504.
43. C. A. Bail, L. P. Argyle, T. W. Brown, et al. "Exposure to opposing views on social media can increase political polarization". In: *Proceedings of the National Academy of Sciences* 115.37 (2018). Publisher: National Academy of Sciences _eprint: https://www.pnas.org/content/115/37/9216.full.pdf, pp. 9216–9221. ISSN: 0027–8424. https://doi.org/10.1073/pnas.1804840115.
44. A. Bakarov. "A Survey of Word Embeddings Evaluation Methods". In: *arXiv:1801.09536 [cs]* (2018-01). URL: http://arxiv.org/abs/1801.09536 (visited on 2020-09-19).
45. R. Baly, G. Karadzhov, J. An, et al. "What Was Written vs. Who Read It: News Media Profiling Using Text Analysis and Social Media Context". In: *Proc. Ann. Meeting Association for Computational Linguistics (ACL)*. event-place: Online. Online: Association for Computational Linguistics, 2020-07, pp. 3364–3374. https://doi.org/10.18653/v1/2020.acl-main.308.
46. R. Baly, G. Karadzhov, A. Saleh, J. Glass, and P. Nakov. *Multi-Task Ordinal Regression for Jointly Predicting the Trustworthiness and the Leading Political Ideology of News Media*. Issue: arXiv:1904.00542. 2019-03-31. URL: http://arxiv.org/abs/1904.00542 (visited on 2022-08-01).
47. R. Baly, G. D. S. Martino, J. Glass, and P. Nakov. *We Can Detect Your Bias: Predicting the Political Ideology of News Articles*. Issue: arXiv:2010.05338. 2020-10-11. URL: http://arxiv.org/abs/2010.05338 (visited on 2022-08-01).
48. J. A. Banas and S. A. Rains. "A meta-analysis of research on inoculation theory". In: *Communication Monographs* 77.3 (2010). Number: 3, pp. 281–311. URL: https://doi.org/10.1080/03637751003758193.
49. M. Barnidge, A. C. Gunther, J. Kim, et al. "Politically Motivated Selective Exposure and Perceived Media Bias". In: *Communication Research* 47.1 (2020-02), pp. 82–103. ISSN: 0093-6502, 1552-3810. https://doi.org/10.1177/0093650217713066.
50. J. J. Bartko. "The Intraclass Correlation Coefficient as a Measure of Reliability". In: *Psychological Reports* 19.1 (1966). _eprint: https://doi.org/10.2466/pr0.1966.19.1.3, pp. 3–11. https://doi.org/10.2466/pr0.1966.19.1.3.
51. M. E. Basiri, S. Nemati, M. Abdar, E. Cambria, and U. R. Acharya. "ABCDM: An Attention-based Bidirectional CNN-RNN Deep Model for sentiment analysis". In: *Fu-*

ture *Generation Computer Systems* 115 (2021), pp. 279–294. ISSN: 0167-739X. https://doi.org/10.1016/j.future.2020.08.005.
52. C. Batailler, S. M. Brannon, P. E. Teas, and B. Gawronski. "A Signal Detection Approach to Understanding the Identification of Fake News". In: *Perspectives on Psychological Science* 17.1 (2022). _eprint: https://doi.org/10.1177/1745691620986135, pp. 78–98. URL: https://doi.org/10.1177/1745691620986135.
53. L. Bauer, K. Gopalakrishnan, S. Gella, Y. Liu, M. Bansal, and D. Hakkani-Tur. "Analyzing the Limits of Self-Supervision in Handling Bias in Language". In: (2021). https://doi.org/10.48550/ARXIV.2112.08637.
54. M. A. Baum and P. Gussin. "In the Eye of the Beholder: How Information Shortcuts Shape Individual Perceptions of Bias in the Media". In: *Quarterly Journal of Political Science* 3.1 (2008). Number: 1, pp. 1–31. ISSN: 1554-0626. https://doi.org/10.1561/100.00007010.
55. E. Baumer, E. Elovic, Y. Qin, F. Polletta, and G. Gay. "Testing and Comparing Computational Approaches for Identifying the Language of Framing in Political News". In: *Proc. Ann. Meeting Association for Computational Linguistics (ACL)*. Denver, Colorado: Association for Computational Linguistics, 2015, pp. 1472–1482. https://doi.org/10.3115/v1/N15-1171.
56. I. Beltagy, K. Lo, and A. Cohan. "SciBERT: A Pretrained Language Model for Scientific Text". In: *Proceedings of the 2019 Conference on Empirical Methods in Natural Language Processing and the 9th International Joint Conference on Natural Language Processing (EMNLP-IJCNLP)*. Hong Kong, China: Association for Computational Linguistics, 2019-11, pp. 3615–3620. https://doi.org/10.18653/v1/D19-1371.
57. C. Bentéjac, A. Csörgo, and G. Martínez-Muñoz. "A Comparative Analysis of XGBoost". In: *ArXiv:abs/1911.01914* (2019).
58. J. Berant, I. Dagan, M. Adler, and J. Goldberger. "Efficient Tree-based Approximation for Entailment Graph Learning". In: *Proc. Ann. Meeting Association for Computational Linguistics (ACL)*. Jeju Island, Korea: Association for Computational Linguistics, 2012-07, pp. 117–125. URL: https://aclanthology.org/P12-1013.
59. E. van den Berg and K. Markert. "Context in Informational Bias Detection". In: *Proceedings of the 28th International Conference on Computational Linguistics*. eventplace: Barcelona, Spain (Online). International Committee on Computational Linguistics, 2020, pp. 6315–6326. https://doi.org/10.18653/v1/2020.colingmain.556.
60. C. J. Beukeboom and C. Burgers. "Linguistic Bias". In: *Oxford Research Encyclopedia of Communication*. Oxford University Press, 2017-07. ISBN: 978-0-19-022861-3. https://doi.org/10.1093/acrefore/9780190228613.013.439.
61. R. Bhardwaj, N. Majumder, and S. Poria. "Investigating Gender Bias in BERT". In: *Cognitive Computation* 13.4 (2021-07). Number: 4, pp. 1008–1018. ISSN: 1866-9956, 1866-9964. https://doi.org/10.1007/s12559-021-09881-2.
62. M. M. Bhuiyan, C. A. Bautista Isaza, T. Mitra, and S. W. Lee. "OtherTube: Facilitating Content Discovery and Reflection by Exchanging YouTube Recommendations with Strangers". In: *Proceedings of the 2022 CHI Conference on Human Factors in Computing Systems*. event-place: New Orleans, LA, USA. New York, NY, USA: Association for Computing Machinery, 2022. https://doi.org/10.1145/3491102.3502028.
63. J. J. Bird, A. Ekárt, and D. R. Faria. "Chatbot Interaction with Artificial Intelligence: human data augmentation with T5 and language transformer ensemble for text classification". In: *Journal of Ambient Intelligence and Humanized Computing* (2021). https://doi.org/10.1007/s12652-021-03439-8.

Bibliography of Publications, Submissions & Talks 219

64. S. Bird, E. Loper, and E. Klein. *Natural Language Processing with Python*. O'Reilly Media Inc, 2009.
65. C. Blackledge and A. Atapour-Abarghouei. "Transforming fake news: Robust generalisable news classification using transformers". In: *2021 IEEE international conference on big data (big data)*. Los Alamitos, CA, USA: IEEE Computer Society, 2021-12, pp. 3960–3968. https://doi.org/10.1109/BigData52589.2021.9671970.
66. C. Blackledge and A. Atapour-Abarghouei. *Transforming fake news: Robust generalisable news classification using transformers*. 2021.
67. F. Blanco. "Cognitive Bias". In: *Encyclopedia of Animal Cognition and Behavior*. Cham: Springer International Publishing, 2017, pp. 1–7. ISBN: 978-3-319-47829-6. https://doi.org/10.1007/978-3-319-47829-6_1244-1.
68. C. A. Bodian, G. Freedman, S. Hossain, J. B. Eisenkraft, and Y. Beilin. "The Visual Analog Scale for Pain: Clinical Significance in Postoperative Patients". In: *Anesthesiology* 95.6 (2001), pp. 1356–1361. ISSN: 0003-3022. https://doi.org/10.1097/00000542-200112000-00013.
69. T. Bolsen and J. N. Druckman. "Counteracting the politicization of science". In: *Journal of Communication* 65.5 (2015). Publisher: Oxford University Press, pp. 745–769. https://doi.org/10.1111/jcom.12171.
70. H. Boomgaarden, M. Boukes, and A. Iorgoveanu. "Image Versus Text: How Newspaper Reports Affect Evaluations of Political Candidates". In: *International Journal of Communication* 10.0 (2016). ISSN: 1932-8036. URL: https://ijoc.org/index.php/ijoc/article/view/4250.
71. S. Bordia and S. R. Bowman. "Identifying and Reducing Gender Bias in Word-Level Language Models". In: *Proceedings of the 2019 Conference of the North*. event-place: Minneapolis, Minnesota. Association for Computational Linguistics, 2019, pp. 7–15. https://doi.org/10.18653/v1/N19-3002.
72. D. Bourgeois, J. Rappaz, and K. Aberer. "Selection Bias in News Coverage: Learning it, Fighting it". In: *Companion of the The Web Conference 2018 on The Web Conference 2018—WWW '18*. event-place: Lyon, France. ACM Press, 2018, pp. 535–543. https://doi.org/10.1145/3184558.3188724.
73. S. R. Bowman, G. Angeli, C. Potts, and C. D. Manning. "A large annotated corpus for learning natural language inference". *In: Proceedings of the 2015 Conference on Empirical Methods in Natural Language Processing*. Lisbon, Portugal: Association for Computational Linguistics, 2015-09, pp. 632–642. https://doi.org/10.18653/v1/D15-1075.
74. P. Branco, Torgo, and R. Ribeiro. "A Survey of Predictive Modelling under Imbalanced Distributions". In: *ArXiv:1505.1658* (2015). Number: 01658.
75. N. M. Brashier, G. Pennycook, A. J. Berinsky, and D. G. Rand. "Timing matters when correcting fake news". In: *Proceedings of the National Academy of Sciences* 118.5 (2021-02-02), e2020043118. ISSN: 0027-8424, 1091-6490. https://doi.org/10.1073/pnas.2020043118.
76. P. Brereton, B. A. Kitchenham, D. Budgen, M. Turner, and M. Khalil. "Lessons from applying the systematic literature review process within the software engineering domain". In: *Journal of Systems and Software* 80.4 (2007). Number: 4, pp. 571–583. ISSN: 0164-1212. https://doi.org/10.1016/j.jss.2006.07.009.
77. M. W. Browne. "Cross-Validation Methods". In: *J. Math. Psychol.* 44.1 (2000-03). Number: 1 Place: USA Publisher: Academic Press, Inc., pp. 108–132. ISSN: 0022-2496. https://doi.org/10.1006/jmps.1999.1279.

78. E. Bruni, N. K. Tran, and M. Baroni. "Multimodal Distributional Semantics". In: *Journal of Artificial Intelligence Research* (2014), pp. 1–47.
79. C. Budak, S. Goel, and J. M. Rao. "Fair and Balanced? Quantifying Media Bias through Crowdsourced Content Analysis". In: *Public Opinion Quarterly* 80 (S1 2016-04). Number: S1, pp. 250–271. ISSN: 0033-362X. https://doi.org/10.1093/poq/nfw007.
80. D. G. Bystrom, T. A. Robertson, and M. C. Banwart. "Framing the Fight: An Analysis of Media Coverage of Female and Male Candidates in Primary Races for Governor and U.S. Senate in 2000". In: *American Behavioral Scientist* 44.12 (2001-08). Number: 12, pp. 1999–2013. ISSN: 0002-7642, 1552-3381. https://doi.org/10.1177/00027640121958456.
81. A. Caliskan, J. J. Bryson, and A. Narayanan. "Semantics derived automatically from language corpora contain human-like biases". In: *Science* 356.6334 (2017-04). Number: 6334, pp. 183–186. ISSN: 0036-8075, 1095-9203. https://doi.org/10.1126/science.aal4230.
82. J. Camacho-Collados and M. T. Pilehvar. "On the Role of Text Preprocessing in Neural Network Architectures: An Evaluation Study on Text Categorization and Sentiment Analysis". In: *BlackboxNLP@EMNLP*. 2018. https://doi.org/10.18653/v1/W18-5406.
83. L. Castro, D. N. Hopmann, and L. Nir. "Whose media are hostile? The spillover effect of interpersonal discussions on media bias perceptions". In: *Communications* 46.4 (2021). Number: 4 Publisher: De Gruyter, pp. 540–563. https://doi.org/10.1515/commun-2019-0140.
84. T. Castro Ferreira, C. Gardent, N. Ilinykh, et al. "The 2020 Bilingual, Bi-Directional WebNLG+ Shared Task Overview and Evaluation Results (WebNLG+ 2020)". In: *Proceedings of the 3rd WebNLG Workshop on Natural Language Generation from the Semantic Web (WebNLG+ 2020)*. Dublin, Ireland (Virtual): Association for Computational Linguistics, 2020, pp. 55–76.
85. D. Cer, M. Diab, E. Agirre, I. Lopez-Gazpio, and L. Specia. "SemEval-2017 Task 1: Semantic Textual Similarity Multilingual and Crosslingual Focused Evaluation". In: *Proceedings of the 11th International Workshop on Semantic Evaluation (SemEval-2017)*. Vancouver, Canada: Association for Computational Linguistics, 2017, pp. 1–14. https://doi.org/10.18653/v1/S17-2001.
86. T. Chakrabarty, C. Hidey, and S. Muresan. *ENTRUST: Argument Reframing with Language Models and Entailment*. arXiv: 2103.06758, 2021.
87. A. Chakraborty, B. Paranjape, S. Kakar, and N. Ganguly. "Stop Clickbait: Detecting and preventing clickbaits in online news media". In: *2016 IEEE/ACM International Conference on Advances in Social Networks Analysis and Mining (ASONAM*. 2016, pp. 9–16.
88. J. Chapman and N. Nuttall. *Journalism Today: A Themed History*. John Wiley & Sons, 2011.
89. S. Chen, Y. Zhang, and Q. Yang. "Multi-Task Learning in Natural Language Processing: An Overview". In: arXiv:2109.09138 *[cs]* (2021-09). URL: http://arxiv.org/abs/2109.09138 (visited on 2022-01-14).
90. T. Chen and C. Guestrin. "XGBoost: A Scalable Tree Boosting System". In: *Proceedings of the 22nd ACM SIGKDD International Conference on Knowledge Discovery and Data Mining*. 2016.
91. W.-F. Chen, K. Al Khatib, B. Stein, and H. Wachsmuth. "Detecting Media Bias in News Articles using Gaussian Bias Distributions". In: *Proc. Ann. Meeting Association for*

Computational Linguistics (ACL). event-place: Online. Association for Computational Linguistics, 2020, pp. 4290–4300. https://doi.org/10.18653/v1/2020.findings-emnlp.383.
92. W.-F. Chen, K. Al Khatib, H. Wachsmuth, and B. Stein. "Analyzing Political Bias and Unfairness in News Articles at Different Levels of Granularity". In: *Proceedings of the Fourth Workshop on Natural Language Processing and Computational Social Science*. Online: Association for Computational Linguistics, 2020, pp. 149–154. https://doi.org/10.18653/v1/2020.nlpcss-1.16.
93. W. Chen, D. Pacheco, K.-C. Yang, and F. Menczer. "Neutral bots probe political bias on social media". In: *Nature Communications* 12.1 (2021-12). Number: 1, p. 5580. ISSN: 2041-1723. https://doi.org/10.1038/s41467-021-25738-6.
94. X. Chen, J. Cheng, J. Liu, et al. "A Survey of Multi-label Text Classification Based on Deep Learning". In: *Artificial Intelligence and Security*. Cham: Springer International Publishing, 2022, pp. 443–456. https://doi.org/10.1007/978-3-031-06794-5_36.
95. L. Chiazor, G. d. Mel, G. White, G. Newton, J. Pavitt, and R. J. Tomsett. "An Automated Framework to Identify and Eliminate Systemic Racial Bias in the Media". In: *CEUR Workshop Proceedings* 2812 (2021-02), pp. 32–36. ISSN: 1613-0073. URL: http://ceur-ws.org/Vol-2812/.
96. U. Chitra and C. Musco. "Analyzing the Impact of Filter Bubbles on Social Network Polarization". In: *Proceedings of the 13th International Conference on Web Search and Data Mining*. event-place: Houston TX USA. ACM, 2020-01-20, pp. 115–123. https://doi.org/10.1145/3336191.3371825.
97. K. Clark, M.-T. Luong, Q. V. Le, and C. D. Manning. "ELECTRA: Pre-training Text Encoders as Discriminators Rather Than Generators". In: *ICLR*. 2020. URL: https://openreview.net/pdf?id=r1xMH1BtvB.
98. J. Cook, S. Lewandowsky, and U. K. H. Ecker. "Neutralizing misinformation through inoculation: Exposing misleading argumentation techniques reduces their influence". In: *PLOS ONE* 12.5 (2017-05). Publisher: Public Library of Science, pp. 1–21. https://doi.org/10.1371/journal.pone.0175799.
99. L. A. Cornelissen, L. I. Daly, Q. Sinandile, H. de Lange, and R. J. Barnett. "A Computational Analysis of News Media Bias: A South African Case Study". In: *Proceedings of the South African Institute of Computer Scientists and Information Technologists 2019 on ZZZ—SAICSIT '19*. event-place: Skukuza, South Africa. ACM Press, 2019, pp. 1–10. https://doi.org/10.1145/3351108.3351134.
100. J. Correll, S. J. Spencer, and M. P. Zanna. "An affirmed self and an open mind: Self-affirmation and sensitivity to argument strength". In: *Journal of Experimental Social Psychology* 40.3 (2004), pp. 350–356. ISSN: 0022-1031. https://doi.org/10.1016/j.jesp.2003.07.001.
101. M. R. Costa-jussà. "An analysis of gender bias studies in natural language processing". In: *Nature Machine Intelligence* 1.11 (2019-11-01). Number: 11, pp. 495–496. ISSN: 2522-5839. https://doi.org/10.1038/s42256-019-0105-5.
102. A. F. Cruz, G. Rocha, and H. L. Cardoso. "On document representations for detection of biased news articles". In: *Proceedings of the 35th Annual ACM Symposium on Applied Computing*. event-place: Brno Czech Republic. ACM, 2020-03-30, pp. 892–899. https://doi.org/10.1145/3341105.3374025.
103. R. Cuéllar-Hidalgo, J. d. J. Guerrero-Zambrano, D. Forest, G. Reyes-Salgado, and J.-M. Torres-Moreno. *LUC at ComMA-2021 Shared Task: Multilingual Gender Biased and Communal Language Identification without using linguistic features*. Issue:

arXiv:2112.10189. 2021-12-19. URL: http://arxiv.org/abs/2112.10189 (visited on 2022-08-01).
104. D. D'Alessio. "An Experimental Examination of Readers' Perceptions of Media Bias". In: *Journalism & Mass Communication Quarterly* 80.2 (2003-06), pp. 282–294. ISSN: 1077-6990. https://doi.org/10.1177/107769900308000204.
105. D. D'Alessio and M. Allen. "Media Bias in Presidential Elections: A Meta-Analysis". In: *Journal of Communication* 50.4 (2000-12-01), pp. 133–156. ISSN: 0021-9916, 1460-2466. https://doi.org/10.1111/j.1460-2466.2000.tb02866.x.
106. S. D'Alonzo and M. Tegmark. *Machine-Learning media bias*. Issue: arXiv:2109.00024. 2021-08-31. URL: http://arxiv.org/abs/2109.00024 (visited on 2022-08-01).
107. J. Dacon and H. Liu. "Does Gender Matter in the News? Detecting and Examining Gender Bias in News Articles". In: *Companion Proceedings of the Web Conference 2021*. New York, NY, USA: Association for Computing Machinery, 2021-06, pp. 385–392. https://doi.org/10.1145/3442442.3452325.
108. A. Dallmann, F. Lemmerich, D. Zoller, and A. Hotho. "Media Bias in German Online Newspapers". In: *Proceedings of the 26th ACM Conference on Hypertext and Social Media*. event-place: Guzelyurt, Northern Cyprus. New York, NY, USA: Association for Computing Machinery, 2015, pp. 133–137. https://doi.org/10.1145/2700171.2791057.
109. R. J. Dalton, P. A. Beck, and R. Huckfeldt. "Partisan Cues and the Media: Information Flows in the 1992 Presidential Election". In: *The American Political Science Review* 92.1 (1998). Number: 1 Publisher: [American Political Science Association, Cambridge University Press], pp. 111–126. ISSN: 0003-0554. URL: http://www.jstor.org/stable/2585932.
110. T. Davidson, D. Warmsley, M. Macy, and I. Weber. "Automated hate speech detection and the problem of offensive language". In: *Proceedings of the International AAAI Conference on Web and Social Media*. Vol. 11. Issue: 1. 2017.
111. G. De Arruda, N. Roman, and A. Monteiro. "Analysing Bias in Political News". In: *JUCS—Journal of Universal Computer Science* 26.2 (2020-02-28), pp. 173–199. ISSN: 0948-6968, 0948-695X. https://doi.org/10.3897/jucs.2020.011.
112. P.-T. De Boer, D. P. Kroese, S. Mannor, and R. Y. Rubinstein. "A tutorial on the cross-entropy method". In: *Annals of operations research* 134.1 (2005). Publisher: Springer, pp. 19–67.
113. A. Dechêne, C. Stahl, J. Hansen, and M. Wanke. "The truth about the truth: A meta-analytic review of the truth effect". In: *Personality and Social Psychology Review* 14.2 (2010). Number: 2 Publisher: Sage Publications Sage CA: Los Angeles, CA, pp. 238–257. https://doi.org/10.1177/1088868309352251.
114. S. DellaVigna and E. Kaplan. "The Fox News Effect: Media Bias and Voting*". In: *The Quarterly Journal of Economics* 122.3 (2007-08), pp. 1187–1234. ISSN: 0033-5533. https://doi.org/10.1162/qjec.122.3.1187.
115. J. Deriu, A. Lucchi, V. De Luca, et al. "Leveraging large amounts of weakly supervised data for multilanguage sentiment classification". In: *Proceedings of the 26th international conference on world wide web*. Number of pages: 8 Place: Perth, Australia. Republic and Canton of Geneva, CHE: International World Wide Web Conferences Steering Committee, 2017, pp. 1045–1052. https://doi.org/10.1145/3038912.3052611.
116. J. Devlin, M.-W. Chang, K. Lee, and K. Toutanova. "BERT: Pre-training of Deep Bidirectional Transformers for Language Understanding". In: *Proc. Ann. Meeting Association for Computational Linguistics (ACL)*. Minneapolis, Minnesota: Association for

Computational Linguistics, 2019-06, pp. 4171–4186. https://doi.org/10.18653/v1/N19-1423.
117. T. G. Dietterich. "Approximate statistical tests for comparing supervised classification learning algorithms". In: *Neural computation* 10.7 (1998). Publisher: MIT Press One Rogers Street, Cambridge, MA 02142-1209, USA journals-info ..., pp. 1895–1923. https://doi.org/10.1162/089976698300017197.
118. T. V. Dijk. "Chapter 12 Discourse and Racism". In: 2007.
119. Y. Dinkov, A. Ali, I. Koychev, and P. Nakov. "Predicting the Leading Political Ideology of YouTube Channels Using Acoustic, Textual, and Metadata Information". In: *Interspeech 2019*. ISCA, 2019-09-15, pp. 501–505. https://doi.org/10.21437/Interspeech.2019-2965.
120. C. Dong, Y. Li, H. Gong, et al. "A Survey of Natural Language Generation". In: *ACM Comput. Surv.* (2022-07). Place: New York, NY, USA Publisher: Association for Computing Machinery. ISSN: 0360-0300. https://doi.org/10.1145/3554727.
121. M. Dragojevic, A. Sink, and D. Mastro. "Evidence of Linguistic Intergroup Bias in U.S. Print News Coverage of Immigration". In: *Journal of Language and Social Psychology* 36.4 (2017-09). Number: 4 _eprint: https://doi.org/10.1177/0261927X16666884, pp. 462–472. ISSN: 0261-927X, 1552-6526. https://doi.org/10.1177/0261927X16666884.
122. R. Dror, G. Baumer, S. Shlomov, and R. Reichart. "The Hitchhiker's Guide to Testing Statistical Significance in Natural Language Processing". In: *Proc. Ann. Meeting Association for Computational Linguistics (ACL)*. Melbourne, Australia: Association for Computational Linguistics, 2018-07, pp. 1383–1392. https://doi.org/10.18653/v1/P18-1128.
123. J. N. Druckman, M. S. Levendusky, and A. McLain. "No Need to Watch: How the Effects of Partisan Media Can Spread via Interpersonal Discussions". In: *American Journal of Political Science* 62.1 (2018). Number: 1 Publisher: [Midwest Political Science Association, Wiley], pp. 99–112. ISSN: 0092-5853. https://doi.org/10.7910/DVN/TJKIWN.
124. J. N. Druckman and M. Parkin. "The Impact of Media Bias: How Editorial Slant Affects Voters". In: *The Journal of Politics* 67.4 (2005-11). Number: 4 Publisher: Cambridge University Press New York, USA, pp. 1030–1049. ISSN: 0022-3816. https://doi.org/10.1111/j.1468-2508.2005.00349.x.
125. Z. Drus and H. Khalid. "Sentiment Analysis in Social Media and Its Application: Systematic Literature Review". In: *Procedia Computer Science* 161 (2019), pp. 707–714. ISSN: 1877-0509. https://doi.org/10.1016/j.procs.2019.11.174.
126. A. D. Dubey. *Twitter Sentiment Analysis during COVID-19 Outbreak*. 2020-04. https://doi.org/10.2139/ssrn.3572023.
127. E. Dubois and G. Blank. "The echo chamber is overstated: the moderating effect of political interest and diverse media". In: *Information, Communication & Society* 21.5 (2018). Number: 5 Publisher: Routledge _eprint: https://doi.org/10.1080/1369118X.2018.1428656, pp. 729–745. ISSN: 1369-118X, 1468-4462. https://doi.org/10.1080/1369118X.2018.1428656.
128. S. Dvir-Gvirsman, R. K. Garrett, and Y. Tsfati. "Why Do Partisan Audiences Participate? Perceived Public Opinion as the Mediating Mechanism". In: *Communication Research* 45.1 (2018-02). Number: 1 _eprint: https://doi.org/10.1177/0093650215593145, pp. 112–136. ISSN: 0093-6502, 1552-3810. https://doi.org/10.1177/0093650215593145.
129. U. K. H. Ecker, S. Lewandowsky, and D. T. W. Tang. "Explicit warnings reduce but do not eliminate the continued influence of misinformation". In: *Memory & Cognition* 38.8 (2010), pp. 1087–1100. URL: https://doi.org/10.3758/MC.38.8.1087.

130. J. L. Egelhofer and S. Lecheler. "Fake news as a two-dimensional phenomenon: a framework and research agenda". In: *Annals of the International Communication Association* 43.2 (2019-04-03). Number: 2 Publisher: Routledge _eprint: https://doi.org/10.1080/23808985.2019.1602782, pp. 97–116. ISSN: 2380-8985, 2380-8977. https://doi.org/10.1080/23808985.2019.1602782.
131. C. Enders and D. Tofighi. "Centering Predictor Variables in Cross-Sectional Multilevel Models: A New Look at An Old Issue". In: *Psychological Methods* 12.2 (2007), pp. 121–138. https://doi.org/10.1037/1082-989X.12.2.121.
132. K. C. Enevoldsen and L. Hansen. "Analysing Political Biases in Danish Newspapers Using Sentiment Analysis". In: *Journal of Language Works – Sprogvidenskabeligt Studentertidsskrift* 2.2 (2017-07), pp. 87–98. URL: https://tidsskrift.dk/lwo/article/view/96014.
133. R. M. Entman. "Media framing biases and political power: Explaining slant in news of Campaign 2008". In: *Journalism* 11.4 (2010). Number: 4 Publisher: Sage Publications Sage UK: London, England, pp. 389–408.
134. R. M. Entman. "Framing Bias: Media in the Distribution of Power". In: *Journal of Communication* 57.1 (2007-02). Number: 1 _eprint: https://academic.oup.com/joc/article-pdf/57/1/163/22326478/jjnlcom0163.pdf, pp. 163–173. ISSN: 0021-9916. https://doi.org/10.1111/j.1460-2466.2006.00336.x.
135. W. P. Eveland and D. V. Shah. "The Impact of Individual and Interpersonal Factors on Perceived News Media Bias". In: *Political Psychology* 24.1 (2003), pp. 101–117. ISSN: 1467-9221. https://doi.org/10.1111/0162-895X.00318.
136. L. R. Fabrigar and D. T. Wegener. *Exploratory factor analysis*. Oxford University Press, 2011.
137. J. C. Fagan. "An Evidence-Based Review of Academic Web Search Engines, 2014-2016: Implications for Librarians' Practice and Research Agenda". In: *Information Technology and Libraries* 36.2 (2017-06). Number: 2, pp. 7–47. https://doi.org/10.6017/ital.v36i2.9718.
138. T. Fagni and S. Cresci. "Fine-grained Prediction of Political Leaning on Social Media with Unsupervised Deep Learning". In: *Journal of Artificial Intelligence Research* 73 (2022-02-18), pp. 633–672. ISSN: 1076-9757. https://doi.org/10.1613/jair.1.13112.
139. L. Fan, M. White, E. Sharma, et al. *In Plain Sight: Media Bias Through the Lens of Factual Reporting*. 2019-09. https://doi.org/10.48550/arXiv.1909.02670.
140. E. Fast, T. Vachovsky, and M. S. Bernstein. "Shirtless and dangerous: Quantifying linguistic signals of gender bias in an online fiction writing community". In: *Tenth International AAAI Conference on Web and Social Media*. 2016.
141. L. Feldman. "Partisan differences in opinionated news perceptions: A test of the hostile media effect". In: *Political Behavior* 33.3 (2011-09), pp. 407–432. ISSN: 0190-9320. https://doi.org/10.1007/s11109-010-9139-4.
142. C. Fellbaum. *WordNet: An electronic lexical database and some of its applications*. 1998.
143. X. Ferrer, T. van Nuenen, J. M. Such, and N. Criado. "Discovering and Categorising Language Biases in Reddit". In: (2020). https://doi.org/10.48550/ARXIV.2008.02754.
144. L. Festinger. *A theory of cognitive dissonance*. Vol. 2. Stanford University Press, 1957.
145. A. Field and Y. Tsvetkov. "Unsupervised Discovery of Implicit Gender Bias". In: *Proceedings of the 2020 Conference on Empirical Methods in Natural Language Processing (EMNLP)*. event-place: Online. Association for Computational Linguistics, 2020, pp. 596–608. https://doi.org/10.18653/v1/2020.emnlp-main.44.

146. L. Finkelstein, E. Gabrilovich, Y. Matias, et al. "Placing Search in Context: The Concept Revisited". In: *Proceedings of the 10th international conference on World Wide Web* (2001), pp. 406–414.
147. P. Fischer, E. Jonas, D. Frey, and S. Schulz-Hardt. "Selective exposure to information: the impact of information limits". In: *European Journal of Social Psychology* 35.4 (2005-07). Number: 4 _eprint: https://onlinelibrary.wiley.com/doi/pdf/10.1002/ejsp.264, pp. 469–492. ISSN: 0046-2772, 1099-0992. https://doi.org/10.1002/ejsp.264.
148. J. L. Fleiss. "Measuring nominal scale agreement among many raters." In: *Psychological bulletin* 76.5 (1971). Number: 5 Publisher: American Psychological Association, p. 378. https://doi.org/10.1037/h0031619.
149. T. Foltýnek, N. Meuschke, and B. Gipp. "Academic Plagiarism Detection: A Systematic Literature Review". In: *ACM Computing Surveys* 52.6 (2020-11-30), pp. 1–42. ISSN: 0360-0300, 1557-7341. https://doi.org/10.1145/3345317.
150. J. Galtung and M. H. Ruge. "The Structure of Foreign News: The Presentation of the Congo, Cuba and Cyprus Crises in Four Norwegian Newspapers". In: *Journal of Peace Research* 2.1 (1965). Number: 1 _eprint: https://doi.org/10.1177/002234336500200104, pp. 64–90. https://doi.org/10.1177/002234336500200104.
151. R. R. R. Gangula, S. R. Duggenpudi, and R. Mamidi. "Detecting Political Bias in News Articles Using Headline Attention". In: *Proceedings of the 2019 ACL Workshop BlackboxNLP: Analyzing and Interpreting Neural Networks for NLP*. Florence, Italy: Association for Computational Linguistics, 2019-08, pp. 77–84. https://doi.org/10.18653/v1/W19-4809.
152. S. Ganguly, J. Kulshrestha, J. An, and H. Kwak. "Empirical Evaluation of Three Common Assumptions in Building Political Media Bias Datasets". In: *Proceedings of the International AAAI Conference on Web and Social Media*. Vol. 14. AAAI Press, 2020, pp. 939–943. URL: https://ojs.aaai.org/index.php/ICWSM/article/view/7362.
153. Z. Gao, A. Feng, X. Song, and X. Wu. "Target-Dependent Sentiment Classification With BERT". In: *IEEE Access* 7 (2019), pp. 154290–154299. ISSN: 2169-3536. https://doi.org/10.1109/ACCESS.2019.2946594.
154. R. K. Garrett. "Politically Motivated Reinforcement Seeking: Reframing the Selective Exposure Debate". In: *Journal of Communication* 59.4 (2009-12), pp. 676–699. ISSN: 0021-9916. https://doi.org/10.1111/j.1460-2466.2009.01452.x.
155. B. Gawronski. "Partisan bias in the identification of fake news". In: *Trends in Cognitive Sciences* 25.9 (2021-09), pp. 723–724. ISSN: 1364-6613. https://doi.org/10.1016/j.tics.2021.05.001.
156. S. Gearhart, A. Moe, and B. Zhang. "Hostile media bias on social media: Testing the effect of user comments on perceptions of news bias and credibility". In: *Human Behavior and Emerging Technologies* 2 (2020-03). https://doi.org/10.1002/hbe2.185.
157. GERALD KI WEI HUANG and JUN CHOI LEE. "Hyperpartisan News Classification with ELMo and Bias Feature". In: *Journal of Information Science and Engineering* 37.5 (2021-09-01). Number: 5. https://doi.org/10.6688/JISE.202109_37(5).0013.
158. A. S. Gerber, D. Karlan, and D. Bergan. "Does the Media Matter? A Field Experiment Measuring the Effect of Newspapers on Voting Behavior and Political Opinions". In: *American Economic Journal: Applied Economics* 1.2 (2009-04). Number: 2, pp. 35–52. ISSN: 1945-7782, 1945-7790. https://doi.org/10.1257/app.1.2.35.
159. S. Gershon. "When Race, Gender, and the Media Intersect: Campaign News Coverage of Minority Congresswomen". In: *Journal of Women, Politics & Policy* 33.2

(2012-05). Number: 2 Publisher: Routledge _eprint: https://doi.org/10.1080/1554477X. 2012.667743, pp. 105–125. ISSN: 1554-477X, 1554-4788. https://doi.org/10.1080/1554477X.2012.667743.

160. B. T. Gervais. "Incivility Online: Affective and Behavioral Reactions to Uncivil Political Posts in a Webbased Experiment". In: *Journal of Information Technology & Politics* 12.2 (2015-04-03). Number: 2 Publisher: Routledge _eprint: https://doi.org/10.1080/19331681.2014.997416, pp. 167–185. ISSN: 1933-1681, 1933-169X. https://doi.org/10.1080/19331681.2014.997416.

161. H. Giese, H. Neth, M. Moussa"ıd, C. Betsch, and W. Gaissmaier. "The echo in fluvaccination echo chambers: Selective attention trumps social influence". In: *Vaccine* 38.8 (2020), pp. 2070–2076. URL: https://doi.org/10.1016/j.vaccine.2019.11.038.

162. C. J. Glynn and M. E. Huge. "How Pervasive Are Perceptions of Bias? Exploring Judgments of Media Bias in Financial News". In: *International Journal of Public Opinion Research* 26.4 (2014). Number: 4 _eprint: https://academic.oup.com/ijpor/article-pdf/26/4/543/2191013/edu004.pdf, pp. 543–553. ISSN: 0954-2892. https://doi.org/10.1093/ijpor/edu004.

163. A. Go, R. Bhayani, and L. Huang. "Twitter sentiment classification using distant supervision". In: *CS224N project report, Stanford* 1.12 (2009). Number: 12, p. 2009.

164. S. K. Goldman and D. C. Mutz. "The Friendly Media Phenomenon: A Cross-National Analysis of Cross-Cutting Exposure". In: *Political Communication* 28.1 (2011-02-09). Number: 1 Publisher: Routledge _eprint: https://doi.org/10.1080/10584609.2010.544280, pp. 42–66. ISSN: 1058-4609, 1091-7675. https://doi.org/10.1080/10584609.2010.544280.

165. J. Graham, J. Haidt, and B. Nosek. "Liberals and conservatives rely on different sets of moral foundations". In: *Journal of personality and social psychology* 96 (2009), pp. 1029–1046. https://doi.org/10.1037/a0015141.

166. M. C. Green and T. C. Brock. "Persuasiveness of Narratives". In: *Persuasion: Psychological insights and perspectives, 2nd ed.* Thousand Oaks, CA, US: Sage Publications, Inc, 2005, pp. 117–142. ISBN: 978-0-7619-2809-6.

167. S. Greene and P. Resnik. "More than Words: Syntactic Packaging and Implicit Sentiment". In: *Proc. Ann. Meeting Association for Computational Linguistics (ACL)*. Boulder, Colorado: Association for Computational Linguistics, 2009-06, pp. 503–511. URL: https://aclanthology.org/N09-1057.

168. A. Gron. *Hands-On Machine Learning with Scikit-Learn and TensorFlow: Concepts, Tools, and Techniques to Build Intelligent Systems*. O'Reilly Media, Inc, 2017.

169. T. Groseclose and J. Milyo. "A social-science perspective on media bias". In: *Critical Review* 17.3 (2005). Publisher: Routledge _eprint: https://doi.org/10.1080/08913810508443641, pp. 305–314. https://doi.org/10.1080/08913810508443641.

170. S. S. Guimarães, J. C. S. Reis, M. Vasconcelos, and F. Benevenuto. "Characterizing political bias and comments associated with news on Brazilian Facebook". In: *Social Network Analysis and Mining* 11.1 (2021-12), p. 94. ISSN: 1869-5450, 1869-5469. https://doi.org/10.1007/s13278-021-00806-3.

171. A. C. Gunther and J. L. Liebhart. "Broad Reach or Biased Source? Decomposing the Hostile Media Effect". In: *Journal of Communication* 56.3 (2006). _eprint: https://onlinelibrary.wiley.com/doi/pdf/10.1111/j.1460-2466.2006.00295.x, pp. 449–466. https://doi.org/10.1111/j.1460-2466.2006.00295.x.

172. A. C. Gunther, B. McLaughlin, M. R. Gotlieb, and D. Wise. "Who Says What to Whom: Content Versus Source in the Hostile Media Effect". In: *International Journal of Public Opinion Research* 29.3 (2017-09), pp. 363–383. ISSN: 0954-2892. https://doi.org/10.1093/ijpor/edw009.
173. A. C. Gunther, N. Miller, and J. L. Liebhart. "Assimilation and Contrast in a Test of the Hostile Media Effect". In: *Communication Research* 36.6 (2009). Number: 6, pp. 747–764. ISSN: 0093-6502. https://doi.org/10.1177/0093650209346804.
174. A. C. Gunther and K. Schmitt. "Mapping Boundaries of the Hostile Media Effect". In: *Journal of Communication* 54.1 (2004), pp. 55–70. ISSN: 1460-2466. https://doi.org/10.1111/j.1460-2466.2004.tb02613.x.
175. S. Guo and K. Q. Zhu. *Modeling Multi-level Context for Informational Bias Detection by Contrastive Learning and Sentential Graph Network*. Issue: arXiv:2201.10376. 2022-01-25. URL: http://arxiv.org/abs/2201.10376 (visited on 2022-08-01).
176. S. Gupta, S. Bolden, J. Kachhadia, A. Korsunska, and J. Stromer-Galley. "PoliBERT: Classifying political social media messages with BERT". In: *Social, Cultural and Behavioral Modeling (SBP-BRIMS 2020)* conference. Washington, DC. 2020.
177. S. Gururangan, A. Marasovic, S. Swayamdipta, et al. "Don't Stop Pretraining: Adapt Language Models to Domains and Tasks". In: *CoRR* abs/2004.10964 (2020). URL: https://arxiv.org/abs/2004.10964.
178. J. Haidt and J. Craig. "Intuitive ethics: how innately prepared intuitions generate culturally variable virtues". In: *Daedalus* 133.4 (2004-10), pp. 55–66. ISSN: 0011-5266. https://doi.org/10.1162/0011526042365555.
179. J. Hainmueller, D. Hopkins, and T. Yamamoto. "Causal inference in conjoint analysis: Understanding multidimensional choices via stated preference experiments". In: *Political Analysis* 22 (2014), pp. 1–30. https://doi.org/10.1093/pan/mpt024.
180. F. Hamborg and K. Donnay. "NewsMTSC: A Dataset for (Multi-)Target-dependent Sentiment Classification in Political News Articles". In: *Proc. Ann. Meeting Association for Computational Linguistics (ACL)*. event-place: Online. Online: Association for Computational Linguistics, 2021, pp. 1663–1675. https://doi.org/10.18653/v1/2021.eacl-main.142.
181. F. Hamborg, K. Donnay, and B. Gipp. "Automated identification of media bias in news articles: an interdisciplinary literature review". In: *International Journal on Digital Libraries* 20.4 (2019-12-01), pp. 391–415. ISSN: 1432-5012, 1432-1300. https://doi.org/10.1007/s00799-018-0261-y.
182. J. Han, Y. Lee, J. Lee, and M. Cha. "The Fallacy of Echo Chambers: Analyzing the Political Slants of User-Generated News Comments in Korean Media". In: *Proceedings of the 5th Workshop on Noisy User-generated Text (W-NUT 2019)*. event-place: Hong Kong, China. Association for Computational Linguistics, 2019, pp. 370–374. https://doi.org/10.18653/v1/D19-5548.
183. X. Han and J. Eisenstein. "Unsupervised Domain Adaptation of Contextualized Embeddings for Sequence Labeling". In: *Proceedings of the 2019 Conference on Empirical Methods in Natural Language Processing and the 9th International Joint Conference on Natural Language Processing (EMNLP-IJCNLP)*. Hong Kong, China: Association for Computational Linguistics, 2019-11, pp. 4238–4248. https://doi.org/10.18653/v1/D19-1433.
184. A. Hannousse. "Searching relevant papers for software engineering secondary studies: Semantic Scholar coverage and identification role". In: *IET Software* 15.1 (2021).

Number: 1 _eprint: https://ietresearch.onlinelibrary.wiley.com/doi/pdf/10.1049/sfw2. 12011, pp. 126–146. https://doi.org/10.1049/sfw2.12011.
185. G. J. Hansen and H. Kim. "Is the Media Biased Against Me? A Meta-Analysis of the Hostile Media Effect Research". In: *Communication Research Reports* 28.2 (2011-04), pp. 169–179. ISSN: 0882-4096. https://doi.org/10.1080/08824096.2011.565280.
186. T. Hartmann and M. Tanis. "Examining the hostile media effect as an intergroup phenomenon: The role of ingroup identification and status". In: *Journal of Communication* 63.3 (2013). Number: 3 Publisher: Oxford University Press, pp. 535–555. https://doi.org/10.1111/jcom.12031.
187. Z. He, B. P. Majumder, and J. McAuley. "Detect and Perturb: Neutral Rewriting of Biased and Sensitive Text via Gradient-based Decoding". In: *Proc. Ann. Meeting Association for Computational Linguistics (ACL)*. event-place: Punta Cana, Dominican Republic. Association for Computational Linguistics, 2021, pp. 4173–4181. https://doi.org/10.18653/v1/2021.findings-emnlp.352.
188. A. Hernández and J. M. Amigó. "Attention Mechanisms and Their Applications to Complex Systems". In: *Entropy* 23.3 (2021). Number: 3. ISSN: 1099-4300. https://doi.org/10.3390/e23030283.
189. G. E. Hinton, S. Osindero, and Y.-W. Teh. "A Fast Learning Algorithm for Deep Belief Nets". In: *Neural Computation* 18.7 (2006-07), pp. 1527–1554. ISSN: 0899-7667, 1530-888X. https://doi.org/10.1162/neco.2006.18.7.1527.
190. J. D. Hmielowski, S. Staggs, M. J. Hutchens, and M. A. Beam. "Talking Politics: The Relationship Between Supportive and Opposing Discussion With Partisan Media Credibility and Use". In: *Communication Research* 49.2 (2022-03). Number: 2 _eprint: https://doi.org/10.1177/0093650220915041, pp. 221–244. ISSN: 0093-6502, 1552-3810. https://doi.org/10.1177/0093650220915041.
191. S. S. Ho, A. R. Binder, A. B. Becker, et al. "The Role of Perceptions of Media Bias in General and Issue-Specific Political Participation". In: *Mass Communication and Society* 14.3 (2011), pp. 343–374. ISSN: 1520-5436. https://doi.org/10.1080/15205436.2010.491933.
192. V. Hofmann, X. Dong, J. B. Pierrehumbert, and H. Schütze. *Modeling Ideological Salience and Framing in Polarized Online Groups with Graph Neural Networks and Structured Sparsity*. 2021. https://doi.org/10.48550/ARXIV2104.08829.
193. M. Hönnibal and I. Montani. *spaCy 2: Natural language understanding with Bloom embeddings, convolutional neural networks and incremental parsing*. 2017.
194. J. B. Hooper. "On Assertive Predicates". In: *Syntax and Semantics Vol. 4*. Leiden, Niederlande: Brill, 1975, pp. 91–124. ISBN: 978-90-04-36882-8. https://doi.org/10.1163/9789004368828_005.
195. J. B. Houston, G. J. Hansen, and G. S. Nisbett. "Influence of User Comments on Perceptions of Media Bias and Third-Person Effect in Online News". In: *Electronic News* 5.2 (2011-06), pp. 79–92. ISSN: 1931-2431. https://doi.org/10.1177/1931243111407618.
196. J. Howard and S. Ruder. "Universal Language Model Fine-tuning for Text Classification". In: *Proc. Ann. Meeting Association for Computational Linguistics (ACL)*. Melbourne, Australia: Association for Computational Linguistics, 2018-07, pp. 328–339. https://doi.org/10.18653/v1/P18-1031.
197. J. J. Hox. *Multilevel analysis: Techniques and applications*. 2nd ed. New York, NY: Routledge, 2010. 1–392. ISBN: 978-1-84872-845-5.

198. M. Hu and B. Liu. "Mining and Summarizing Customer Reviews". In: *Proceedings of the Tenth ACM SIGKDD International Conference on Knowledge Discovery and Data Mining*. event-place: Seattle, WA, USA. New York, NY, USA: Association for Computing Machinery, 2004, pp. 168–177. https://doi.org/10.1145/1014052.1014073.
199. C. Hube. "Methods for detecting and mitigating linguistic bias in text corpora". In: (2020). https://doi.org/10.15488/9873.
200. C. Hube and B. Fetahu. "Detecting Biased Statements in Wikipedia". In: *Companion of the The Web Conference 2018 on The Web Conference 2018—WWW '18*. Lyon, France: ACM Press, 2018, pp. 1779–1786. https://doi.org/10.1145/3184558.3191640.
201. C. Hube and B. Fetahu. "Neural Based Statement Classification for Biased Language". In: *Proceedings of the Twelfth ACM International Conference on Web Search and Data Mining*. event-place: Melbourne VIC, Australia. New York, NY, USA: Association for Computing Machinery, 2019-01-30, pp. 195–203. https://doi.org/10.1145/3289600.3291018.
202. P.-L. Huguet Cabot, D. Abadi, A. Fischer, and E. Shutova. "Us vs. Them: A Dataset of Populist Attitudes, News Bias and Emotions". In: *Proc. Ann. Meeting Association for Computational Linguistics (ACL)*. event-place: Online. Association for Computational Linguistics, 2021, pp. 1921–1945. https://doi.org/10.18653/v1/2021.eacl-main.165.
203. H. Huo and M. Iwaihara. "Utilizing BERT Pretrained Models with Various Fine-Tune Methods for Subjectivity Detection". In: *Asia-Pacific Web (APWeb) and Web-Age Information Management (WAIM) Joint International Conference on Web and Big Data*. Springer, 2020, pp. 270–284.
204. K. Hyland. *Metadiscourse: Exploring Interaction in Writing*. 1st. Bloomsbury Classics in Linguistics. London: Bloomsbury Academic, 2018. ISBN: 978-1-350-06361-7. https://doi.org/10.5040/9781350063617.
205. R. Ibrahim and M. O. Shafiq. "Explainable Convolutional Neural Networks: A Taxonomy, Review, and Future Directions". In: *ACM Comput. Surv.* (2022-08). Place: New York, NY, USA Publisher: Association for Computing Machinery. ISSN: 0360-0300. https://doi.org/10.1145/3563691.
206. K. Ikeda, G. Hattori, C. Ono, H. Asoh, and T. Higashino. "Twitter user profiling based on text and community mining for market analysis". In: *Knowledge-Based Systems* 51 (2013), pp. 35–47. ISSN: 0950-7051. https://doi.org/10.1016/j.knosys.2013.06.020.
207. S. Jia, T. Lansdall-Welfare, and N. Cristianini. "Measuring Gender Bias in News Images". In: *Proceedings of the 24th International Conference on World Wide Web*. event-place: Florence, Italy. New York, NY, USA: Association for Computing Machinery, 2015, pp. 893–898. https://doi.org/10.1145/2740908.2742007.
208. Y. Jiang, J. Petrak, X. Song, K. Bontcheva, and D. Maynard. "Team Bertha von Suttner at SemEval-2019 Task 4: Hyperpartisan News Detection using ELMo Sentence Representation Convolutional Network". In: *Proceedings of the 13th International Workshop on Semantic Evaluation*. Minneapolis, Minnesota, USA: Association for Computational Linguistics, 2019-06, pp. 840–844. https://doi.org/10.18653/v1/S19-2146.
209. Y. Jiang, Y. Wang, X. Song, and D. Maynard. "Comparing Topic-Aware Neural Networks for Bias Detection of News". In: *ECAI 2020—24th European Conference on Artificial Intelligence, 29 August-8 September 2020, Santiago de Compostela, Spain, August 29—September 8, 2020 - Including 10th Conference on Prestigious Applications of Artificial Intelligence (PAIS 2020)*. Vol. 325. IOS Press, 2020, pp. 2054–2061. https://doi.org/10.3233/FAIA200327.

210. Z. Jianqiang and G. Xiaolin. "Comparison Research on Text Pre-processing Methods on Twitter Sentiment Analysis". In: *IEEE Access* 5 (2017), pp. 2870–2879. https://doi.org/10.1109/ACCESS.2017.2672677.
211. V. Jóhannsdóttir and Þ. Einarsdóttir. "Gender Bias in the Media: The Case of Iceland". In: *Stjórnmál og Stjórnsýsla* 11.2 (2015). Number: 2 ISBN: 16706803, pp. 207–230. URL: https://www.proquest.com/scholarly-journals/gender-bias-media-case-iceland/docview/1752862035/se-2?accountid=11898.
212. D. M. Kahan. "Misconceptions, misinformation, and the logic of identity-protective cognition". In: (2017). Publisher: Cultural Cognition Project Working Paper Series. https://doi.org/10.2139/SSRN.2973067.
213. L. Kameswari and R. Mamidi. "Towards Quantifying Magnitude of Political Bias in News Articles Using a Novel Annotation Schema". In: *Proceedings of the International Conference on Recent Advances in Natural Language Processing (RANLP 2021), Held Online, 1–3 September, 2021*. INCOMA Ltd., 2021, pp. 671–678. URL: https://aclanthology.org/2021.ranlp-1.76.
214. L. Kameswari, D. Sravani, and R. Mamidi. "Enhancing Bias Detection in Political News Using Pragmatic Presupposition". In: *Proceedings of the Eighth International Workshop on Natural Language Processing for Social Media*. event-place: Online. Online: Association for Computational Linguistics, 2020, pp. 1–6. https://doi.org/10.18653/v1/2020.socialnlp-1.1.
215. L. Karttunen. "Implicative Verbs". In: *Language* 47.2 (1971). Number: 2 Publisher: Linguistic Society of America, pp. 340–358. ISSN: 0097-8507. URL: http://www.jstor.org/stable/412084.
216. G. Karypis and V. Kumar. "METIS—unstructured graph partitioning and sparse matrix ordering system, version 2.0. Technical report". In: *University of Minnesota, Department of Computer Science, Minneapolis*, MN 55455 (1995-01).
217. A. Kastenmüller, T. Greitemeyer, E. Jonas, P. Fischer, and D. Frey. "Selective exposure: The impact of collectivism and individualism". In: *British Journal of Social Psychology* 49.4 (2010), pp. 745–763. URL: https://doi.org/10.1348/014466609X478988.
218. A. Kause, T. Townsend, and W. Gaissmaier. "Framing Climate Uncertainty: Frame Choices Reveal and Influence Climate Change Beliefs". In: *Weather, Climate, and Society* 11.1 (2019). Number: 1, pp. 199–215. ISSN: 1948-8327. https://doi.org/10.1175/WCAS-D-18-0023.1
219. C. Kelly. "Political identity and perceived intragroup homogeneity". In: *British Journal of Social Psychology* 28.3 (1989). Publisher: Wiley Online Library, pp. 239–250. https://doi.org/10.1111/j.2044-8309.1989.tb00866.x.
220. J. Kiesel, M. Mestre, R. Shukla, et al. "SemEval-2019 Task 4: Hyperpartisan News Detection". In: *Proceedings of the 13th International Workshop on Semantic Evaluation. Minneapolis, Minnesota, USA: Association for Computational Linguistics*, 2019-06, pp. 829–839. https://doi.org/10.18653/v1/S19-2145.
221. K. Kim. "The Hostile Media Phenomenon: Testing the Effect of News Framing on Perceptions of Media Bias". In: *Communication Research Reports* 36.1 (2019-01-01). Number: 1 Publisher: Routledge _eprint: https://doi.org/10.1080/08824096.2018.1555659, pp. 35–44. ISSN: 0882-4096, 1746-4099. https://doi.org/10.1080/08824096.2018.1555659.
222. M. Kim. "Partisans and Controversial News Online: Comparing Perceptions of Bias and Credibility in News Content From Blogs and Mainstream Media". In: *Mass Com-*

munication and Society 18.1 (2015-01), pp. 17–36. ISSN: 1520-5436. https://doi.org/10.1080/15205436.2013.877486.
223. M. Kim. "The Role of Partisan Sources and Audiences' Involvement in Bias Perceptions of Controversial News". In: *Media Psychology* 19.2 (2016-04), pp. 203–223. ISSN: 1521-3269. https://doi.org/10.1080/15213269.2014.1002941.
224. D. P. Kingma and J. Ba. "Adam: A Method for Stochastic Optimization". In: *arXiv e-prints* (2014-12). _eprint: 1412.6980, arXiv:1412.6980.
225. W. Kinnally. "Reactance and the hostile media effect: Placing the effect within the theory". PhD thesis. ProQuest Information & Learning, 2009.
226. B. Kitchenham. *Procedures for Performing Systematic Reviews*. Keele University. Technical Report TR/SE- 0401. Department of Computer Science, Keele University, UK, 2004.
227. J. T. Klapper. "The effects of mass communication." In: (1960). Publisher: Free Press.
228. J. Kleinnijenhuis, T. Hartmann, M. Tanis, and A. M. J. van Hoof. "Hostile Media Perceptions of Friendly Media Do Reinforce Partisanship". In: *Communication Research* 47.2 (2020-03). Number: 2 _eprint: https://doi.org/10.1177/0093650219836059, pp. 276–298. ISSN: 0093-6502, 1552-3810. https://doi.org/10.1177/0093650219836059.
229. S. Knobloch-Westerwick and Jingbo Meng. "Looking the Other Way: Selective Exposure to Attitude-Consistent and Counterattitudinal Political Information". In: *Communication Research* 36.3 (2009-06). Number: 3 _eprint: https://doi.org/10.1177/0093650209333030, pp. 426–448. ISSN: 0093-6502, 1552-3810. https://doi.org/10.1177/0093650209333030.
230. K. Krippendorff. "Computing Krippendorff's alpha-reliability". In: *Departmental Papers (ASC); University of Pennsylvania (2011)*. URL: https://repository.upenn.edu/cgi/viewcontent.cgi?article=1043&context=asc_papers.
231. M. Krommyda, A. Rigos, K. Bouklas, and A. Amditis. "An Experimental Analysis of Data Annotation Methodologies for Emotion Detection in Short Text Posted on Social Media". In: *Informatics* 8.1 (2021-03-12), p. 19. ISSN: 2227-9709. https://doi.org/10.3390/informatics8010019.
232. A. C. Kroon, D. Trilling, and T. Raats. "Guilty by Association: Using Word Embeddings to Measure Ethnic Stereotypes in News Coverage". In: *Journalism & Mass Communication Quarterly* 98.2 (2021-06). Number: 2, pp. 451–477. ISSN: 1077-6990, 2161-430X. https://doi.org/10.1177/1077699020932304.
233. R. Kühne, C. Poggiolini, and W. Wirth. "The differential effects of related and unrelated emotions on judgments about media messages". In: *Communications* 0.0 (2020-04-04). ISSN: 1613-4087, 0341-2059. https://doi.org/10.1515/commun-2020-2091.
234. R. Kumar, S. Ratan, S. Singh, et al. "ComMA@ICON: *Multilingual gender biased and communal language identification task at ICON-2021*". In: *Proceedings of the 18th international conference on natural language processing: Shared task on multilingual gender biased and communal language identification*. NIT Silchar: NLP Association of India (NLPAI), 2021-12, pp. 1–12. URL: https://aclanthology.org/2021.iconmultigen.1.
235. H. Kwak, J. An, and Y.-Y. Ahn. "A Systematic Media Frame Analysis of 1.5 Million New York Times Articles from 2000 to 2017". In: *12th ACM Conference on Web Science*. Southampton United Kingdom: ACM, 2020-07, pp. 305–314. https://doi.org/10.1145/3394231.3397921.
236. H. Kwak, J. An, E. Jing, and Y.-Y. Ahn. "FrameAxis: characterizing microframe bias and intensity with word embedding". In: PeerJ Computer Science 7 (2021). Publisher: PeerJ, e644. https://doi.org/10.7717/peerj-cs.644.

237. J. R. Landis and G. G. Koch. "The Measurement of Observer Agreement for Categorical Data". In: *Biometrics* 33.1 (1977). Number: 1 Publisher: [Wiley, International Biometric Society], pp. 159–174. ISSN: 0006-341X. URL: http://www.jstor.org/stable/2529310.
238. K. Lazaridou, A. Löser, M. Mestre, and F. Naumann. "Discovering Biased News Articles Leveraging Multiple Human Annotations". In: *Proceedings of The 12th Language Resources and Evaluation Conference, LREC 2020, Marseille, France, May 11-16, 2020*. Marseille, France: European Language Resources Association, 2020, pp. 1268–1277. URL: https://aclanthology.org/2020.lrec-1.159/.
239. P. F. Lazarsfeld, B. Berelson, and H. Gaudet. *The people's choice*. Columbia University Press, 1944. URL: https://doi.org/10.1007/978-3-531-90400-9_62.
240. S. Leavy. *Uncovering Gender Bias in Media Coverage of Politicians with Machine Learning*. Issue: arXiv:2005.07734. 2020-05-15. URL: http://arxiv.org/abs/2005.07734 (visited on 2022-08-01).
241. S. Leavy. "Uncovering gender bias in newspaper coverage of Irish politicians using machine learning". In: *Digital Scholarship in the Humanities* 34.1 (2018-06), pp. 48–63. ISSN: 2055-7671. https://doi.org/10.1093/llc/fqy005.
242. E.-J. Lee. "That's Not the Way It Is: How User-Generated Comments on the News Affect Perceived Media Bias". In: *Journal of Computer-Mediated Communication* 18.1 (2012-10). Number: 1 _eprint: https://academic.oup.com/jcmc/article-pdf/18/1/32/19492053/jjcmcom0032.pdf, pp. 32–45. ISSN: 1083-6101. https://doi.org/10.1111/j.1083-6101.2012.01597.x.
243. J. Lee, W. Yoon, S. Kim, et al. "BioBERT: a pre-trained biomedical language representation model for biomedical text mining". In: *Bioinformatics* 36.4 (2020). Publisher: Oxford University Press, pp. 1234–1240.
244. N. Lee, Y. Bang, A. Madotto, and P. Fung. "Mitigating Media Bias through Neutral Article Generation". In: *CoRR* abs/2104.00336 (2021). _eprint: 2104.00336. https://doi.org/10.48550/arXiv.2104.00336.
245. N. Lee, Y. Bang, T. Yu, A. Madotto, and P. Fung. NeuS: *Neutral Multi-News Summarization for Mitigating Framing Bias*. Issue: arXiv:2204.04902. 2022-05-03. URL: http://arxiv.org/abs/2204.04902 (visited on 2022-08-01).
246. T.-T. Lee. "The Liberal Media Myth Revisited: An Examination of Factors Influencing Perceptions of Media Bias". In: *Journal of Broadcasting & Electronic Media* 49.1 (2005), pp. 43–64. ISSN: 0883-8151. https://doi.org/10.1207/s15506878jobem4901_4.
247. K. Lerman, X. Yan, and X. Z. Wu. "The "majority illusion" in social networks". In: *PLoS ONE* 11.2 (2016). Number: 2 _eprint: 1506.03022, pp. 1–13. ISSN: 1932-6203. https://doi.org/10.1371/journal.pone.0147617.
248. M. Levendusky and N. Malhotra. "Does Media Coverage of Partisan Polarization Affect Political Attitudes?" In: *Political Communication* 33.2 (2016), pp. 283–301. https://doi.org/10.1080/10584609.2015.1038455.
249. B. Levin. *English verb classes and alternations: a preliminary investigation*. London;Chicago: University of Chicago Press, 1993. ISBN: 0-226-47533-6.
250. O. Levy, Y. Goldberg, and I. Dagan. "Improving Distributional Similarity with Lessons Learned from Word Embeddings". In: *Transactions of the Association for Computational Linguistics* 3 (2015), pp. 211–225. ISSN: 2307-387X. https://doi.org/10.1162/tacl_a_00134.
251. M. Lewis, Y. Liu, N. Goyal, et al. "BART: Denoising Sequence-to-Sequence Pretraining for Natural Language Generation, Translation, and Comprehension". In: *Proc.*

Ann. Meeting Association for Computational Linguistics (ACL). Online: Association for Computational Linguistics, 2020-07, pp. 7871–7880. https://doi.org/10.18653/v1/2020.acl-main.703.
252. C. Li and D. Goldwasser. "Encoding Social Information with Graph Convolutional Networks forPolitical Perspective Detection in News Media". In: *Proc. Ann. Meeting Association for Computational Linguistics (ACL)*. Florence, Italy: Association for Computational Linguistics, 2019-07, pp. 2594–2604. https://doi.org/10.18653/v1/P19-1247.
253. C. Li and D. Goldwasser. "Using Social and Linguistic Information to Adapt Pretrained Representations for Political Perspective Identification". In: *Proc. Ann. Meeting Association for Computational Linguistics (ACL)*. event-place: Online. Association for Computational Linguistics, 2021, pp. 4569–4579. https://doi.org/10.18653/v1/2021.findings-acl.401.
254. S. Lim, A. Jatowt, and M. Yoshikawa. *DEIM Forum 2018 C1-3 Towards Bias Inducing Word Detection by Linguistic Cue Analysis in News Articles*. 2018.
255. S. Lim, A. Jatowt, and M. Yoshikawa. "Towards Bias Inducing Word Detection by Linguistic Cue Analysis in News". In: *DEIM Forum 2018* C1-3 (2018).
256. S. Lim, A. Jatowt, M. Färber, and M. Yoshikawa. "Annotating and Analyzing Biased Sentences in News Articles using Crowdsourcing". In: *Proceedings of the Twelfth Language Resources and Evaluation Conference*. Marseille, France: European Language Resources Association, 2020-05, pp. 1478–1484. ISBN: 979-10-95546-34-4. URL: https://aclanthology.org/2020.lrec-1.184.
257. S. Lim, A. Jatowt, and M. Yoshikawa. "Understanding Characteristics of Biased Sentences in News Articles". In: *CIKM Workshops*. 2018.
258. T. Lin, Y. Wang, X. Liu, and X. Qiu. "A Survey of Transformers". In: *CoRR* abs/2106.04554 (2021). URL: https://arxiv.org/abs/2106.04554.
259. S. van der Linden, A. Leiserowitz, S. Rosenthal, and E. Maibach. "Inoculating the public against misinformation about climate change". In: *Global Challenges (Hoboken, NJ)* 1.2 (2017). URL: https://doi.org/10.1002/gch2.201600008.
260. S. van der Linden. "Misinformation: susceptibility, spread, and interventions to immunize the public". In: *Nature Medicine* 28.3 (2022-03-01). Number: 3 ISBN: 1546-170X, pp. 460–467. https://doi.org/10.1038/s41591-022-01713-6.
261. R. Liu, C. Jia, and S. Vosoughi. "A Transformer-based Framework for Neutralizing and Reversing the Political Polarity of News Articles". In: *Proceedings of the ACM on Human-Computer Interaction* 5 (CSCW1 2021-04-13), pp. 1–26. ISSN: 2573-0142. https://doi.org/10.1145/3449139.
262. R. Liu, C. Jia, J. Wei, G. Xu, L. Wang, and S. Vosoughi. "Mitigating Political Bias in Language Models Through Reinforced Calibration". In: *ArXiv:abs/2104.14795* (2021).
263. R. Liu, L. Wang, C. Jia, and S. Vosoughi. "Political Depolarization of News Articles Using Attribute-aware Word Embeddings". In: (2021). https://doi.org/10.48550/ARXIV.2101.01391.
264. X. Liu, P. He, W. Chen, and J. Gao. "Multi-Task Deep Neural Networks for Natural Language Understanding". In: *Proc. Ann. Meeting Association for Computational Linguistics (ACL)*. Florence, Italy: Association for Computational Linguistics, 2019-07, pp. 4487–4496. URL: https://www.aclweb.org/anthology/P19-1441.
265. Y. Liu, M. Ott, N. Goyal, et al. "RoBERTa: A Robustly Optimized BERT Pretraining Approach". In: *CoRR* abs/1907.11692 (2019). _eprint: 1907.11692. URL: http://arxiv.org/abs/1907.11692.

266. Y. Liu, X. F. Zhang, D. Wegsman, N. Beauchamp, and L. Wang. "POLITICS: Pretraining with Same-story Article Comparison for Ideology Prediction and Stance Detection". In: (2022). https://doi.org/10.48550/ARXIV.2205.00619.
267. M. Lovett, S. Bajaba, M. Lovett, and M. Simmering. "Data quality from crowdsourced surveys: A mixed method inquiry into perceptions of amazon's mechanical turk masters". In: *Applied Psychology* 67 (2018), pp. 339–366. https://doi.org/10.1111/apps.12124.
268. A. L. Maas, R. E. Daly, P. T. Pham, D. Huang, A. Y. Ng, and C. Potts. "Learning Word Vectors for Sentiment Analysis". In: *Proc. Ann. Meeting Association for Computational Linguistics (ACL)*. Portland, Oregon, USA: Association for Computational Linguistics, 2011-06, pp. 142–150. URL: https://www.aclweb.org/anthology/P11-1015.
269. A. Maass, D. Salvi, L. Arcuri, and G. Semin. "Language use in intergroup contexts: The linguistic intergroup bias". In: *Journal of Personality and Social Psychology* 67.6 (1989). Number: 6, pp. 981–993. https://doi.org/10.1037/0022-3514.57.6.981.
270. K. Madanagopal and J. Caverlee. "Towards Ongoing Detection of Linguistic Bias on Wikipedia". In: *Companion Proceedings of the Web Conference 2021*. event-place: Ljubljana Slovenia. ACM, 2021-04-19, pp. 629–631. https://doi.org/10.1145/3442442.3452353.
271. T. Manzini, L. Yao Chong, A. W. Black, and Y. Tsvetkov. "Black is to Criminal as Caucasian is to Police: Detecting and Removing Multiclass Bias in Word Embeddings". In: *Proc. Ann. Meeting Association for Computational Linguistics (ACL)*. Minneapolis, Minnesota: Association for Computational Linguistics, 2019-06, pp. 615–621. https://doi.org/10.18653/v1/N19-1062.
272. G. Marks and N. Miller. "Ten years of research on the false-consensus effect: An empirical and theoretical review." In: Psychological Bulletin 102.1 (1987). Number: 1, pp. 72–90. ISSN: 0033-2909. https://doi.org/10.1037//0033-2909.102.1.72.
273. B. Mathew, P. Saha, S. M. Yimam, C. Biemann, P. Goyal, and A. Mukherjee. "HateXplain: A Benchmark Dataset for Explainable Hate Speech Detection". In: (2020). https://doi.org/10.48550/ARXIV.2012.10289.
274. B. Mathew, P. Saha, S. M. Yimam, C. Biemann, P. Goyal, and A. Mukherjee. "HateXplain: A Benchmark Dataset for Explainable Hate Speech Detection". In: *Proceedings of the AAAI Conference on Artificial Intelligence* 35.17 (2021-05), pp. 14867–14875. ISSN: 2374-3468, 2159-5399. https://doi.org/10.1609/aaai.v35i17.17745.
275. J. Matthes, J. Knoll, and C. v. Sikorski. "The "Spiral of Silence" Revisited: A Meta-Analysis on the Relationship Between Perceptions of Opinion Support and Political Opinion Expression". In: *Communication Research* 45.1 (2018). Number: 1 _eprint: https://doi.org/10.1177/0093650217745429, pp. 3–33. https://doi.org/10.1177/0093650217745429.
276. J. Matthes, D. Schmuck, and C. von Sikorski. "In the Eye of the Beholder: A Case for the Visual Hostile Media Phenomenon". In: *Communication Research* (2021-06-01), p. 009365022110185. ISSN: 0093-6502, 1552-3810. https://doi.org/10.1177/00936502211018596.
277. K. J. McCarthy and W. Dolfsma. "Neutral media? Evidence of media bias and its economic impact". In: *Review of Social Economy* 72.1 (2014-02), pp. 42–54. ISSN: 0034-6764. https://doi.org/10.1080/00346764.2013.806110.
278. R. McChesney. "The Problem of the Media: U.S". In: *Communication Politics in the Twenty-First Century*. New York: Monthly Review Press, 2004.

279. W. J. McGuire. "The effectiveness of supportive and refutational defenses in immunizing and restoring beliefs against persuasion". In: *Sociometry* 24.2 (1961), pp. 184–197.
280. L. McInnes, J. Healy, N. Saul, and L. Großberger. "UMAP: Uniform manifold approximation and projection". In: *Journal of Open Source Software* 3.29 (2018). Publisher: The Open Journal, p. 861. https://doi.org/10.21105/joss.00861.
281. B. W. McKeever, D. Riffe, and F. D. Carpentier. "Perceived Hostile Media Bias, Presumed Media Influence, and Opinions About Immigrants and Immigration". In: *Southern Communication Journal* 77.5 (2012-11), pp. 420–437. ISSN: 1041-794X. https://doi.org/10.1080/1041794X.2012.691602.
282. "Mean Squared Error". In: *Encyclopedia of Machine Learning*. Boston, MA: Springer US, 2010, pp. 653–653. ISBN: 978-0-387-30164-8. https://doi.org/10.1007/978-0-387-30164-8_528.
283. *Media Bias Rating Methods | How AllSides Rates Media Bias*. 2021-03-30. URL: https://www.allsides.com/media-bias/media-bias-rating-methods (visited on 2021-03-30).
284. J. Mendelsohn, Y. Tsvetkov, and D. Jurafsky. "A Framework for the Computational Linguistic Analysis of Dehumanization". In: *Frontiers in Artificial Intelligence* 3 (2020-08), p. 55. ISSN: 2624-8212. https://doi.org/10.3389/frai.2020.00055.
285. J. Meneghello, N. Thompson, K. Lee, K. W. Wong, and B. Abu-Salih. "Unlocking Social Media and User Generated Content as a Data Source for Knowledge Management". In: *International Journal of Knowledge Management (IJKM)* 16.1 (2020), pp. 101–122. https://doi.org/10.4018/IJKM.2020010105.
286. T. Mikolov, K. Chen, G. Corrado, and J. Dean. "Efficient Estimation of Word Representations in Vector Space". In: *arXiv:1301.3781 [cs]* (2013-09-06). URL: http://arxiv.org/abs/1301.3781 (visited on 2020-09-19).
287. G. A. Miller. "WordNet: A Lexical Database for English". In: *Communications of the ACM* 38.11 (1995). Number: 11, pp. 39–41. https://doi.org/10.1145/219717.219748.
288. S.-J. Min and J. C. Feaster. "Missing Children in National News Coverage: Racial and Gender Representations of Missing Children Cases". In: *Communication Research Reports* 27.3 (2010-08), pp. 207–216. ISSN: 0882-4096. https://doi.org/10.1080/08824091003776289.
289. J. Mitrović. "Crowdsourcing and its application". In: *INFOtheca* 14.1 (2013-06). Number: 1, Volume XIV, pp. 37–46.
290. M. Mladenović, J. Mitrović, and C. Krstev. "A language-independent model for introducing a new semantic relation between adjectives and nouns in a WordNet". In: *Proceedings of 8th Global WordNet Conference*. 2016, pp. 218–225. ISBN: 978-606-714-239-6.
291. N. Mokhberian, A. Abeliuk, P. Cummings, and K. Lerman. "Moral Framing and Ideological Bias of News". In: vol. 12467. 2020, pp. 206–219. https://doi.org/10.1007/978-3-030-60975-7_16.
292. M. Mozafari, R. Farahbakhsh, and N. Crespi. "Hate speech detection and racial bias mitigation in social media based on BERT model". In: *PLOS ONE* 15.8 (2020-08-27). Number: 8 Publisher: Public Library of Science San Francisco, CA USA, e0237861. ISSN: 1932-6203. https://doi.org/10.1371/journal.pone.0237861.
293. N. S. Mullah and W. M. N. W. Zainon. "Advances in machine learning algorithms for hate speech detection in social media: A review". In: *IEEE access : practical innovations, open solutions* 9 (2021), pp. 88364–88376. https://doi.org/10.1109/ACCESS.2021.3089515.

294. S. Mullainathan and A. Shleifer. *Media Bias*. Harvard Institute of Economic Research-Working Papers 1981. Harvard—Institute of Economic Research, 2002. URL: https://EconPapers.repec.org/RePEc:fth:harver:1981.
295. S. Munson, S. Lee, and P. Resnick. "Encouraging Reading of Diverse Political Viewpoints with a Browser Widget". In: *Proceedings of the International AAAI Conference on Web and Social Media* 7.1 (2021-08). Number: 1, pp. 419–428. URL: https://ojs.aaai.org/index.php/ICWSM/article/view/14429.
296. S. Munson and P. Resnick. "Encouraging Reading of Diverse Political Viewpoints with a Browser Widget". In: *Proceedings of the 7th International Conference on Weblogs and Social Media*, ICWSM 2013. 2013-07.
297. M. Nadeem, A. Bethke, and S. Reddy. "StereoSet: Measuring stereotypical bias in pretrained language models". In: *Proc. Ann. Meeting Association for Computational Linguistics (ACL)*. event-place: Online. Association for Computational Linguistics, 2021, pp. 5356–5371. https://doi.org/10.18653/v1/2021.acl-long.416.
298. P. Nakov, H. T. Sencar, J. An, and H. Kwak. "A Survey on Predicting the Factuality and the Bias of News Media". In: *ArXiv:abs/2103.12506* (2021).
299. N. Newman, D. R. Fletcher, D. A. Schulz, D. S. Andi, D. C. T. Robertson, and P. R. K. Nielsen. "Reuters Institute Digital News Report 2021". In: *Reuters Institute for the Study of Journalism (RIS)* 10 (2021). Place: Oxford, UK. URL: https://reutersinstitute.politics.ox.ac.uk/sites/default/files/2021-06/Digital_News_Report_2021_FINAL.pdf.
300. T. T. H. Nguyen, A. Jatowt, M. Coustaty, and A. Doucet. "Survey of Post-OCR Processing Approaches". In: *ACM Comput. Surv.* 54.6 (2021-07). Number: 6 Place: New York, NY, USA Publisher: Association for Computing Machinery. ISSN: 0360-0300. https://doi.org/10.1145/3453476.
301. R. S. Nickerson. "Confirmation Bias: A Ubiquitous Phenomenon in Many Guises". In: *Review of General Psychology* 2.2 (1998-06), pp. 175–220. ISSN: 1089-2680, 1939-1552. https://doi.org/10.1037/1089-2680.2.2.175.
302. D. Nikolov, M. Lalmas, A. Flammini, and F. Menczer. "Quantifying biases in online information exposure". In: *Journal of the Association for Information Science and Technology* 70.3 (2019). Number: 3 Publisher: Wiley Online Library, pp. 218–229. https://doi.org/10.1002/asi.24121.
303. G. Nisbett. "Political Humor and Third-Person Perception". In: (2011). URL: https://sharcuk.my/handle/11244/319387 (visited on 21/21/17 16).
304. T. Niven and H.-Y. Kao. "Measuring Alignment to Authoritarian State Media as Framing Bias". In: *Proceedings of the 3rd NLP4IF Workshop on NLP for Internet Freedom: Censorship, Disinformation, and Propaganda*. event-place: Barcelona, Spain (Online). International Committee on Computational Linguistics (ICCL), 2020, pp. 11–21. URL: https://aclanthology.org/2020.nlp4if-1.2.
305. B. P. O'connor. "SPSS and SAS programs for determining the number of components using parallel analysis and Velicer's MAP test". In: *Behavior Research Methods, Instruments, & Computers* 32.3 (2000-09-01), pp. 396–402. ISSN: 1532-5970. https://doi.org/10.3758/BF03200807.
306. R. Ookalkar, K. V. Reddy, and E. Gilbert. "Pop: Bursting News Filter Bubbles on Twitter Through Diverse Exposure". In: *Conference Companion Publication of the 2019 on Computer Supported Cooperative Work and Social Computing*. event-place: Austin, TX, USA. New York, NY, USA: Association for Computing Machinery, 2019, pp. 18–22. https://doi.org/10.1145/3311957.3359513.

307. M. Orbach, Y. Bilu, A. Toledo, et al. "Out of the Echo Chamber: Detecting Countering Debate Speeches". In: *Proc. Ann. Meeting Association for Computational Linguistics (ACL)*. event-place: Online. Association for Computational Linguistics, 2020, pp. 7073–7086. https://doi.org/10.18653/v1/2020.acl-main.633.
308. M. Osmundsen, A. Bor, P. B. Vahlstrup, A. Bechmann, and M. B. Petersen. "Partisan polarization is the primary psychological motivation behind political fake news sharing on twitter". In: *American Political Science Review* 115.3 (2021). Publisher: Cambridge University Press, pp. 999–1015. https://doi.org/10.1017/S0003055421000290.
309. M. Ostendorff, T. Ruas, M. Schubotz, G. Rehm, and B. Gipp. "Pairwise Multi-Class Document Classification for Semantic Relations between Wikipedia Articles". In: *Proceedings of the ACM/IEEE Joint Conference on Digital Libraries in 2020*. Virtual Event China: ACM, 2020-08, pp. 127–136. https://doi.org/10.1145/3383583.3398525.
310. B. Pang and L. Lee. "A Sentimental Education: Sentiment Analysis Using Subjectivity Summarization Based on Minimum Cuts". In: *Proc. Ann. Meeting Association for Computational Linguistics (ACL)*. event-place: Barcelona, Spain. USA: Association for Computational Linguistics, 2004, 271–es. https://doi.org/10.3115/1218955.1218990.
311. K. Pant, T. Dadu, and R. Mamidi. "Towards Detection of Subjective Bias using Contextualized Word Embeddings". In: *Companion Proceedings of the Web Conference 2020*. event-place: Taipei Taiwan. ACM, 2020-04-20, pp. 75–76. https://doi.org/10.1145/3366424.3382704.
312. O. Papakyriakopoulos, S. Hegelich, J. C. M. Serrano, and F. Marco. "Bias in word embeddings". In: *Proceedings of the 2020 Conference on Fairness, Accountability, and Transparency*. event-place: Barcelona Spain. ACM, 2020-01-27, pp. 446–457. https://doi.org/10.1145/3351095.3372843.
313. E. Pariser. *The filter bubble: What the Internet is hiding from you*. Penguin, UK, 2011.
314. E. H. Park and V. C. Storey. "Emotion Ontology Studies: A Framework for Expressing Feelings Digitally and Its Application to Sentiment Analysis". In: *ACM Comput. Surv.* (2022-08). Place: New York, NY, USA Publisher: Association for Computing Machinery. ISSN: 0360-0300. https://doi.org/10.1145/3555719.
315. S. Park, J. Ko, H. Choi, and J. Song. "NewsCube 2.0: an exploratory design of a social news website for media bias mitigation". In: *Workshop on Social Recommender Systems*. 2011.
316. S. Park, S. Kang, S. Chung, and J. Song. "NewsCube: delivering multiple aspects of news to mitigate media bias". In: *Proceedings of the 27th international conference on Human factors in computing systems*—CHI 09. event-place: Boston, MA, USA. Boston, MA, USA: ACM Press, 2009, p. 443. https://doi.org/10.1145/1518701.1518772.
317. E. Pavlick and C. Callison-Burch. "Tense Manages to Predict Implicative Behavior in Verbs". In: *EMNLP*. 2016. https://doi.org/10.18653/v1/D16-1240.
318. F. Pedregosa, G. Varoquaux, A. Gramfort, et al. "Scikit-learn: Machine Learning in Python". In: *Journal of Machine Learning Research* 12 (2011), pp. 2825–2830.
319. Y. Peng. "Same Candidates, Different Faces: Uncovering Media Bias in Visual Portrayals of Presidential Candidates with Computer Vision". In: *Journal of Communication* 68.5 (2018), pp. 920–941. ISSN: 0021-9916. https://doi.org/10.1093/joc/jqy041.
320. J. Pennebaker, R. Boyd, K. Jordan, and K. Blackburn. *The Development and Psychometric Properties of LIWC2015*. 2015. https://doi.org/10.15781/T29G6Z.
321. J. W. Pennebaker, M. E. Francis, and R. J. Booth. "Linguistic inquiry and word count: LIWC 2001". In: *Mahway: Lawrence Erlbaum Associates* 71.2001 (2001). Number: 2001, p. 2001.

322. G. Pennycook, A. Bear, E. T. Collins, and D. G. Rand. "The Implied Truth Effect: Attaching Warnings to a Subset of Fake News Headlines Increases Perceived Accuracy of Headlines Without Warnings". In: *Management Science* 66.11 (2020-11), pp. 4944–4957. ISSN: 0025-1909, 1526-5501. https://doi.org/10.1287/mnsc.2019.3478.
323. G. Pennycook, Z. Epstein, M. Mosleh, A. A. Arechar, D. Eckles, and D. G. Rand. "Shifting attention to accuracy can reduce misinformation online". In: *Nature* 592.7855 (2021-04-01). Number: 7855, pp. 590–595. ISSN: 1476-4687. https://doi.org/10.1038/s41586-021-03344-2.
324. G. Pennycook and D. G. Rand. "Lazy, not biased: Susceptibility to partisan fake news is better explained by lack of reasoning than by motivated reasoning". In: *Cognition* 188 (2019), pp. 39–50. ISSN: 0010-0277. https://doi.org/10.1016/j.cognition.2018.06.011.
325. G. Pennycook and D. G. Rand. "The Psychology of Fake News". In: *Trends in Cognitive Sciences* 25.5 (2021). Number: 5, pp. 388–402. ISSN: 1364-6613. https://doi.org/10.1016/j.tics.2021.02.007.
326. R. M. Perloff. "A Three-Decade Retrospective on the Hostile Media Effect". In: *Mass Communication and Society* 18.6 (2015-11-02). Number: 6, pp. 701–729. ISSN: 1520-5436, 1532-7825. https://doi.org/10.1080/15205436.2015.1051234.
327. M. Pfau, K. Tusing, A. Koerner, et al. "Enriching the inoculation construct: The role of critical components in the process of resistance". In: *Human Communication Research* 24.2 (1997), pp. 187–215. URL: https://doi.org/10.1111/j.1468-2958.1997.tb00413.x.
328. G. Piccinini. "The First Computational Theory of Cognition: McCulloch and Pitts's "A Logical Calculus of the Ideas Immanent in Nervous Activity"". In: *Neurocognitive Mechanisms: Explaining Biological Cognition*. Oxford University Press, 2020-11-12. ISBN: 978-0-19-886628-2. URL: https://doi.org/10.1093/oso/9780198866282.003.0006 (visited on 2023-01-25).
329. C. Piñón. "A Finer Look at the Causative-Inchoative Alternation". In: *Semantics and Linguistic Theory* 11 (2001), pp. 346–364.
330. K. Power, L. Rak, and M. Kim. "Women in business media: A Critical Discourse Analysis of Representations of Women in Forbes, Fortune and Bloomberg BusinessWeek, 2015-2017." In: *Critical Approaches to Discourse Analysis Across Disciplines* 11.2 (2019). Number: 2.
331. D. Preoţiuc-Pietro, V. Lampos, and N. Aletras. "An analysis of the user occupational class through Twitter content". In: *Proc. Ann. Meeting Assoc. for Computational Linguistics (ACL)*. Beijing, China. Association for Computational Linguistics, 2015-07, pp. 1754–1764. https://doi.org/10.3115/v1/P15-1169.
332. R. Pryzant, R. D. Martinez, N. Dass, S. Kurohashi, D. Jurafsky, and D. Yang. "Automatically Neutralizing Subjective Bias in Text". In: (2019). https://doi.org/10.48550/ARXIV.1911.09709.
333. R. Pryzant, R. D. Martinez, N. Dass, S. Kurohashi, D. Jurafsky, and D. Yang. "Automatically neutralizing subjective bias in text". In: *Proceedings of the aaai conference on artificial intelligence*. Vol. 34. Issue: 01. 2020, pp. 480–489. https://doi.org/10.1609/aaai.v34i01.5385.
334. R. Puglisi and J. M. Snyder. "Chapter 15—Empirical Studies of Media Bias". In: *Handbook of Media Economics*. Vol. 1. Handbook of Media Economics. North-Holland, 2015, pp. 647–667. https://doi.org/10.1016/B978-0-444-63685-0.00015-2.
335. C. Raffel, N. Shazeer, A. Roberts, et al. "Exploring the Limits of Transfer Learning with a Unified Textto- Text Transformer". In: *Journal of Machine Learning Research* 21.140 (2020), pp. 1–67. URL: http://jmlr.org/papers/v21/20-074.html.

336. M. I. Rana, S. Khalid, and M. U. Akbar. "News classification based on their headlines: A review". In: *17th IEEE International Multi Topic Conference 2014*. 2014, pp. 211–216. https://doi.org/10.1109/INMIC.2014.7097339.
337. P. Rao and M. Taboada. "Gender Bias in the News: A Scalable Topic Modelling and Visualization Framework". In: *Frontiers in Artificial Intelligence* 4 (2021-06-16), p. 664737. ISSN: 2624-8212. https://doi.org/10.3389/frai.2021.664737.
338. H. Rashkin, S. Singh, and Y. Choi. "Connotation Frames: A Data-Driven Investigation". In: *Proc. Ann. Meeting Association for Computational Linguistics (ACL)*. Berlin, Germany: Association for Computational Linguistics, 2016-08, pp. 311–321. https://doi.org/10.18653/v1/P16-1030.
339. S. Rathje, J. Roozenbeek, C. Traberg, J. Van Bavel, and S. van der Linden. "Letter to the Editors of Psychological Science: Meta-Analysis Reveals that Accuracy Nudges Have Little to No Effect for U.S. Conservatives: Regarding Pennycook et al. (2020)". In: *Psychological Science* (2022-01). https://doi.org/10.25384/SAGE.12594110.v2.
340. S. Raza, D. J. Reji, and C. Ding. "Dbias: Detecting biases and ensuring Fairness in news articles". In: (2022-02). Publisher: In Review Type: preprint. https://doi.org/10.21203/rs.3.rs-1356281/v1.
341. M. Recasens, C. Danescu-Niculescu-Mizil, and D. Jurafsky. "Linguistic Models for Analyzing and Detecting Biased Language". In: *Proc. Ann. Meeting Association for Computational Linguistics (ACL)*. Vol. 1. Sofia, Bulgaria: Association for Computational Linguistics, 2013-08, pp. 1650–1659. URL: https://www.aclweb.org/anthology/P13-1162 (visited on 2020-06-13).
342. S. A. Reid. "A Self-Categorization Explanation for the Hostile Media Effect". In: *Journal of Communication* 62.3 (2012). _eprint: https://doi.org/10.1111/j.1460-2466.2012.01647.x, pp. 381–399. https://doi.org/10.1111/j.1460-2466.2012.01647.x.
343. F. Ribeiro, L. Henrique, F. Benevenuto, et al. "Media Bias Monitor: Quantifying Biases of Social Media News Outlets at Large-Scale." In: *Proceedings of the International AAAI Conference on Web and Social Media*. Vol. 12. Issue: 1. 2018, pp. 290–299.
344. E. Riloff and J. Wiebe. "Learning Extraction Patterns for Subjective Expressions". In: *Proceedings of the 2003 Conference on Empirical Methods in Natural Language Processing*. 2003, pp. 105–112. URL: https://aclanthology.org/W03-1014.
345. A. Rodríguez, C. Argueta, and Y.-L. Chen. "Automatic Detection of Hate Speech on Facebook Using Sentiment and Emotion Analysis". In: *2019 International Conference on Artificial Intelligence in Information and Communication (ICAIIC)*. 2019, pp. 169–174. https://doi.org/10.1109/ICAIIC.2019.8669073.
346. M. Rodríguez-Ibánez, A. Casánez-Ventura, F. Castejón-Mateos, and P.-M. Cuenca-Jiménez. "A review on sentiment analysis from social media platforms". In: *Expert Systems with Applications* 223 (2023), p. 119862. ISSN: 0957-4174. https://doi.org/10.1016/j.eswa.2023.119862.
347. H. Rojas. ""Corrective" Actions in the Public Sphere: How Perceptions of Media and Media Effects Shape Political Behaviors". In: *International Journal of Public Opinion Research* 22.3 (2010). Number: 3, pp. 343–363. ISSN: 0954-2892. https://doi.org/10.1093/ijpor/edq018.
348. J. Roozenbeek, C. S. Traberg, and S. van der Linden. "Technique-based inoculation against real-world misinformation". In: *Royal Society Open Science* 9.5 (2022), p. 211719. https://doi.org/10.1098/rsos.211719.

349. L. Ross, D. Greene, and P. House. "The "false consensus effect": An egocentric bias in social perception and attribution processes". In: *Journal of Experimental Social Psychology* 13.3 (1977-05). Number: 3, pp. 279–301. ISSN: 0022-1031. https://doi.org/10.1016/0022-1031(77)90049-X.
350. Q. Ruan, B. Mac Namee, and R. Dong. "Pseudo-labelling Enhanced Media Bias Detection". In: (2021). https://doi.org/10.48550/ARXIV.2107.07705.
351. Q. Ruan, B. M. Namee, and R. Dong. "Bias Bubbles: Using Semi-Supervised Learning to Measure How Many Biased News Articles Are Around Us". In: *The 29th Irish Conference on Artificial Intelligence and Cognitive Science 2021, Dublin, Republic of Ireland, December 9–10, 2021*. Vol. 3105. CEUR-WS.org, 2021, pp. 153–164. URL: http://ceur-ws.org/Vol-3105/paper40.pdf.
352. M. Rubin and C. Badea. "Why Do People Perceive Ingroup Homogeneity on Ingroup Traits and Outgroup Homogeneity on Outgroup Traits?" In: *Personality and Social Psychology Bulletin* 33.1 (2007-01). Number: 1 _eprint: https://doi.org/10.1177/0146167206293190, pp. 31–42. ISSN: 0146-1672, 1552-7433. https://doi.org/10.1177/0146167206293190.
353. S. Ruder. "An Overview of Multi-Task Learning in Deep Neural Networks". In: *CoRR* abs/1706.05098 (2017). _eprint: 1706.05098. URL: http://arxiv.org/abs/1706.05098.
354. D. Saez-Trumper, C. Castillo, and M. Lalmas. "Social Media News Communities: Gatekeeping, Coverage, and Statement Bias". In: *Proceedings of the 22nd ACM International Conference on Information & Knowledge Management*. New York, NY, USA: Association for Computing Machinery, 2013, pp. 1679–1684. https://doi.org/10.1145/2505515.2505623.
355. B. J. Sagarin, R. B. Cialdini, W. E. Rice, and S. B. Serna. "Dispelling the illusion of invulnerability: The motivations and mechanisms of resistance to persuasion". In: *Journal of personality and social psychology* 83.3 (2002), pp. 526–541. URL: https://doi.org/10.1037/0022-3514.83.3.526.
356. N. F. Saleh, J. Roozenbeek, F. A. MakkiAKKI, W. P. MCClanahan, and S. van der Linden. "Active inoculation boosts attitudinal resistance against extremist persuasion techniques: a novel approach towards the prevention of violent extremism". In: *Behavioural Public Policy* (2021). Publisher: Cambridge University Press, pp. 1–24. https://doi.org/10.1017/bpp.2020.60.
357. H. Salehinejad, S. Sankar, J. Barrett, E. Colak, and S. Valaee. *Recent advances in recurrent neural networks*. 2018.
358. A. Sales, A. Zehe, L. B. Marinho, A. Veloso, A. Hotho, and J. Omeliyanenko. "Assessing Media Bias in Cross- Linguistic and Cross-National Populations". In: *Proceedings of the Fifteenth International AAAI Conference on Web and Social Media, ICWSM 2021, held virtually, June 7–10, 2021*. AAAI Press, 2021, pp. 561–572. URL: https://ojs.aaai.org/index.php/ICWSM/article/view/18084.
359. M. B. Salwen and P. D. Driscoll. "Consequences of third-person perception in support of press restrictions in the O. J. Simpson trial". In: *Journal of Communication* 47.2 (1997), pp. 60–78. ISSN: 1460-2466. https://doi.org/10.1111/j.1460-2466.1997.tb02706.x.
360. V. Sanh, L. Debut, J. Chaumond, and T. Wolf. "DistilBERT, a distilled version of BERT: smaller, faster, cheaper and lighter". In: *CoRR* abs/1910.01108 (2019). _eprint: 1910.01108. URL: http://arxiv.org/abs/1910.01108.
361. M. Sap, D. Card, S. Gabriel, Y. Choi, and N. A. Smith. "The Risk of Racial Bias in Hate Speech Detection". In: *Proc. Ann. Meeting Association for Computational Linguistics*

(ACL). Florence, Italy: Association for Computational Linguistics, 2019-07, pp. 1668–1678. https://doi.org/10.18653/v1/P19-1163.
362. E. Sapiro-Gheiler. "Examining Political Trustworthiness through Text-Based Measures of Ideology". In: *Proceedings of the AAAI Conference on Artificial Intelligence* 33 (2019-07-17), pp. 10029–10030. ISSN: 2374- 3468, 2159-5399. https://doi.org/10.1609/aaai.v33i01.330110029.
363. I. H. Sarker. "Deep Learning: A Comprehensive Overview on Techniques, Taxonomy, Applications and Research Directions". In: *SN Computer Science* 2.6 (2021-08-18), p. 420. ISSN: 2661–8907. https://doi.org/10.1007/s42979-021-00815-1.
364. K. M. Schmitt, A. C. Gunther, and J. L. Liebhart. "Why Partisans See Mass Media as Biased". In: *Communication Research* 31.6 (2004-12). Number: 6 _eprint: https://doi.org/10.1177/0093650204269390, pp. 623–641. ISSN: 0093-6502, 1552-3810. https://doi.org/10.1177/0093650204269390.
365. A. Schulz, W. Wirth, and P. Müller. "We Are the People and You Are Fake News: A Social Identity Approach to Populist Citizens' False Consensus and Hostile Media Perceptions". In: *Communication Research* 47.2 (2020-03). Number: 2 _eprint: https://doi.org/10.1177/0093650218794854, pp. 201–226. ISSN: 0093-6502, 1552-3810. https://doi.org/10.1177/0093650218794854.
366. *Second conference internationale sur le traitement automatique des langues, COLING 1967, grenoble, france, august 1967.* tex.bibsource: dblp computer science bibliography, https://dblp.orgtex.timestamp:Fri, 06 Aug 2021 00:39:46 +0200. 1967 URL: https://aclanthology.org/volumes/C67-1/.
367. G. R. Semin and K. Fiedler. "The cognitive functions of linguistic categories in describing persons: Social cognition and language". In: *Journal of Personality and Social Psychology* 54.4 (1988). Number: 4, pp. 558–568. https://doi.org/10.1037/0022-3514.54.4.558.
368. T. Serre. "Deep learning: The good, the bad, and the ugly". In: Annual Review of Vision Science 5.1 (2019). tex.eprint: https://doi.org/10.1146/annurev-vision-091718-014951, pp. 399–426. https://doi.org/10.1146/annurevvision-091718-014951.
369. A. Severyn and A. Moschitti. "UNITN: Training Deep Convolutional Neural Network for Twitter Sentiment Classification". In: *Proceedings of the 9th International Workshop on Semantic Evaluation (SemEval 2015)*. Denver, Colorado: Association for Computational Linguistics, 2015-06, pp. 464–469. https://doi.org/10.18653/v1/S15-2079.
370. U. Shahid, B. Di Eugenio, A. Rojecki, and E. Zheleva. "Detecting and understanding moral biases in news". In: *Proceedings of the First Joint Workshop on Narrative Understanding, Storylines, and Events.* event-place: Online. Association for Computational Linguistics, 2020, pp. 120–125. https://doi.org/10.18653/v1/2020.nuse-1.15.
371. M. Sinha and T. Dasgupta. "Determining Subjective Bias in Text through Linguistically Informed Transformer based Multi-Task Network". In: *Proceedings of the 30th ACM International Conference on Information & Knowledge Management.* event-place: Virtual Event Queensland Australia. ACM, 2021-10-26, pp. 3418–3422. https://doi.org/10.1145/3459637.3482084.
372. B. Sinno, B. Oviedo, K. Atwell, M. Alikhani, and J. J. Li. *Political Ideology and Polarization of Policy Positions: A Multi-dimensional Approach.* Issue: arXiv:2106.14387. 2022-05-03. URL: http://arxiv.org/abs/2106.14387 (visited on 2022-08-01).
373. T. D. Smedt, G. D. Pauw, and P. V. Ostaeyen. *Automatic Detection of Online Jihadist Hate Speech.* Publication Title: CoRR Volume: abs/1803.04596 _eprint: 1803.04596. 2018.

374. S. M. Smith, L. R. Fabrigar, and M. E. Norris. "Reflecting on Six Decades of Selective Exposure Research: Progress, Challenges, and Opportunities". In: *Social and Personality Psychology Compass* 2.1 (2008). Number: 1 _eprint: https://doi.org/10.1111/j.1751-9004.2007.00060.x, pp. 464–493. https://doi.org/10.1111/j.1751-9004.2007.00060.x.
375. A. Soliman, J. Hafer, and F. Lemmerich. "A Characterization of Political Communities on Reddit". In: *Proceedings of the 30th ACM Conference on Hypertext and Social Media* (2019).
376. T. Spinde, S. Hinterreiter, F. Haak, et al. "Introducing the Media Bias Framework. An Interdisciplinary Literature Review on the Perception And Detection of Media Bias". In: *ACM Computing Surveys (in preparation)* (2022).
377. D. Spohr. "Fake news and ideological polarization: Filter bubbles and selective exposure on social media". In: Business Information Review 34.3 (2017). Publisher: SAGE Publications Sage UK: London, England, pp. 150–160.
378. P. Stefanov, K. Darwish, A. Atanasov, and P. Nakov. "Predicting the Topical Stance and Political Leaning of Media using Tweets". In: *Proc. Ann. Meeting Association for Computational Linguistics (ACL)*. event-place: Online. Association for Computational Linguistics, 2020, pp. 527–537. https://doi.org/10.18653/v1/2020.aclmain.50.
379. C. Sun, X. Qiu, Y. Xu, and X. Huang. "How to Fine-Tune BERT for Text Classification?" In: *CoRR* abs/1905.05583 (2019). URL: http://arxiv.org/abs/1905.05583.
380. Y. Sun, S. Wang, Y.-K. Li, et al. "ERNIE 2.0: A Continual Pre-Training Framework for Language Understanding". In: *Proceedings of the AAAI Conference on Artificial Intelligence* 34 (2020-04), pp. 8968–8975. https://doi.org/10.1609/aaai.v34i05.6428.
381. C. R. Sunstein. *Going to extremes: How like minds unite and divide*. Oxford University Press, 2009.
382. B. Swire-Thompson, J. DeGutis, and D. Lazer. "Searching for the Backfire Effect: Measurement and Design Considerations". In: *Journal of Applied Research in Memory and Cognition* 9.3 (2020). Number: 3, pp. 286–299. ISSN: 2211-3681. https://doi.org/10.1016/j.jarmac.2020.06.006.
383. H. Tajfel, J. C. Turner, W. G. Austin, and S. Worchel. "An integrative theory of intergroup conflict". In: *Organizational identity: A reader* 56.65 (1979), pp. 9780203505984–16.
384. E. C. Tandoc Jr. "The facts of fake news: A research review". In: *Sociology Compass* 13.9 (2019), e12724. ISSN: 1751-9020. https://doi.org/10.1111/soc4.12724.
385. D. Tang, F. Wei, N. Yang, M. Zhou, T. Liu, and B. Qin. "Learning Sentiment-Specific Word Embedding for Twitter Sentiment Classification". In: Proc. Ann. Meeting Association for Computational Linguistics (ACL). Baltimore, Maryland: Association for Computational Linguistics, 2014, pp. 1555–1565. https://doi.org/10.3115/v1/P14-1146.
386. M. Tran. "How biased are American media outlets? A framework for presentation bias regression". In: *2020 IEEE International Conference on Big Data (Big Data)*. event-place: Atlanta, GA, USA. IEEE, 2020-12-10, pp. 4359–4364. https://doi.org/10.1109/BigData50022.2020.9377987.
387. M. Tully, E. K. Vraga, and A.-B. Smithson. "News media literacy, perceptions of bias, and interpretation of news". In: *Journalism* 21.2 (2020-02). Number: 2 _eprint: https://doi.org/10.1177/1464884918805262, pp. 209–226. ISSN: 1464-8849, 1741-3001. https://doi.org/10.1177/1464884918805262.
388. J. C. Turner. *Social influence*. Thomson Brooks/Cole Publishing Co, 1991.
389. R. Vallone, L. Ross, and M. Lepper. "The Hostile Media Phenomenon: Biased Perception and Perceptions of Media Bias in Coverage of the Beirut Massacre". In: *Journal of*

personality and social psychology 49.3 (1985-09). Number: 3 Publisher: American Psychological Association, pp. 577–585. ISSN: 0022-3514. https://doi.org/10.1037//0022-3514.49.3.577.
390. A. Vaswani, N. Shazeer, N. Parmar, et al. "Attention is All you Need". In: *Proc. Ann. Conf. Neural Information Processing Systems (NeurIPS)*. 2017, pp. 5998–6008. URL: https://proceedings.neurips.cc/paper/2017/hash/3f5ee243547dee91fbd053c1c4a845aa-Abstract.html.
391. M. D. Vicario, A. Bessi, F. Zollo, et al. "The spreading of misinformation online". In: *Proceedings of the National Academy of Sciences* 113.3 (2016), pp. 554–559. https://doi.org/10.1073/pnas.1517441113.
392. J. Vig, S. Gehrmann, Y. Belinkov, et al. "Investigating Gender Bias in Language Models Using Causal Mediation Analysis". In: *Proc. Ann. Conf. Neural Information Processing Systems (NeurIPS)*. Vol. 33. Curran Associates, Inc., 2020, pp. 12388–12401. URL: https://proceedings.neurips.cc/paper/2020/file/92650b2e92217715fe312e6fa7b90d82-Paper.pdf.
393. G. Villa, G. Pasi, and M. Viviani. "Echo chamber detection and analysis: A topology- and content-based approach in the COVID-19 scenario". In: *Social Network Analysis and Mining* 11.1 (2021-12). Number: 1, p. 78. ISSN: 1869-5450, 1869-5469. https://doi.org/10.1007/s13278-021-00779-3.
394. E. K. Vraga and M. Tully. "Media literacy messages and hostile media perceptions: Processing of nonpartisan versus partisan political information". In: *Mass Communication and Society* 18.4 (2015), pp. 422–448. URL: https://doi.org/10.1080/08838151.2016.1273923.
395. C. H. de Vreese. "News framing: Theory and typology". In: *Information Design Journal* 13.1 (2005). Number: 1 Publisher: John Benjamins Type: Journal Article, pp. 51–62. ISSN: 0142-5471. https://doi.org/10.1075/idjdd.13.1.06vre.
396. J. P. Wahle, N. Ashok, T. Ruas, N. Meuschke, T. Ghosal, and B. Gipp. "Testing the Generalization of Neural Language Models for COVID-19 Misinformation Detection". In: (2021). Publisher: *arXiv Version Number*: 5. https://doi.org/10.48550/ARXIV.2111.07819.
397. J. P. Wahle, T. Ruas, N. Meuschke, and B. Gipp. "Are Neural Language Models Good Plagiarists? A Benchmark for Neural Paraphrase Detection". In: *ACM/IEEE Joint Conference on Digital Libraries (JCDL)*, 2021. 2021-03. URL: https://arxiv.org/pdf/2103.12450.pdf (visited on 2021-04-29).
398. J. P. Wahle, T. Ruas, N. Meuschke, and B. Gipp. "Incorporating Word Sense Disambiguation in Neural Language Models". In: arXiv:2106.07967 *[cs]* (2021-06). URL: https://arxiv.org/pdf/2106.07967.pdf (visited on 2021-06-19).
399. A. Wang, A. Singh, J. Michael, F. Hill, O. Levy, and S. Bowman. "GLUE: A Multi-Task Benchmark and Analysis Platform for Natural Language Understanding". In: *Proceedings of the 2018 EMNLP Workshop BlackboxNLP: Analyzing and Interpreting Neural Networks for NLP*. Brussels, Belgium: Association for Computational Linguistics, 2018-11, pp. 353–355. https://doi.org/10.18653/v1/W18-5446.
400. J. Wang and B. Yu. "News2PubMed: A Browser Extension for Linking Health News to Medical Literature". In: *Proceedings of the 44th International ACM SIGIR Conference on Research and Development in Information Retrieval*. event-place: Virtual Event, Canada. New York, NY, USA: Association for Computing Machinery, 2021, pp. 2605–2609. https://doi.org/10.1145/3404835.3462788.

401. Z. Waseem. "Are You a Racist or Am I Seeing Things? Annotator Influence on Hate Speech Detection on Twitter". In: *Proceedings of the First Workshop on NLP and Computational Social Science*. Austin, Texas: Association for Computational Linguistics, 2016-11, pp. 138–142. https://doi.org/10.18653/v1/W16-5618.
402. Z.Waseem and D. Hovy. "Hateful Symbols or Hateful People? Predictive Features for Hate Speech Detection on Twitter". In: *Proc. Conf. North American Chapter Association for Computaitonal Linguistics: Human Language Technology (NAACL-HLT)*. San Diego, California: Association for Computational Linguistics, 2016-06, pp. 88–93. https://doi.org/10.18653/v1/N16-2013.
403. A. Webson, Z. Chen, C. Eickhoff, and E. Pavlick. "Are "Undocumented Workers" the Same as "Illegal Aliens"? Disentangling Denotation and Connotation in Vector Spaces". In: *Proceedings of the 2020 Conference on Empirical Methods in Natural Language Processing (EMNLP)*. Online: Association for Computational Linguistics, 2020-11, pp. 4090–4105. https://doi.org/10.18653/v1/2020.emnlp-main.335.
404. B. E. Weeks, D. S. Lane, D. H. Kim, S. S. Lee, and N. Kwak. "Incidental Exposure, Selective Exposure, and Political Information Sharing: Integrating Online Exposure Patterns and Expression on Social Media". In: *Journal of Computer-Mediated Communication* 22.6 (2017-11-01). Number: 6 Publisher: Oxford University Press Oxford, UK, pp. 363–379. ISSN: 1083-6101. https://doi.org/10.1111/jcc4.12199.
405. M. Wessel, T. Horych, T. Ruas, A. Aizawa, B. Gipp, and T. Spinde. "Introducing MBIB—the first Media Bias Identification Benchmark Task and Dataset Collection". In: *Proceedings of 46th international ACM SIGIR conference on research and development in information retrieval (SIGIR '23)*. 2023.
406. M. Wevers. "Using Word Embeddings to Examine Gender Bias in Dutch Newspapers, 1950–1990". In: *Proceedings of the 1st International Workshop on Computational Approaches to Historical Language Change*. event-place: Florence, Italy. Association for Computational Linguistics, 2019, pp. 92–97. https://doi.org/10.18653/v1/W19-4712.
407. D. M. White. "The "Gate Keeper": A Case Study in the Selection of News". In: *Journalism Quarterly* 27.4 (1950-09), pp. 383–390. ISSN: 0022-5533. https://doi.org/10.1177/107769905002700403.
408. A. Williams. "Unbiased Study of Television News Bias". In: *Journal of Communication* 25 (1975), pp. 190–199.
409. T. Wilson, J. Wiebe, and P. Hoffmann. "Recognizing Contextual Polarity in Phrase-Level Sentiment Analysis". In: *Proceedings of the Conference on Human Language Technology and Empirical Methods in Natural Language Processing*. event-place: Vancouver, British Columbia, Canada. USA: Association for Computational Linguistics, 2005, pp. 347–354. https://doi.org/10.3115/1220575.1220619.
410. T. Wolf, L. Debut, V. Sanh, et al. "Transformers: State-of-the-Art Natural Language Processing". In: *Proceedings of the 2020 Conference on Empirical Methods in Natural Language Processing: System Demonstrations*. Online: Association for Computational Linguistics, 2020-10, pp. 38–45. URL: https://www.aclweb.org/anthology/2020.emnlp-demos.6.
411. S. Wolton. *Are Biased Media Bad for Democracy? Microeconomics: Asymmetric & Private Information eJournal*, 2017. https://doi.org/10.2139/ssrn.2285854.
412. S. Wolton. "Are Biased Media Bad for Democracy?" In: *American Journal of Political Science* 63.3 (2019-07), pp. 548–562. ISSN: 0092-5853, 1540-5907. https://doi.org/10.1111/ajps.12424.

413. J. Worsham and J. Kalita. "Multi-task learning for natural language processing in the 2020s: Where are we going?" In: *Pattern Recognition Letters* 136 (2020-08), pp. 120–126. ISSN: 0167-8655. https://doi.org/10/gmgb3j.
414. Z. Xiao, W. Song, H. Xu, Z. Ren, and Y. Sun. "TIMME: Twitter Ideology-detection via Multi-task Multirelational Embedding". In: *Proceedings of the 26th ACM SIGKDD International Conference on Knowledge Discovery & Data Mining*. event-place: Virtual Event CA USA. ACM, 2020-08-23, pp. 2258–2268. https://doi.org/10.1145/3394486.3403275.
415. C. Xiong, Z. Liu, J. Callan, and T.-Y. Liu. "Towards Better Text Understanding and Retrieval through Kernel Entity Salience Modeling". In: *The 41st International ACM SIGIR Conference on Research & Development in Information Retrieval*. event-place: Ann Arbor, MI, USA. New York, NY, USA: Association for Computing Machinery, 2018, pp. 575–584. https://doi.org/10.1145/3209978.3209982.
416. Z. Yang, Z. Dai, Y. Yang, J. Carbonell, R. R. Salakhutdinov, and Q. V. Le. "XLNet: Generalized Autoregressive Pretraining for Language Understanding". In: *Proc. Ann. Conf. Neural Information Processing Systems (NeurIPS)*. Vol. 32. Curran Associates, Inc., 2019. URL: https://proceedings.neurips.cc/paper/2019/file/dc6a7e655d7e5840e66733e9ee67cc69-Paper.pdf.
417. T. Yano, P. Resnik, and N. Smith. "Shedding (a Thousand Points of) Light on Biased Language". In: *Proc. Conf. North American Chapter Association for Computaitonal Linguistics: Human Language Technology (NAACL-HLT)*. 2010.
418. X. Ying. "An Overview of Overfitting and its Solutions". In: *Journal of Physics: Conference Series* 1168.2 (2019-02). Publisher: IOP Publishing, pp. 1–7. https://doi.org/10.1088/1742-6596/1168/2/022022.
419. G. W. Yun, S.-Y. Park, S. Lee, and M. A. Flynn. "Hostile Media or Hostile Source? Bias Perception of Shared News". In: *Social Science Computer Review* 36.1 (2018-02), pp. 21–35. ISSN: 0894-4393. https://doi.org/10.1177/0894439316684481.
420. A. Zahid, M. Nasir Khan, A. Latif Khan, F. Kamiran, and B. Nasir. "Modeling, Quantifying and Visualizing Media Bias on Twitter". In: *IEEE Access* 8 (2020), pp. 81812–81821. ISSN: 2169-3536. https://doi.org/10.1109/ACCESS.2020.2990800.
421. S. Zannettou, M. Elsherief, E. Belding, S. Nilizadeh, and G. Stringhini. "Measuring and Characterizing Hate Speech on News Websites". In: *12th ACM Conference on Web Science*. event-place: Southampton United Kingdom. New York, NY, USA: ACM, 2020-07-06, pp. 125–134. https://doi.org/10.1145/3394231.3397902.
422. Y. Zhang and Q. Yang. "A Survey on Multi-Task Learning". In: *IEEE Transactions on Knowledge and Data Engineering* (2021), pp. 1–1. https://doi.org/10.1109/TKDE.2021.3070203.
423. F. Zhou, X. Xu, G. Trajcevski, and K. Zhang. "A Survey of Information Cascade Analysis: Models, Predictions, and Recent Advances". In: *ACM Comput. Surv.* 54.2 (2021-03). Place: New York, NY, USA Publisher: Association for Computing Machinery. ISSN: 0360-0300. https://doi.org/10.1145/3433000.
424. X. Zhou, H. Elfardy, C. Christodoulopoulos, T. Butler, and M. Bansal. "Hidden Biases in Unreliable News Detection Datasets". In: *Proc. Ann. Meeting Association for Computational Linguistics (ACL)*. event-place: Online. Association for Computational Linguistics, 2021, pp. 2482–2492. https://doi.org/10.18653/v1/2021.eaclmain.211.
425. Y. Zhou, R. Ji, J. Su, and J. Yao. "Uncovering Media Bias via Social Network Learning". In: *ACM Transactions on Intelligent Systems and Technology* 12.1 (2021-02-28). Number: 1, pp. 1–12. ISSN: 2157-6904, 2157-6912. https://doi.org/10.1145/3422181.

426. Y. Zhu, R. Kiros, R. Zemel, et al. "Aligning books and movies: Towards story-like visual explanations by watching movies and reading books". In: *Proceedings of the IEEE international conference on computer vision*. 2015, pp. 19–27. https://doi.org/10.1109/iccv.2015.11.
427. D. Zimbra, A. Abbasi, D. Zeng, and H. Chen. "The State-of-the-Art in Twitter Sentiment Analysis: A Review and Benchmark Evaluation". In: *ACM Transactions on Management Information Systems (TMIS)* 9.2 (2018-08). Number: 2 Place: New York, NY, USA Publisher: Association for Computing Machinery. ISSN: 2158-656X. https://doi.org/10.1145/3185045.
428. F. J. Zuiderveen Borgesius, D. Trilling, J. Möller, B. Bodó, C. H. De Vreese, and N. Helberger. "Should we worry about filter bubbles?" In: *Internet Policy Review* 5.1 (2016). Number: 1, pp. 1–16. ISSN: 2197-6775. https://doi.org/10.14763/2016.1.401.

The manufacturer's authorised representative in the EU is Springer Nature Customer Service Centre GmbH, Europaplatz 3, 69115 Heidelberg, Germany. If you have any concerns regarding our products, please contact ProductSafety@springernature.com

Printed and bound by CPI Group (UK) Ltd, Croydon, CR0 4YY
26/03/2026
02078969-0001